RACINE'S MID-CAREER TRAGEDIES

RACINE'S
MID-CAREER
TRAGEDIES

TRANSLATED INTO ENGLISH RHYMING VERSE

WITH INTRODUCTIONS BY

LACY LOCKERT

PRINCETON

PRINCETON UNIVERSITY PRESS

1958

COPYRIGHT © 1958, PRINCETON UNIVERSITY PRESS

LONDON : OXFORD UNIVERSITY PRESS

L. C. CARD 58-6105

135977

PRINTED AT THE PRINCETON UNIVERSITY PRESS

PRINCETON, NEW JERSEY, U.S.A.

CONTENTS

PAGE

PREFACE ix

BÉRÉNICE 1

    INTRODUCTION 3

    BERENICE 19

BAJAZET 89

    INTRODUCTION 91

    BAJAZET 105

MITHRIDATE 183

    INTRODUCTION 185

    MITHRIDATES 199

IPHIGÉNIE 273

    INTRODUCTION 275

    IPHIGENIA 291

PREFACE

THE four tragedies of Racine which this book contains have an interesting significance as a group. Written one after another in immediate succession, they may be said to represent "a dramatist's progress." That progress, the circumstances and the nature of it, I have explained in the Introduction to *Britannicus* in my first volume of translations of Racine's plays, and repeated this explanation in my study of *Bérénice* which was published in *The Romanic Review* for February, 1939, and which (with slight changes) serves as the Introduction to the translation of *Bérénice* in the present volume.

As to the merits of these four dramas, the consensus of critical opinion for upwards of a century, at least, has been that they are inferior to what are generally called Racine's "four masterpieces"—*Andromaque, Britannicus, Phèdre*, and *Athalie*. There are dissenting appraisals, however, by individual critics. I have commented upon what is practically a cult of admirers of *Bérénice* in modern times; Jules Lemaître ranked it and *Bajazet* among their author's very best tragedies. Sainte-Beuve at one period of his life regarded *Iphigénie* as equalled or surpassed only by *Athalie*. But, on the other hand, not a few authorities have rated *Bérénice* below all the others, and Lemaître rated *Iphigénie* the lowest of all![1] My own view is that there was a steady improvement in the quality of Racine's work from *Bérénice* to *Iphigénie*, though really not much to choose between *Bajazet* and *Mithridate*. I state in discussing *Iphigénie* that I think it rivals *Andromaque* in merit—but then I dissent from the customary estimate of *Andromaque* as a masterpiece like *Britannicus, Phè-*

[1] Such statements do not, of course, include Racine's first, unimportant plays, *la Thébaïde* and *Alexandre,* nor his *Esther.*

dre, and *Athalie*. Yet even if not "great" plays, *Bérénice*, *Bajazet, Mithridate*, and *Iphigénie* are—all of them—good plays, celebrated plays, deservedly famous among the notable dramas of the world's literature. They are well worth knowing, both in themselves and for what they show us of the development, amidst adverse circumstances, of the great dramatist who wrote them.

My introduction to each of these plays, especially *Bérénice*, is not such as usually accompanies a translated drama, dwelling upon its excellences and lightly passing over its defects. But the "progress" of Racine, from the pseudo-classical conventionalism so markedly present in *Bérénice* to the truly classical quality of so much of *Iphigénie*, seems to me what most needs to be pointed out in regard to these four significant tragedies, which come mid-way in their author's career, after his early development culminating in *Britannicus* and before his final great achievements, *Phèdre* and *Athalie*.

I am again indebted to Miss Louise Allen, Dr. C. Maxwell Lancaster, and Dr. Philip W. Timberlake for their aid in connection with this book as with previous books of mine.

LACY LOCKERT

BÉRÉNICE
(BERENICE)

INTRODUCTION

THE almost simultaneous appearance of Racine's *Béré-nice* and Corneille's *Tite et Bérénice* was explained by an old story, which told that Henrietta of England, Louis XIV's sister-in-law, suggested to these dramatists that each should write a play, in competition with the other, about the parting of Titus and Berenice. This story went unchallenged until 1907, when Gustave Michaut exposed its unsubstantial basis in his book, *la Bérénice de Racine*, and offered an alternative explanation to account for what occurred.

It was at this time, 1670, said Michaut, that the feud between the two poets was bitterest. Their relations had first become strained when Corneille declared, after reading *Alexandre*, that Racine's proper field was not drama. With the sensational success of *Andromaque*, Corneille's partisans, jealous of his eclipse, were heard belittling the achievement of his young rival, who, they said, could write a pretty play about love but had not the virile power and broad historical grasp of their own idol; such criticism led Racine to choose a theme from Roman history, and involving political motives, for his next tragedy and thus to vie with Corneille in his own peculiar domain; and when this play, *Britannicus*, encountered a disappointing reception, he laid the blame upon Corneille himself. Then, while his real or fancied wrongs rankled sorest within him, Racine must have learned, in some way, that his foe was at work on the drama *Tite et Bérénice*. Here, Racine felt, was a subject which he could treat more successfully than Corneille. He would write upon it, also; he would work with all possible speed and have his version of it completed as soon as the other one; produced at the same time, the two plays would decide, by their respective fortunes, who was the greatest tragic poet of France. Thus he would at once exalt himself and discomfit the man he hated. It is a matter of record that he did.

But Michaut did not stop with formulating this plausible hypothesis to account for the *Bérénice* of Racine. He maintained that if such a hypothesis be accepted, *Bérénice* becomes of capital importance among the works of its author. Its subject was taken by Racine because it was appropriate to his dramatic system—because better than any other it gave him a chance to exhibit the theory of that system and to apply it effectively. That he should be victorious in the contest which he had initiated was imperative; for a new defeat, after *Britannicus*, would definitely relegate him to the second rank and confirm the supremacy of his rival; his whole future as a dramatist and the future of his conception of drama were at stake. Therefore is it not clear, said Michaut, that he mustered all his powers and made every effort of which he was capable, and that thus *Bérénice* must be the most carefully wrought, the most perfect, the most Racinian of the plays of Racine?

It is indeed clear that on this occasion Racine must have tried his hardest to surpass Corneille; but the rest of Michaut's deductions are unwarranted and unreasonable. To surpass Corneille: that was Racine's object, whether he initiated the contest himself or was forced into it by the Princess Henrietta; and success, as Michaut rightly pointed out, was absolutely vital to him. Such being the case, he surely would use any methods that seemed most likely to accomplish his aim, even though they consorted ill with his literary ideals. In this play, above all others, he was attempting to win the plaudits of his immediate audience, not of posterity. It is, of all his plays, the one in which we should least expect to see him trying to exemplify his dramatic theory instead of trying solely to be popular; it is the one in which we should most expect him to compromise with current tastes and fashions, however little he relished them at heart. If he himself chose this subject for competition with Corneille, he did so because he believed it one which he could handle in a way that would please the public better than Corneille could—and not because it was peculiarly suited to illustrate his conception of what a tragedy should be. A *pièce de combat* is not the place where one exhibits ideals and illustrates theories. The public to be courted is little concerned with such things.

It is not likely, then, that *Bérénice* should be the best embodiment of Racine's dramatic creed. That it is the most perfect of his plays is also improbable, *a priori*, because of the haste of its composition and the objective it had. Michaut himself admitted that the subjects of pure passion, such as Racine found in his master Euripides, from which his rivalry with Corneille long diverted him, were better suited to his genius. But the merits of a drama should not be determined by *a priori* arguments of probability, but by an investigation of the drama itself.

"Your true Racinian of the inner circle sets *Bérénice* above all other plays," observes the author of a popular biography of Racine in English.[1] That alleged fact, even if it be a fact, is of no critical importance. People who do not stop at intelligent appreciation of a writer, but form a cult to bow down and worship him, may be expected to be blind to his characteristic defects and perhaps actually relish them, or else they would not make a fetish of him; in consequence they are likely to feel especial admiration for those of his works in which these defects are most prominent. Thus the typical Dante cultist considers the *Paradiso* his masterpiece; scarcely otherwise explainable was Quiller-Couch's amazing opinion that *The Tempest* is a more precious literary treasure than *Hamlet*

[1] Mary Duclaux, *The Life of Racine*, New York, n.d., p. 99.

or *Othello* or *King Lear* (or the *Odyssey* or the *Divine Comedy*); and a Wordsworthian shows marked partiality for such poems as "The Character of the Happy Warrior" and "She was a Phantom of Delight."

Bérénice enjoyed a notable success when first produced, and in modern times Jules Lemaître in France and G. Lytton Strachey in England have praised it highly. The economy of its plot, whereby an entire drama has been made out of such meagre material, and the easy, changing flow of its verse from colloquial simplicity to extreme poetic beauty are justly celebrated. On the other hand, neither the great Sainte-Beuve nor N. M. Bernardin, of later critics one of the best grounded in the dramatic literature of the seventeenth century, rated it among Racine's masterpieces, or even among his plays of the second rank along with *Bajazet* and *Mithridate*; and more recently still, Pierre Brisson and Martin Turnell have expressed a rather poor opinion of it. From the time of its original performance to the present day it has been thought by many to possess too slight a theme—to be, indeed, an elegy in dramatic form rather than a tragedy. Such a view may be justified; but *Bérénice* has faults which are far worse than that. These faults are obscured by its traditional fame as a classic; but a candid examination will discover that, however congenial to that immediate public to which it was addressed, the characters and codes of conduct to be found in it are such as must greatly lessen its permanent appeal and thereby the estimate of its worth.

The effectiveness of the play depends primarily on our admiration and sympathy for its three principal figures, Titus, Berenice, and Antiochus. The tone and treatment throughout make it impossible for us to find artistic satisfaction in contemplating the anguish of these characters with ironical cynicism, as we are meant to contemplate the writhings of the weak or base dramatis personae in some plays of the modern naturalistic school. Berenice herself shows in her words of last farewell how the author intended us to regard the story which he put upon the stage.

> Let us all three
> Unto the whole world an example be
> Of the tenderest and the most unhappy love
> That it can treasure the sad history of.

The love of Titus and Berenice was, traditionally, one of the great loves of all time; as such it was known to Racine, and as such he made it the subject of his drama. Now a truly great love, a love which in its frustration fills us with the sense of human dignity and lofty pathos and piteous waste so that the tragic emotion is aroused, can proceed only from great souls—that is, from essentially noble souls.[2] There is

[2] On this point, Henry Carrington Lancaster expressed (in his *History of French Dramatic Literature in the Seventeenth Century*, Part IV, Baltimore, 1940, p. 74, note) his complete dissent. He then says: "The appeal of Titus and Berenice, like that of Phèdre or of Eriphile, is the greater because their failings bring them nearer to average humanity."

The "Eriphile" of Racine's *Iphigénie* is an effective character in the unlovely part that she plays; but surely very few people would consider her an appealing figure. The heroine of *Phèdre* is indeed appealing, but she is far from being petty or ignoble or contemptible; and it is pettiness and baseness (not imperfection, not the possession of human failings even if they result in great wrongdoing) which are the opposite of nobility or greatness of soul.

As to whether noble feelings and greatness of soul are necessary in the characters *in such a play as Bérénice* if the proper tragic effect is to be had, we know the authoritative opinion of Racine himself, stated in his preface to this drama: "It is not absolutely requisite that there should be blood and dead bodies in a tragedy; it is enough that the action should be great and the characters heroic, that one's emotions should be stirred and that one should feel, throughout, that majestic sadness which constitutes the whole pleasure of tragedy." And as to the question of whether it is possible, or not, for an essentially petty or ignoble person to feel a truly great love, the answer should seem axiomatic. "Do men gather grapes of thorns, or figs of thistles?"

material for very moving, powerful drama in the theme of two such lovers placed in circumstances which compel, on grounds of transcendent importance, their renunciation of each other. But the Titus and Berenice of Racine are emphatically not great and noble souls, and the moral issues which confront them are somewhat nebulous.

A man's choice between the claims of empire, to which his own worth and a nation's preference call him, and of a deeply beloved and deeply loving woman involves, in itself, no easy struggle. Many people to-day, if not in Racine's day, would sympathize with, and commend, a decision in favour of the latter alternative. But the dramatist throws added weight into that scale of the wavering balances. For five long years his Titus has assured Berenice that no considerations of State shall part them, and thus has encouraged her to let her love for him grow without restraint and without fear that his choice will one day be against her; only on his actual accession to the throne, with its sobering sense of responsibility, does his resolve weaken and change. We may well question whether Berenice is not correct in maintaining that a man who has so thoroughly committed himself has no right to draw back. Moreover, it may reasonably be argued that the obligation of Titus to employ his ability to serve the Roman commonwealth is vitiated or even quite cancelled by the fact that he owes that ability entirely to Berenice; it was her love which inspired him to be no longer a profligate; the valour and benevolence of Titus are her creation, and *she* owes no debt to Rome, being a foreign queen—rather is Rome in *her* debt for the services which Titus has already rendered to his country.

It would have been easy for Racine to present more compelling grounds for the lovers' sacrifice. With scant departure from history he could, for example, have brought out the point that if Titus should renounce the imperial diadem it would fall to his brother Domitian, a monster like Nero, whose reign would cause untold suffering.[3] He has not chosen, however, to do anything of the sort. On the contrary, it would seem that he has deliberately made the case for Berenice as strong, and the case for Rome as weak, as possible in order to show that even thus the claims of empire are paramount.[4] His opinion may not be our own, but we can understand it —at least in some measure. It is a corollary of the doctrine of the Divine Right of Kings, which was then current. If a monarch rules by divine right, he is God's chosen one for the task of ruling, and to decline that task would be to flout God's will—would be, in Dante's phrase, to make the great refusal, an act at once cowardly and impious. But the divine call to the throne does not seem to have been looked upon merely as imposing the practical obligation to govern a State; it was viewed as something like a challenge to a man's own self-respect. With kingship was imagined to come a noble ambition to reign, which none but a dastard would disregard. Empire must be yielded only with life. Everything else must give way to it in importance. Again and again Titus speaks of

[3] In reality, Titus might have appointed some other heir, but the author could have assumed, as he does throughout *Britannicus* and as his audience would assume, that the succession was hereditary, just as it was in France. Yet even in that situation, so great a claim had Berenice upon her lover's loyalty that some of us would feel that the right thing for Titus to do was to put the question squarely before the Roman people whether they would accept him with Berenice or take another ruler, and if, in their prejudice against a queen and a foreigner, they chose the latter alternative, the consequences of their choice would justly be on their own heads. But a submission of the matter to the public would probably have resulted in a divided vote and the horrors of civil war.

[4] Titus even puts to himself the question, implying a negative answer:

Do I see the State
Tottering upon the brink of an abyss?
Can nothing save it but this sacrifice?

his *gloire*, which compels him to take the step he finally takes; *gloire* has indeed something of the sense of "duty" or "obligation," but not wholly nor alone that sense; it can better be rendered by "honour" or "glory" or "reputation"—often best by the old phrase "fair fame."

Now, if an author conforms to the moral concepts of his own age, he does reasonably well; but if he is true to moral concepts of permanent validity, he does still better—as he needs must do to achieve anything really great. If the moral concepts implicit in his work are not of permanent validity, his work is to that extent a thing of his own age, not of all time. There are, of course, different degrees of validity and of universality. The self-imposed task of Sophocles' Antigone does not seem to us a duty, but there is nothing evil in it—only nobility and love—and we can imaginatively conceive of her feelings about it and sympathize with them and with her. But the *gloire* of Racine's Titus makes him break his plighted word to a woman who loves him, and it is not so much duty to others as it is a pride which is dependent upon conformity to ideas now obsolete.

To make matters worse, the dramatist shows that Berenice herself cannot understand Titus's viewpoint.[5] She eventually appreciates some of the considerations by which he is constrained, but never his notion of *gloire*; it seems to be a concept which a sovereign fully grasps only after he is invested with sovereignty, and is hence a specimen not of universal morality but of that "private morality" which Lemaître con-

---

[5] Till she learns his decision from his own lips, she believes his *gloire* compels him to cleave to her. She says: "Il ne me quitte point, il y va de sa gloire" ("His honour is at stake; he will not leave me"). Later she says to him: "Hé bien! régnez, cruel; contentez votre gloire" ("Well then, reign, cruel man! Have thy fair fame"), and goes on to speak of his broken oaths to her and of his "injustice." It is hard for her to realize that he still loves her.

demns in the characters of Corneille in his decline and of
all of the other playwrights of the period except Racine.[6]
That such is its nature is proved by the fact that Titus in his
hour of deepest despair thinks of suicide as an honourable
way out of his troubles. If his *gloire* were an intelligible duty
towards his country to discharge the task of ruling it which
has been committed to him, his suicide would be no less a
flight from that duty than his abdication would be; it would
have all the disadvantages of abdication and none of its ad-
vantages; it would make both Rome and Berenice lose him,
instead of only one or the other of them. Plainly, then, either
his *gloire* is an artificial "point of honour," according to
which it would be disgraceful to live without the crown if
one has the opportunity to live with it;[7] or else his impulse
to kill himself is so pusillanimous and so silly that he appears
abject instead of nobly "sympathetic" as his role requires
him to be.

But indeed all three of the major characters in the play are
anything but sympathetic—Titus and Berenice and Antiochus

[6] See his *Jean Racine,* Paris, 1908, pp. 131-134; also his article on Pierre
Corneille in L. Petit de Julleville's *Histoire de la Langue et de la Littéra-
ture française,* Paris, 1897, vol. iv, p. 295.

[7] Titus, however, is sure that he cannot live long when separated from
his beloved. He tells her that he will only briefly (the literal meaning of
the French is "not so many *days*") have to keep a weary reckoning of the
time of their absence from each other, and that soon the tidings of his
death will force her, he hopes, to realize how much he has loved her.
But obviously, if his loss of Berenice will speedily bring him to the grave,
his sacrifice of himself and her will be of no real benefit to Rome. She
interrupts his words with the very sensible question: "Ah, sire, if this be
true, why part us?" Her logic is wasted because it is not the good of his
country which chiefly concerns Titus, but the figure he himself will cut.
His *gloire* requires that, while life is his, he shall cling to the sceptre
which has been placed in his hands; how long he may do so is as heaven
shall dispose, but he can at least
>   Leave an example to posterity
>   Which nowise can be rivaled easily.

alike. When Titus resolves to break with Berenice, he shirks
at first the final interview and leave-taking which common
decency demands of him, and asks Antiochus instead to acquaint her with his decision. He is afraid, he says, that he
will weaken if he sees her again; and the fact is that he has
already shown himself too weak to make the necessary explanations to her when the right opportunity was offered him
to do so. Then Antiochus in his turn comes presently to the
conclusion that he is unwilling to be the bearer of such evil
tidings to the woman he himself has in secret loved long and
hopelessly. He reflects that it will cause him fresh pangs to
behold, in her tears, the evidence of how much she loves
another; so he plans to slip away without discharging the
task entrusted to him or informing Titus that he will not
discharge it, for "plenty of other people will come to apprise
her of her misfortune." When he sees her, he cannot refrain
from saying that he knows she is disappointed in not encountering Titus instead of him; he hints that there are very
distressing things which he might tell her, but he will not
tell them.

> I dread thy grief more than thine anger; fain
> Would I displease thee, rather than cause thee pain.
> Thou wilt approve my choice before this day
> Ends. Farewell, madam.

Berenice, already alarmed by the manner in which Titus
has avoided her, now fears anything and everything. She
protests that to leave her thus in terrified suspense is more
cruel than the ghastliest revelation could be. (This fact should
have been apparent to any one!) She implores Antiochus to
speak out, and finally, with entire justice, threatens him with
her eternal hatred if he will not. When, thus constrained, he
breaks the sad news to her in as kindly a manner as possible,

she refuses to believe him, declares it all an infamous falsehood intended to cause dissension between her and Titus, and
bids him, *even if he has not lied to her*, never to come into
her presence again. The more clearly the situation is com-
prehended, the worse her conduct at this moment is seen
to be. She has always in long years of trial found Antiochus
a man of stainless honour who has put self behind him in his
unwavering devotion to her interests (for she knew nothing
of his design to flee from the task of enlightening her, and
Racine of course did not mean this to be a baseness in him) ;
she does not really believe the outrageous charges which she
flings in his face, but only wants to believe them, as she ad-
mits to Phenice a moment later; she is going instantly to
Titus, she says, and she might at least wait to learn the truth
from his own lips before making those charges. But no :
what she has heard stabs her to the heart; and in blind anger
at her pain, and in blind craving to assuage that pain (even
by self-deception, and by cruelty and injustice to the mortal
who has seemed most loyal to her) she strikes out at the un-
offending messenger—"naturally," says Lemaître, and the
tenderness with which other critics treat her indicates that
they share his opinion. "Naturally," beyond doubt, if by
"naturally" one means in accord with the nature of some
kinds of people. But such an act is not natural to any one
whom it is possible to admire or to sympathize with; for
honourable men and women do not lose all sense of rectitude
and fairness, no matter how dire the shock of anguish that
assails them. Shakespeare's Hermione would not have be-
haved like Berenice, nor would Racine's own Junia or Monime.

The one occasion in the play in which Antiochus appears
genuinely to advantage is when he announces that he is cured
of his love by such treatment, but it soon becomes evident

that he is not. For the rest, he vacillates throughout between hope and despair. Titus, also, frequently wavers more or less in his adherence to what he believes to be the only right course for him; and there is a good deal of conscious pose in the things he says and does. As for Berenice, though she has been told by Antiochus that Titus is compelled to renounce her because of the Roman prejudice against queens and that he is half mad with helpless love and sorrow, she instantly concludes that if he leaves her he cares nothing for her. In Act V she at first refuses to see him again; and though she denies that she wishes heaven to avenge her upon him, she says that his own conscience will do so, and she repeatedly charges him with cruelty, indifference, and bad faith. A really great love tends to feel grief rather than anger if it thinks itself abused. But it also has more confidence in the beloved one than Berenice exhibits in Titus; though utterly unprepared for his decision and quite unable to see the rightness of it or to follow his arguments justifying it, she ought to believe him at least sincere, however tragically mistaken he might be—if hers were the love which is natural to the higher type of man or woman. Even before she hears that she and Titus must part, she is prone to find petty, personal explanations for what she cannot understand in her lover's conduct. When she comes to him in the second act and he shows constraint and perturbation and finally rushes from the room with stammered words about Rome and the Empire, she does not account for his strange behaviour in the obvious way, though Phenice has warned her that hostile public sentiment remains to be reckoned with; she imagines instead that Titus has learned of Antiochus's love for her and that he is jealous —a conventional hypothesis which, as Voltaire pointed out, would be entertained by characters on the stage rather than by people in real life—and comforts herself with the conventional idea that if Titus feels jealously, he loves her.[8]

"Conventional"—that word explains a large share of the blemishes of *Bérénice*. Not only was the view held by Titus of what befits a monarch the one which other French tragedies of the period would lead us to expect him to hold, but those tragedies frequently represent lovers as acting in a manner which to-day would be thought despicable. In the eternal discussions of love and its manifestations with which the salons of the seventeenth century busied themselves, it would seem that any ignoble impulse which might be felt by human beings in the grip of that passion was accepted as natural and therefore as legitimate—almost, even, as necessarily present in any love which is sincere. This point of view came by way of the pastoral and "heroic" romances into the stereotyped, artificial drama of that day, which we call pseudo-classical or "romanesque," and so dominated it that its heroes and heroines are often quite beyond the pale of more enlightened sympathies.

No other play of Racine's after *Andromaque* has so much of the flavour of romanesque tragedy as *Bérénice*. Its very subject is, in essence, the one most frequently met with in the dramas of the two Corneilles, Quinault, and their fel-

---

[8] To some of us, Berenice's rebuke of Antiochus for declaring his love to her may seem another exhibition of the unamiable side of her character. But even to-day, for a man to tell a married woman that he loves her is regarded as an act of very doubtful propriety, and Racine's contemporaries evidently felt much the same way in the case of a woman who was betrothed. By drawing this parallel we can better understand the feelings of both Antiochus and Berenice throughout the first act; and it will be apparent that the Queen's behaviour then was dignified and kindly— indeed, quite fine. Nor need we be surprised that when afterwards, in Act III, Antiochus comes again into her presence, she asks him somewhat sharply if he has not yet departed. She at that time fancies that Titus has been offended by the knowledge of his secret passion and its indiscreet avowal.

lows: a conflict between the claims of love and honour, or of love and the State. Each of the principal characters has a confidant, just as each does in *Andromaque*; nowhere else in Racine is the pairing complete and stiffly conventional. Of the three confidants in *Bérénice*, only Paulinus has the slightest individuality; Phenice is stupid even beyond the wont of confidants when she cannot imagine the reason for Titus's flight from her mistress, though it was she herself who insisted that the laws and feelings of Rome remained a serious obstacle. And in no other play after *Andromaque* is the conventional love-language of gallantry so jarringly in evidence.

There is perhaps a reason for all this, quite beyond the exigencies of a contest with Corneille. More familiar than any other author of his times with the great tragedies of ancient Greece, Racine appears to have been actuated, throughout his career as a dramatist, by two ambitions: to write plays as nearly like those of Sophocles and Euripides as would be possible in seventeenth-century France, and to write plays that would be universally admired. *La Thébaïde* contains few pseudo-classical elements. Save for Creon's love for Antigone, it is a straightforward attempt to put the story of the children of Oedipus as told by Seneca and the Greeks into the form of a French tragedy; its faults are for the most part merely those of inexperience. It enjoyed a very creditable success for a maiden effort, but nothing like the success that Racine had hoped for. Very well, he must have said to himself, if people did not care for what *he* preferred, he would show that he could give them what *they* preferred; and he wrote the wholly romanesque *Alexandre*, which was extremely popular. He had now proved that he could win favour; perhaps he could win it also with something more nearly to his taste. In *Andromaque* he took a long stride towards naturalness and truth, and both city and Court hailed his daring experiment with the wildest delight. He then went still further in the same direction in *Britannicus*; but this tragedy, though it became after a few years one of the most highly esteemed of his works, was a failure when first presented, until it was saved by the praise which Louis XIV bestowed upon it. *Bérénice* was the next product of Racine's pen; it hence comes at a crucial point in his career.

Two courses lay open to him. He could continue resolutely in the vein of *Britannicus*, hoping that he might at length please the public with that sort of play, whether by more fortunate selection of subject or by educating his audiences to a better appreciation of true dramatic values; or he could revert to the manner of *Andromaque*, in which case he would be certain to acquire fresh laurels. He chose the latter alternative. *Bérénice* has little less of pseudo-classical convention than has *Andromaque*,[9] and it scored a triumph. Thereafter, Racine again made progress away from the romanesque and towards a purer form of art, but this time slowly and cautiously, through *Bajazet* and *Mithridate* to an *Iphigénie* which in large part is of genuine classical inspiration, and thence, doubtless reassured by the applause that had greeted each step, to the transcendent achievement of *Phèdre*.

[9] This fact was remarked upon by Bernardin in his edition of *Bajazet* (*Théâtre complet de Jean Racine*, vol. iii, Paris, n. d.) p. 54, note 12: ". . . in *Bérénice* and *Bajazet* Racine went back completely to romanesque tragedy, from which he had seemed to want to break away in *Britannicus*"; but no one, apparently, has hitherto pointed out the reason for it.

CHARACTERS IN THE PLAY

Titus, *Emperor of Rome.*
Berenice, *Queen of Palestine.*
Antiochus, *King of Commagene.*
Paulinus, *confidant of Titus.*
Arsaces, *confidant of Antiochus.*
Phenice, *lady-in-waiting of Berenice.*
Rutilus, *a Roman.*
Retinue of Titus.

The scene is laid in the Imperial Palace at Rome in a room between the apartments of Titus and those of Berenice.

The names "Antiochus," "Paulinus," "Arsaces," and "Phenice" are accented on the second syllable; the others on the first syllable. "Berenice," as a familiar modern name of three syllables, is pronounced thus (as Dante's "Beatrice" usually is in English translations); but in "Phenice" the classical pronunciation of the final "e" is preserved.

BERENICE

ACT I

Enter ANTIOCHUS *and* ARSACES.

ANTIOCHUS.

Let us stop here a moment. I can see,
Arsaces, that such pomp is new to thee.
Oft hath this sumptuous and private room
Held Titus' secrets. Hither he doth come
At whiles, from Court withdrawing, to declare
His love unto the Queen. This doorway here
Leadeth to his apartments, and that one
Yonder to hers. Do thou go and make known
To her that, although loath to vex her, I
Venture to beg a private colloquy.

ARSACES.

Thou, my lord, vex her? Thou, that friend so dear
Who hast watched o'er her with devoted care?
Thou, that Antiochus who didst love her once?
Thou, whom the East among its kings accounts
One of the greatest? What! already is
Her coming marriage with Titus an abyss
Between you?

ANTIOCHUS.

      Go, I say. Seek but to learn
If I may talk with her alone; concern
Thyself no further.

                         [*Exit* ARSACES.

  (*To himself*) Antiochus, art thou e'er
The same? Couldst without trembling say to her,

"I love thee"? Nay, I tremble now. Distraught
Of soul, I fear this moment that I have sought.
Berenice robbed me of hope long ago.
She imposed eternal silence on me. Lo,
Five years I have kept silent. Till this day
'Neath friendship's veil I have hid my love away.
Can I believe that when about to be
The bride of Titus, she will hearken to me
More than in Palestine? He weds her. Do
I choose this hour to speak my love anew?
What will my rash avowal bring me? Since
We must part, let us part without offense!
Let us begone, and naught disclosing, fly
Far from her sight, forget her, or else die. . . .
        What! suffer always pangs to her unknown!
Always shed tears which I must swallow down!
What! even in losing her am I to fear
Her anger? Fair queen, what offends thee here?
Have I now come to ask thee to forego
Empire, or love me? nay, to make thee know
But this: that having long beguiled my heart
With hope some obstacle might rise to thwart
My rival's love, to-day when he hath power
O'er all,—when now draws near your marriage hour,—
A sad example of long constancy
After five years of love and vain hope, I
Go forth, still true, when I may hope no further.
Instead of anger, she might give me, rather,
Her pity. In any case, speak out I shall.
I have restrained myself enough, withal.
What can a hopeless lover dread, alas,
Who is resolved to see no more her face?

                              [*Re-enter* ARSACES.

Arsaces, may we enter?

ARSACES.

Sir, I have seen,
Though it was hard to gain her sight, the Queen;
I had to pierce such throngs for ever new
Of folk whom her approaching grandeur drew
To worship at her feet. After eight days
Of strict seclusion, Titus finally stays
His weeping for Vespasian, his sire;
This lover turns again to love's desire;
And if I am to heed Court-gossip, 'tis
Likely, my lord, the happy Berenice
Ere nightfall will exchange the name of Queen
For that of Empress.

ANTIOCHUS.

Ah me!

ARSACES.

What! Herein
Findest thou something to displease thee?

ANTIOCHUS.

So
I cannot, then, have speech with her with no
Witnesses.

ARSACES.

Thou shalt see her, sire. 'Tis known
To Berenice thou wouldst talk with her alone
And unattended. She vouchsafed a glance
To me which said that what thou beggest she grants;
And doubtless she awaits a favourable
Time to escape the courtiers' throngs.

ANTIOCHUS.

'Tis well.
But hast thou not neglected any of those
Important things thou'rt charged with?

ARSACES.

My lord knows
My promptness to obey. Ships, speedily
Fitted out, even now at Ostia lie,
Ready at any hour to leave the port,
Awaiting only thy command to start.
But who is it whom thou art sending home
To Commagene?

ANTIOCHUS.

The hour will have come
At which to go, when I have seen the Queen,
Arsaces.

ARSACES.

Who will go?

ANTIOCHUS.

I.

ARSACES.

Thou, sir?

ANTIOCHUS.

When
I leave the palace, I leave Rome, and I
Leave it for ever.

ARSACES.

I am certainly
Surprised to hear this, sire, and rightly so.

After Queen Berenice so long ago
Took thee, sire, from the midst of thy domain,—
After she hath been able to detain
Thee for three years in Rome,—and now when she,
Sure of her triumph, wishes thee to see
Her splendid nuptials, and when in his love
Titus, about to be the husband of
This queen, prepares for her such pomp and state
That in their glory thou wilt participate . . .

ANTIOCHUS.

Let her enjoy, Arsaces, her glad lot,
And end thy talk thereof; it likes me not.

ARSACES.

I understand now, sire. These honours make
The Queen forget thy goodness for her sake.
Hate comes when friendship proveth faithless.

ANTIOCHUS.

Nay.
I never hated her less than to-day.

ARSACES.

What, then? Doth the new emperor, given o'er
To thoughts of greatness, know thee now no more?
Or doth some hint of coldness yet to come
Cause thee to shun his presence far from Rome?

ANTIOCHUS.

Titus hath shown towards me a friend's true heart.
Wrongly would I complain.

ARSACES.

Then why depart?
What caprice makes thee thine own enemy?

Heaven enthrones a prince who loveth thee,—
A prince who formerly hath seen thee fight,—
Seen thee seek death and glory, following right
Behind him, who did by thine aid reduce
To wear his yoke at last the rebel Jews.
    He recollects that famous, direful day
Whereon it was decided in which way
The long and doubtful siege would end. The foe,
Safe on their triple walls and feeling no
Anxiety, watched our vain assaults. We plied
The battering-ram to no avail outside.
Thou, thou alone, sire, didst then seize upon
A ladder, and unto those ramparts, won
Thus by thy valour, bring death. On thine own
That same day's light, however, almost shone.
Titus embraced thee as thou layest, it seemed,
Dead in mine arms; and the whole army deemed
That thou wert dead, and in their victory wept.
    This is the time, sire, when thou shouldst accept
Rewards for all the blood men saw thee shed.
If, longing to behold thy realm instead,
Thou'dst live no longer where thou dost not reign,
Must the Euphrates see thee come again
Thither with no increase of honours? Wait
To go till Caesar sends thee home in state,
Laden with gifts and titles Rome confers
To make kings greater who are friends of hers.
Can nothing change thy mind, my lord? . . . Wilt thou
Answer naught?

ANTIOCHUS.

    What wouldst have me say? I now
Await a moment's speech with Berenice.

ARSACES.

And then, my lord?

ANTIOCHUS.

Her destiny it is
That will decide mine own.

ARSACES.

How?

ANTIOCHUS.

I but wait
For her to tell me of her marriage. Then, straight,
If what I hear on all sides is repeated
By her,—if truly she is to be seated
Upon the Caesars' throne,—if Titus so
Hath said, and he will wed her,—I shall go.

ARSACES.

But what doth make this marriage a thing 'tis best
Thou shouldst not see?

ANTIOCHUS.

Thou shalt be told the rest
When we are gone.

ARSACES.

In what confusion sore
Thou leavest my mind!

ANTIOCHUS.

The Queen is here. No more.
Farewell. Do all that I have bidden thee do.
[*Exit* ARSACES. *Enter* BERENICE *and* PHENICE.

BERENICE.

At last, from the forced joy of all the new
Friends my good fortune hath made mine, I can
Escape! I flee their tedious and vain
Show of respect, to find thee here, who art
A friend that speaketh to me from his heart.
'Tis true that I e'en now was blaming thee
In just impatience for thy neglect of me.
"What!" I said, "does Antiochus, whose care
For me both Europe and Asia everywhere
Have witnessed, he whom I have always seen,
Constant through all my trials, follow me in
My fate's vicissitudes unfalteringly,—
To-day when heaven appears to promise me
An honour I would share with him as well,
Does he, this same Antiochus, conceal
Himself from me and leave me for so long
Thus at the mercy of these strangers' throng?

ANTIOCHUS.

Is it, then, true, as thy words seem to prove,
Madam, that marriage will now crown your love?

BERENICE.

Sir, I would fain confess to thee my fears.
These last few days have seen me shed some tears.
The mourning that was on the Court imposed
So long by Titus, kept him, thus engrossed,
From even all secret show of love. No more
Would he reveal that ardour which, before,
He had displayed when he had spent his days
Hanging upon my sight. Silent always
Now, burdened by cares, with tearful eyes,

He ever left me with but farewell sighs.
Judge how I must have suffered, I, whose own
Fondness for him is for himself alone,
As I have often told thee,—I, who would
Have cherished not his greatness but the good
In him and sought only his heart.

ANTIOCHUS.

Hath he
Resumed his former loving ways with thee?

BERENICE.

Thou wert a witness of the past night, when
The Senate, carrying out his pious plan,
Enrolled his father as a deity.
With filial duty satisfied thereby,
He can turn from it, and give thought to her
He loves; and at this very moment, sir,
Though not a word to me hereof he said,
He with the Senate meeteth, which he bade
Assemble. There the bounds he doth extend
Of Palestine, and join Arabia and
All Syria thereto; and if I may
Put faith in what his friends are saying to-day
And in the countless oaths he swore ere this
To me, he wishes to crown Berenice
Queen of so many lands that to no few
Titles he can add that of empress, too.
He will himself come hither soon to tell
Me this.

ANTIOCHUS.

And I have come to say farewell
To thee for ever.

BERENICE.

What is this thou sayst?
Ah heaven! Farewell? What meanest thou? Sore dis-
  tressed,
Pale, and confused, thou seemest, Prince.

ANTIOCHUS.

          I must go—
Must leave thee, madam.

BERENICE.

      What! may I not know
The reason . . .

ANTIOCHUS (*to himself*).

    Better had I gone, and not
Seen her again.

BERENICE.

    What fearest thou? Speak out!
Too long thy silence leaves me in suspense.
What secret lies behind thy going hence?

ANTIOCHUS.

Forget not that I am obeying thee,
And that for the last time thou hearest me.
If ever thou rememberest—at this height
Thou hast attained of glory and of might—
Thy birthplace, madam, thou wilt recall that there
My heart was pierced by the first shafts that e'er
Sped from thine eyes. I fell in love with thee.
I gained thy brother Agrippa's preference. He
Spoke unto thee in my behalf. Perchance
Thou then wouldst have received without offence
My homage. But it was in vain I strove,

For Titus came, saw thee, and won thy love.
Dazzling thy sight, he like a man did come
Who carried in his hands the wrath of Rome.
Judea quailed, and poor Antiochus
Could deem himself his earliest victim, thus.
Soon thy lips bade me urge no more my suit;
But long I did thy stern decree dispute,
And still in place of words I made mine eyes
Speak for me. Everywhere my tears and sighs
Followed thee, until thy severity
At last prevailed and thou requiredst of me
Silence, on pain of exile from thy sight.
I had to promise it, and even to plight
My word thereto with oaths; but since I dare
Finally my soul's real feelings to declare,
Know this, that when thou wrongly didst extort
That pledge from me, I swore within my heart
That I would love thee always, without cease.

BERENICE.

Alas! What tellest thou me?

ANTIOCHUS.

        I held my peace
For five years, madam, and I shall hold it far
Longer henceforth. Unto the field of war
I followed my triumphant rival's spears.
I hoped to shed my blood after my tears,
Or else at least to make thee hear my name—
Since me thou wouldst not hear—borne by the fame
Of countless deeds to thee. Heaven seemed disposed
To end my misery. For my supposed
Death thou didst mourn—alas, I did not die!
O dangers faced in vain! How foiled was I!

Titus outdid what my despair could do.
I must accord his valour its just due.
Though destined emperor of the world was he,—
Though called mankind's delight, though loved by thee,—
He seemed to be a mark for every blow,
While his unhappy rival was to go
(Though hopeless, scorned, tired of life) only where
He led. I see thou lendest an eager ear
Unto my praise of him, and thou dost take
Less umbrage, hearing these words. For Titus' sake
Thou pardonest the others, all too well
Hearkening to the story that I tell
Though grim the memories that around it throng.
    After a siege as cruel as it was long,
He overcame the rebels and subdued
All whom flames, famine, and intestine feud
Had spared of them, bleeding and pale and wild
Of eye, and left their walls in ruins piled.
Ye came to Rome, then. I remained behind.
How in that lonely Eastern land I pined!
Long I abode in Caesarea, to roam
In those dear places where I first had come
To love thee. All through thy forlorn domain
I cried aloud for thee and in my pain
Sought where thy feet had trod. Conquered at last
By grief, I in despair my steps addressed
To Italy, where Fate reserved for me
Her latest blow. Titus, as soon as he
Embraced me, brought me unto thee. A veil
Of friendship deceived him and thee as well;
And I, who loved thee, was the confidant
Of your love. But some hope was always blent
With my despondency and beguiled me still.

Rome and Vespasian both opposed your will;
And Titus, after many victories,
Might have to yield. But lo, Vespasian is
No more, and Titus now is master. Why
Did I not flee at once, then? Because I
Wished to observe for a few days what turn
The new reign was to take. My fate, I learn
Now, is assured. Thy triumph is at hand.
Without me, enough others will attend
All the festivities and come to add
To thine own ecstasies their raptures glad.
I, who could bring thee only tears,—who prove
Always the victim of a fruitless love,—
I go forth, happy in my misery
That I could tell the story blamelessly
Of all my woes to thee who wert their cause,
More in love with thee than I ever was.

BERENICE.

Sir, I would not have thought that on the day
That is to join my destiny for ay
With Caesar's any man could unreproved
Come tell me to my face that I am loved
By him. Thou in my silence hast a token
Of my true friendship. All thy words just spoken
Wrongly to me I for its sake forget.
I did not stop their utterance. With regret,
Moreover, do I hear thee say good-bye.
Heaven knows that midst my many honours I
Yearned for no eyes but thine to see my bliss.
Like every one, I prized thy nobleness.
Titus loved thee, and thou admiredst him;
And oft 'twas very sweet to me to seem

To be with Titus when I was with thee,
His other self.

ANTIOCHUS.

Hence, all too late, I flee.
I flee such converse, in which I can claim
No thoughts of thine,—flee Titus,—flee a name
That drives me mad, that through the livelong day
Is ever on thy lips,—flee (shall I say
Yet more?) thine absent eyes, whose glance doth fall
Upon me without seeing me at all.
Farewell. I go, thine image in my breast,
To wait for death, still loving thee to the last.
But think not that in blind grief I shall go,
Proclaiming unto all the world my woe.
News of that death I long for in my pain
Alone will tell thee that I lived till then.
Farewell.

[*Exit* ANTIOCHUS.

PHENICE.

Oh, how I pity him! Such great
Constancy, madam, deserved a happier fate.
Dost *thou* not pity him?

BERENICE.

His sudden flight
Leaves me a secret sorrow, I admit.

PHENICE.

I would have kept him here.

BERENICE.

Keep him here? I?
Rather should I lose even all memory

Of him. Wouldst thou have me encourage, then,
His mad love?

PHENICE.

Titus hath not yet made plain
What he intends to do. With jealous eye
Rome sees thee here. The inflexibility
Of her stern laws doth fill my heart with dread.
Only with Romans do the Romans wed.
They hate all monarchs, madam, and thou art one.

BERENICE.

The time when I could tremble is now gone,
Phenice. Titus loves me, and all power
Is his. He needeth but to speak, naught more,
And he will see the Senate come to pay
Homage to me, the people crown straightway
With flowers his statues. Have thine eyes beheld
The splendour of last night? Were they not filled
With its great sights: the mighty funeral pyre,
The torches, lighting up the dark with fire,—
The eagles, fasces, soldiers, populace,—
Kings, consuls, senators who flock apace,
All, sharing in my lover's radiance bright,—
The gold and purple, richer in that light
His glory sheds,—those laurels that, to bear
Witness unto his victories, he doth wear,—
The eyes of visitors from every land
Centering their eager gaze upon him, and
His noble bearing and his gracious mien?
Ah, with what reverence and love, within
Their hearts, all pledge to him their loyalty!
Can any see him and not think, like me,
That howsoe'er obscure had been the birth

Which Fate assigned him, surely the whole earth,
Seeing him, would have known him for its lord?
By these fond memories I am overpowered,
Phenice. But all Rome doth even now
Offer to heaven for Titus many a vow
And by her sacrifices celebrate
His reign's beginning. Wherefore should we wait
Here longer? Let us go, to add our prayer
For his success to heaven, which in its care
Guards him. Then shall I, without more delay,
Seek him unsummoned, and when with him say
All that affection, long repressed, inspires
In hearts made one by love and like desires.

                                   [*Exeunt.*

ACT II

Titus, Paulinus, and attendants are discovered.

Titus.

Hath any one yet gone for me unto
The King of Commagene? Doth he know
That I await him?

Paulinus.

        I went to the Queen.
At her apartments he had lately been,
But had gone thence when I arrived there, sire.
I left word telling him of thy desire.

Titus.

'Tis well. And what now is Queen Berenice
Doing?

Paulinus.

      The Queen knows of thy bounteousness
To her, and at this very moment she
Lifts prayers to heaven for thy prosperity.
To do so, she was going forth.

Titus.

              The kind
Princess! Alas!

Paulinus.

       What saddeneth thy mind
For her sake? Almost the entire East, sir,
Will bow beneath her sway. Thou pitiest her?

Titus.

Paulinus, let us be left here alone.

                [Exeunt all but Titus *and* Paulinus.

The course that I have chosen is still unknown
To Rome, Paulinus, which now waits to see
What the Queen's destiny indeed will be.
The secrets of her heart and mine have grown
To be the common talk of every one.
The time has come to make my purpose clear.
What says the public voice—what dost thou hear
Said—of the Queen and me?

PAULINUS.

All men accord
Thy virtues and her beauty praise, my lord.

TITUS.

What do they say of my consuming love?
What is the outcome they expect thereof?

PAULINUS.

Thou art supreme. Love or renounce thy love,
The Court, whate'er thou doest, will approve.

TITUS.

And I have seen this false Court, at all times
Eager to please its lord, commend the crimes
Of Nero, even the most horrible,
And, kneeling, reverence his frenzy's will.
I nowise take for judge a servile Court;
For nobler plaudits I will play my part,
And, to no flatterers' voices paying heed,
Would hear all hearts speak through thy lips instead.
Paulinus, thou hast promised me I shall.
Respect and dread let no complaints at all
Reach me. That I may better hear and see,
I have asked ears and eyes, dear friend, of thee.
I even made their gift my friendship's price,

That I my people's feelings in this wise
Should learn, and truth should pierce through flattery
Unto me, thanks to thy sincerity.
Speak, then! What hope can Berenice possess?
Will Rome be kind to her or merciless?
Must I believe that on the Caesars' throne
This lovely queen could e'er irk any one?

PAULINUS.

Doubt not that Rome—through reason, caprice, or
    both—
To have her made its empress would be loath.
All know her charms; such beauty and such grace,
Thou thinkest, should rule o'er the whole human race.
She hath a Roman woman's heart, 'tis e'en
Said; she hath countless virtues; but a queen
She is, my lord. Rome, with a law which could
Be changed by none, permits no alien blood
To mix with hers, and doth not recognize
The issue of a union which defies
Her precepts. Also, Rome, in banishing
Her kings, linked with the very name of king,
So noble and so sacred theretofore,
A hate so terrible for evermore
That, though she is loyal and obedient
Unto her emperors, this virulent
Hate, the last relic of her pride, lives on
In every heart, when liberty is gone.
Julius, the first who ruled by force of arms
And hushed the voice of Law mid war's alarums,
Loved Cleopatra ardently, but repressed
His love and left her grieving in the East
Alone. Mark Antony, who loved her to

Idolatry, forgetting what was due
Honour and country in her fond embrace,
Never dared call her "wife." Rome went, no less,
To seek him on his siren's knees, nor stayed
Her vengeful fury until both were dead—
He and his mistress, too. Since then, my lord,
Caligula and Nero, those abhorred
Monsters whose names I speak here with regret,
Who, human but in form, trod 'neath their feet
All of the laws of Rome save this alone,
Feared this sole law; and ne'er did either one
Before our faces light the torch for some
Marriage that would be odious to Rome.

    Thou badest me speak frankly. We have seen
Felix, the freedman Pallas' brother, when
He with the brand of Claudius still was scarred,
Become the husband of two queens, my lord;
And—to withhold naught, as thou saidst I should—
These two queens were of Berenice's blood.
Dost think 'twould not shock Rome wert thou to wed
A queen and place her in our Caesars' bed,
When in the East a slave freed from our chains
Had made his way thus to the bed of queens?
I know not if ere this day's end hath come,
The Senate will not, in the name of Rome,
All that which I have said to thee repeat,
And the whole city, falling at thy feet,
Will not like them beg thee to make a choice
Worthy of Rome and thee, as with one voice.
Sire, thou hast time to weigh well thy response.

TITUS.

Ah! what a love they wish me to renounce!

PAULINUS.

That love is great, I must indeed confess.

TITUS.

Greater a thousand times than thou canst guess,
Paulinus. 'Tis my very life to see
Her face each day, love her, make her love me.
Yet more—from thee I keep no secrets—I
Have for her sake oft thanked the gods on high
For having chosen my father when he was
In Idumea and rallied to his cause
The army and the East, and having then
Turned the hearts to him of all other men
And 'neath his peaceful sway brought bleeding Rome.
I even have coveted my father's throne,
Paulinus—I, who would have given my life
A hundred times to make his longer if
Fate had not proved so merciless and had
Been willing that way to extend the thread
Of his existence—such my hope (how ill
A lover knoweth what is in truth his will)
To share with Berenice that throne, repay
Thus her great love and loyalty some day,
And see the whole world at her feet then fall
Like me. Despite her loveliness and all
My love, Paulinus, after vow on vow
Attested by my tears, when I can now
Crown her, when more than e'er before do I
Adore her now, and when the marriage tie
Can join our fortunes and discharge at last
The oaths I swore in all these five years past,
I am about . . . Gods! can I say it?

PAULINUS.

What,

My lord?

TITUS.

Paulinus, I am now about
To part from her eternally. My heart
Shall fail not in this hour. We must part.
If I have made thee speak,—if I desired
To hear thee,—'twas that I might be inspired
Secretly by thee to o'ercome so strong
A love, unwilling to be silenced. Long
Did Berenice keep in doubt my victory;
And if I cleave to honour finally,
Know that to conquer love meant inward fray
From which my heart will bleed for many a day.
　　I loved; I breathed my vows in peace unmarred.
Another had the cares of empire. Lord
Of mine own fate and free to feed love's fires,
I took no thought save of mine own desires.
But scarcely was my father to the skies
Called home than, when my hand had closed his eyes,
Of my fond error I was disabused;
I felt the charge that on me was imposed;
I knew that, far from being my love's thrall,
I must, Paulinus, soon renounce it all,
And that the gods' choice, thwarting my heart's will,
Gave to the world the life-days left me still.
To-day Rome waits to see what will occur.
What shame for me, how ominous for her,
If my first act should all her claims disown
To base my happiness on her laws o'erthrown!
　　Resolved to make this cruel sacrifice,

I would prepare for it poor Berenice.
But how begin? I in the last eight days,
When with her, have tried twenty times to raise
The subject; but each time, at the first word,
My tongue froze in my mouth. Thus she hath heard
Naught. I still hoped my grief, and being so
Confused, would warn her of our coming woe,
But, unsuspecting, she beheld my fears
And with her dear hand sought to dry my tears,
Nor dreamed that anything could be less true
Than that a love would end which was her due.
Finally, this morning I have steeled my heart.
I needs must see her, tell her we must part.
I now await Antiochus, to consign
This treasure to his charge, that can be mine
No more. I want him to conduct her home
Unto her eastern lands. To-morrow Rome
Will see the Queen depart with him. She soon
Will learn the truth from me; for I anon
Shall speak with her for the last time.

PAULINUS.

Naught less

Did I expect from one whose eagerness
For fair fame hath brought victory everywhere.
Captive Judea's still-smoking ramparts bear
Eternal witness to that noble thirst
And have assured me from the very first
That thy heroic soul would not desire
To undo all thou hast accomplished, sire,
And that the conqueror of so many nations
Sooner or later would subdue his passions.

TITUS.

Ah me! What cruel things doth this fair fame
Require by virtue of its own fair name!
How much more fair 'twould seem to my sad gaze
If death were all that it doth bid me face!
What do I say? my very love for it
Berenice first within my bosom lit.
Thou knowest 'tis true. Not always did there shine
Round me the lustre of renown now mine.
Brought up in Nero's court, I went astray
Through bad example, following the way,
In youth, of pleasure down its easy slope.
Then I met Berenice. What will the hope
To please her whom one loves, and win her who
Hath won his heart, not cause a man to do?
I spared not mine own blood, and all gave way
Before my sword. Triumphant, I one day
Returned. But blood and tears were not enough
For me to be found worthy of her love.
I undertook to assuage the wretchedness
Of the unfortunate. In every place
My gifts were lavished. I grew happy then,
And happier than thou canst imagine when
I could appear before her and she was
Swayed by the good I did, which pled my cause.
I owe her all; and what is her reward,
Paulinus, now? I am to disregard
That debt and say to her who made me o'er
In honour's mould: "Depart; see me no more."

PAULINUS.

What, sire! When grants which thou dost on her shower
To the Euphrates will extend her power,—

When so great honours are conferred on her
That they amaze the Senate,—canst thou fear
Thou wilt be thought an ingrate? Berenice
Will rule a hundred peoples whom ere this
She had not ruled.

TITUS.

Mere trifles to beguile
A grief so terrible which she will feel!
Knowing her, I well know—have always known—
Her heart hath ne'er desired aught save mine own.
I loved her, won her love. Since that glad day
(Or "fatal" one, alas! ought I to say?)
Having no aim in loving me but love,
In Rome an alien, in the Court thereof
A stranger, she hath lived, claiming no right
Except that at some certain hour she might
See me, Paulinus, and for that might wait.
And if I sometimes am a little late,—
If at the expected moment aught defers
My coming,—I then find her bathed in tears
And it is long ere I can dry her eyes.
    I am, in short, bound by love's strongest ties:
Tender reproaches, ever fresh delight,
Unstudied charms, fears naught could put to flight,
Her beauty, the high soul and goodness in her.
For five whole years I every day have seen her
Yet feel each time I never have before.
Come, dear Paulinus, let us dwell no more
Upon all this. The more I think and speak
Of it, the more I feel myself grow weak
In my cruel resolution. What a blow,
Ye gods, my news will deal her! Yes, let us go.

I know my duty. To do it, is my task.
Whether I can and live, I do not ask.

[*Enter* RUTILUS.

RUTILUS.

Berenice, sire, hath come to speak with thee.

TITUS.

Ah heaven! Paulinus!

PAULINUS.

What! thus immediately
Thou seekest to draw back? Forget not thou
The brave decision which thou madest. Now,
My lord, 'tis time to act.

TITUS.

So be it; we
Shall see her. Let her enter.

[*Exit* RUTILUS. *Enter* BERENICE *and* PHENICE.

BERENICE.

Do not be
Offended if in my heart's ardour I
Wrongly intrude upon thy privacy.
When all thy Court gathers around me, stirred
By tidings of the gifts thou hast conferred
On me, sire, is it right that I alone
Must in that hour bide voiceless, having known
Nothing myself thereof? My lord—to be
Frank, for I know that touching thee and me
Thou keepest no secrets from this loyal friend—
Naught stayeth thee, thy mourning now hath end,
And yet thou seekest me not, though thou'rt thine own

Master! Thou offerest me another crown,
I have been told; but this thou didst not say
To me thyself. Let us have less display
Of love and less constraint. Canst thou not show
Thy love except before the Senate? Oh,
Titus,—for love no longer will use here
Those titles prompted by respect and fear—
What is the care which on thy love so weighs
That it can give me only provinces?
Since when hast thou believed that I would prize
Greatness? Love's words from thee, love's looks and
      sighs,
Are all the ambition of my heart, love-fraught.
Be with me oftener, and give me naught.
Are all thine hours spent in the Empire's care?
Hast thou, after eight days, nothing whate'er
To tell me? How one word would reassure
My ever-boding spirit! But was not your
Talk of me when I unexpectedly
Came hither? In your private speech was I
Nowise involved, my lord? Or was I not
At the very least, sire, present in thy thought?

Titus.

Ne'er doubt it, madam; and I call the skies
To witness that thine image haunts mine eyes.
Nor time nor absence—this I swear before thee—
Could rob thee of my heart, which doth adore thee.

Berenice.

How now! Thou swearest to me eternal love
And swearest it thus coldly? Wherefore of
Heaven wouldst thou thus invoke the power? Must
Thou needs take oaths to conquer my distrust?

I never meant to charge thee with a lie.
I will believe thee on thy heart's first sigh.

TITUS.

Madam . . .

BERENICE.

Yes, sire? . . . What now! thou answerest naught;
Thou turnest away thine eyes and seemest distraught.
Canst thou but show to me a face of woe?
Over thy father's death dost thou brood so
Without cessation? Can naught charm from thee
This gnawing sorrow?

TITUS.

Would to heaven—ah me!—
My father had not died, were living yet!
How happy I would be!

BERENICE.

Sir, such regret
Is natural to thy filial piety.
But thou hast now honoured his memory
With tears enough. Thou also owest some care
To Rome and to thy glory. I do not dare
To urge mine own claims. Berenice formerly
Could have consoled thee, and more joyfully
Thou wouldst have heard her. I have for thy sake
Been pierced with many sorrows, but thou couldst make
My weeping cease with one word. Thou dost mourn
A father—ah, beside what I have borne
(That memory makes me shudder even yet)
How small a trial is thine! *I* faced the threat
Of being torn from all that I adore,—

I, whose dire anguish and confusion sore
Thou knowest when leaving me for the least while,—
I, who would die the day which brought exile
To me from thee . . .

TITUS.

Alas! what dost thou say,
Madam? Why choose this time? Stop, stop, I pray!
This love o'erwhelmeth an ungrateful man.

BERENICE.

Ungrateful, sire? Canst thou be that? And can
I weary thee, then, with my tenderness?

TITUS.

Nay, madam, since the truth I must confess,
My heart hath never burned more with love's fires.
But . . .

BERENICE.

Yes? Go on.

TITUS.

Ah me!

BERENICE.

Speak!

TITUS.

Rome . . . Th' Em-
pire's . . .

BERENICE.

Yes?

TITUS.

Come, Paulinus. I can tell her naught.
[*Exeunt* TITUS *and* PAULINUS.

BERENICE.

How now! He leaves me without saying aught?
Alas, Phenice! what a meeting—this!
What have I done? What would he? And why is
He mute?

PHENICE.

Like thee, the more I seek the cause
Hereof, the further I am at a loss.
Does nothing come into thy memory,
Madam, that might have moved his heart 'gainst thee?
Look back. Consider.

BERENICE.

Thou canst take my word
For it: I think of all that hath occurred
From the first day I saw him to this same
Sad day, and see that I deserve no blame
Unless for too much love. Thou heardest what
We said just now. Thou must hide from me naught;
Speak out. Did I say anything which could
Displease him? I, perhaps, more than I should—
How do I know?—have scorned his gifts to me
Or censured him for grieving. Can it be,
He dreads the wrath of Rome? He fears perchance—
Yes, fears—to wed a queen, to give offense
So greatly. Alas me! if that were true . . .
Nay, nay, he hath assured my love anew
A hundred times against Rome's cruel laws;
A hundred times . . . Would he would make the cause
Of so unkind a silence clear to me!
I cannot breathe in this uncertainty.
Phenice, could I live if I should deem
He tires of me or I offended him?

Let us, then, follow him . . .
                    But I believe,
Now when I think of it, that I perceive
The reason why he is disturbed in mind,
Phenice. He hath somehow come to find
Out what took place of late. Antiochus'
Love for me well may be what moves him thus.
He now awaiteth, I was told, the King
Of Commagene. In no other thing
Need we, then, seek the source of my distress.
Doubtless the throes which he could not repress
And which have filled my heart with such alarm
Spring from suspicions easy to disarm.
    But of rejecting such a lover I
Will make no boast, dear Titus. Would to high
Heaven that without dishonour unto thee
A mightier one could test my loyalty,
Laying before my feet more realms than thou,—
That he with countless crowns could crown my brow
And thou couldst give me nothing but thy love!
Then to thee in thy triumph I could prove
How precious is thy heart in my fond sight.
    Phenice, come; one word can set all right.
Let us take courage; Titus loves me still.
I deemed that I was the most miserable
Of mortals much too quickly. Yes, if he
Is jealous, he is still in love with me.
                                    [*Exeunt.*

ACT III

Titus.

What, Prince? Thou wert about to leave? What might
So speed thy sudden departure—nay, thy flight?
Wouldst thou have hidden all, till thou didst go
From me? Dost quit this palace as a foe?
What will the Court, Rome, the whole Empire say?
And, as thy friend, what can I *not* say? Pray,
Wherein have I offended? In all things
Hast thou been treated like the other kings?
My heart was thine while yet my sire did live,
But that was the sole gift I then could give;
And now, when like my heart my hand is free,
Thou fleest the favours that awaited thee?
Deemest thou that my past fortunes I forget
And fix my thoughts upon my high estate
While all my friends seem in them most remote,
Strangers to me now that I need them not?
Prince, thou who from my sight wouldst fain have gone,
I need thee more than I have ever done.

Antiochus.

Me?

Titus.

Thee.

Antiochus.

Alas! From one so miserable
What canst thou look for, sire, except good will?

Titus.

Prince, I forget not that my victory

Owed half its greatness to thy bravery;
That Rome hath seen, amid her lengthy trains
Of captives, more than one who wore thy chains;
And that she in the Capitol still views
The spoils thy hand hath taken from the Jews.
Now I expect of thee no warlike deeds;
To borrow but thy voice, will serve my needs.
I know that Berenice owes much to thee
For all thy long care, that she feeleth she
Hath in thee a true friend, and that in Rome
She sees and listens unto thee alone.
Thou sharest with us one heart and one soul.
Now, in the name of such a beautiful
And loyal friendship, use the influence
Which thou hast over her, I beg thee, Prince.
See her for me.

ANTIOCHUS.

Appear before her? I?
I have for ever bidden her good-bye.

TITUS.

For me, thou needs must speak with her again.

ANTIOCHUS.

Plead thine own cause with her, my lord. The Queen
Adores thee. Wherefore shouldst thou at this hour
Deny thyself the bliss 'twould be to pour
Thy heart out to her? She impatiently
Awaits thee, sire, and I will guarantee,
With my last words, she will thy wish obey.
She herself told me that thou wert to-day
Ready to wed her and wouldst come to woo her.

TITUS.

How happy I would be if I might do her
This homage! 'Twould be sweet indeed to vow
My love to her; its ardour fain would now
Burst forth. Yet now, this very day, Prince, I
Must leave her.

ANTIOCHUS.

Leave her? Thou?

TITUS.

      My destiny
It is. For her and Titus, marriage can
No more be thought of. That dear hope in vain
I cherished. To-morrow she must leave the city
With thee.

ANTIOCHUS.

What do I hear? Ah heaven!

TITUS.

       Pity
My greatness, which afflicts me. I decree,
As the world's master, what its fate shall be;
I can make kings, and kings can I depose;
Yet of mine own heart I cannot dispose.
Ever the foe of sovereigns, Rome would scorn
E'en one so fair, if in the purple born.
The lustre of a crown and being descended
From many royal sires hath sore offended
All eyes and brought dishonour on my love.
Anywhere else, my heart is free to rove,
Fearing no murmurers, and kindle to flame
For one of base condition; without shame
Rome would accept even the lowliest

Of the fair daughters nurtured at her breast
As empress, if I chose her for my bride.
Julius himself could not resist that tide
Which sweeps me on. Unless the people see
The Queen go hence to-morrow, straightway she
Will hear them come to me with frenzied cries,
Demanding that she go, before her eyes.
Let us from such disgrace protect our names,
And since we must yield, yield to honour's claims.
My eight days' silence and my face of woe
Will have prepared her for this fatal blow;
And at this moment, restless and o'erwrought,
She fain would have me tell her all my thought.
Soothe a distracted lover's bitter pain.
Spare me th' enlightning of her. Go; explain
Wherefore I have been mute, what is my plight,
And, above all, that I must shun her sight.
Alone behold her tears and my own tears.
Bear her my last farewell, and bring me hers.
Let us both flee, flee from a meeting sure
To be beyond our power to endure.

    Oh, if the hope that she will reign—will live—
Within my soul will cause her not to grieve
So sorely, Prince, in her misfortune, swear
To her that, ever faithful, I shall bear—
With broken heart, an exile more than she—
Unto the very tomb the name with me
Of being her lover. One long banishment
My reign will be, if heaven, not content
With tearing from me my intended wife,
Would fain afflict me with a lengthy life.

    Thou, Prince, whom friendship alone binds to her,
Forsake her not in her affliction, e'er.

Let the East see thee bring her to her home.
Let her in triumph, not flight, appear to come.
Let such true friendship have eternal ties,
And keep me always in your memories.

    To make your kingdoms nearer neighbours, each
Alike shall even to the Euphrates reach.
I know the Senate holds you in such high
Esteem that with one voice 'twill ratify
My gifts to both. Cilicia unto
Thy Commagene do I add.
                    Adieu.
Never desert my princess, my soul's queen,
Who my heart's one desire hath ever been,—
Whom I shall love until my life's last sigh.

                             [*Exit* TITUS.

ARSACES.

So heaven will do thee justice finally.
Thou wilt go hence, sire, but with Berenice.
Thou wilt not have to bear her off; she is
To be consigned to thee.

ANTIOCHUS.

                Give me some chance
To catch my breath. This change is so immense,
Arsaces, my amazement so extreme.
Titus doth yield to me what is to him
All life! Gods! can I credit what I heard?
And if so, should my heart thereat be stirred
To joy?

ARSACES.

          But what must I myself believe,
My lord? What obstacle, dost thou conceive,

Will rise to thwart thy happiness anew?
When, torn with anguish by thy final adieu
And trembling still at having dared to unfold
Thy love to her, thou toldest me how bold
Thou wert, didst thou deceive me? Thou wouldst flee
A marriage which thou couldst not bear to see.
That marriage is broken off; what now affrights thee?
Follow the sweet course to which love invites thee.

ANTIOCHUS.

Arsaces, I am charged to escort her home.
I shall enjoy, for no brief time to come,
Dear converse with her; and her eyes will grow
Used to the sight of mine; and she may know
At length within her breast the difference
'Twixt Titus' coldness and *my* love's permanence.
Here he o'erwhelms me with his grandeur. Dim
My light shines in the splendour here of him.
But though throughout the East resounds his name,
There Berenice will find not small my fame.

ARSACES.

Doubt not, sire, all will speed thy suit.

ANTIOCHUS.

Oh, how
We both love to delude ourselves!

ARSACES.

Sayst thou,
"Delude ourselves"? Nay, wherefore?

ANTIOCHUS.

Could I move
Her heart? Might she no more reject my love?

Would she with any word ease my distress?
Thinkest thou that she in her unhappiness,
Though the whole world should slight her charms, would
        e'er
Let me shed o'er her fate a single tear,
Or that she would so stoop as to receive
Attentions from me which she might believe
Were prompted by my love of her?

ARSACES.

              And who
Could solace her as well as thou couldst do
In her humiliation? Fortune, sir,
Frowns on her. Titus hath deserted her.

ANTIOCHUS.

Alas! I shall but have, from this new turn
Of fortune, added pain when I discern
How much she loves him, by her weeping. I
Shall see her grieve; I shall be made thereby
To pity her myself. The sole reward
Of all my love for her will be the hard
Fate of beholding tears not shed for me.

ARSACES.

Dost thou delight only in ceaselessly
Torturing thyself? Has there been ever known
A noble heart so faint, sire, as thine own?
Open thine eyes and let them see, with me,
Why Berenice will surely wed with thee.
Know that since Titus gives up his design
To marry her, she now must needs be thine.

ANTIOCHUS.

"Must needs"!

ARSACES.

Allow her tears some days to flow.
Let her first agony be vented so.
All works for thee—resentment, a desire
To be revenged, thy presence ever nigh her
And Titus' absence, time itself, the weight
Of her three sceptres, which will be too great
For her weak hand, and the proximity
Of your two realms, which argues they should be
Made one. Self-interest, reason, fondness, then,
Alike unite you.

ANTIOCHUS.

Yes, I breathe again,
Arsaces; thou restorest me to life.
I have sweet hopes that she will be my wife.
Why delay? Let us do what is expected
Of us: seek Berenice, and, as directed,
Make known to her that Titus doth forsake
Her now. . . . But stay! What would I undertake?
Is it for me, Arsaces, to assume
So cruel a task? My heart revolts therefrom,
Whether because of pity, love, or both.
My adored Berenice hear from my mouth
She is cast off? Ah, Queen, who could foresee
Such words would e'er be spoken unto thee!

ARSACES.

Her anger will all be with Titus, sire.
If thou dost speak, 'twill be at her desire.

ANTIOCHUS.

Nay, let us seek her not, not look upon
Her sorrow. Enough others will come soon

To tell her of her misfortune. And is she,
Dost thou consider, not sufficiently
Unfortunate to learn unto what shame
Titus condemns her, without her at the same
Time being by the mortal anguish wrung
Of learning it from his own rival's tongue?
Let us, I say, flee, nor incur the weight,
By such bad news, of her undying hate.

ARSACES.

Here she is, sire. Decide what is thy will.

ANTIOCHUS.

Ah heaven!

[*Enter* BERENICE *and* PHENICE.

BERENICE.

How now, my lord? thou art here still?

ANTIOCHUS.

I see that thou beholdest me with regret
And that 'twas Caesar whom thou soughtest. Yet
Blame only him if, after all good-byes,
I with my presence still offend thine eyes.
I would be now in Ostia, perchance,
Had he not bidden me not to go hence.

BERENICE.

He seeks thee only. All of us doth he
Shun.

ANTIOCHUS.

He detained me but to speak of thee.

BERENICE.

Of me?

ANTIOCHUS.

Yes, madam.

BERENICE.

And what, Prince, did he say?

ANTIOCHUS.

A thousand people, better than I may,
Can tell thee.

BERENICE.

What, sir . . .

ANTIOCHUS.

      Be to wrath more slow.
Other men, far from keeping silent now,
Would triumph, perhaps, and boldly satisfy
This thine impatience with great joy; but I
Trembling always, to whom, as well is known
To thee, thy peace is dearer than mine own—
I dread thy grief more than thine anger; fain
Would I displease thee, rather than cause thee pain.
Thou wilt approve my choice before this day
Ends. Farewell, madam.

BERENICE.

     O heavens! What sayst thou? Stay!
I cannot hide the turmoil, Prince, within
My bosom. Thou seest a distracted queen,
Who, stricken to the heart, implores one word
Of thee. Thou wouldst not have my soul's peace marred,
Thou sayest; yet thy cruel refusal to speak,
So far from sparing me pain, doth only wake
Misery, anger, and enmity in me.
Sir, if my soul's peace is so dear to thee,—

If I was ever precious in thy sight,—
Upon this darkness round me shed some light!
What was it that Titus told thee?

ANTIOCHUS.

In the name
Of heaven, madam . . .

BERENICE.

What! such to thee I am
That thou so little fearest to disobey me?

ANTIOCHUS.

If I did speak, thy hatred would repay me.

BERENICE (*imperiously*).

I bid thee speak!

ANTIOCHUS.

O gods, how great thy violence!
Madam, I say thou wilt commend my silence.

BERENICE.

This moment, Prince, do as I wish; or I
Will surely hate thee till the day I die.

ANTIOCHUS.

After this, madam, I cannot deny thee
Thy will. I must speak out and satisfy thee.
But flatter not thy hopes: I shall declare
Misfortunes to thee of which thou mayst not dare
To think. I know the heart within thy breast.
I am to strike it where 'tis tenderest.
Titus hath ordered me . . .

BERENICE.

What?

ANTIOCHUS.

　　　　　　　　To announce to thee
That thou and he must part eternally.

BERENICE.

Part? Who? From me? Titus from Berenice?

ANTIOCHUS.

I must be just to him in saying this
To thee. All horrors that despair hath bred
In any loving, noble heart, I read
In his. He weeps, he worships thee, but will
It aught avail him that he loves thee still?
No queen can win the Roman Empire's trust.
Ye needs must part, and thou to-morrow must
Go hence.

BERENICE.

　　　　Part! Oh, Phenice!

PHENICE.

　　　　　　　　Thou must show
The greatness of thy soul. This sudden blow
Is indeed cruel, madam, and well may make thee
Quail.

BERENICE.

　　After all his oaths, Titus forsake me!
Titus, who swore . . . Nay, I cannot believe thee.
His honour is at stake; he will not leave me.
Slander is this against his innocence,
A trick to sunder us, a base pretence.
He loves me. He cannot desire my death.
Come; I will seek him, speak with him forthwith.
Let us go.

ANTIOCHUS.

What! thou thinkest I could be . . .

BERENICE.

Too much thou wishest it true, to persuade *me*.
No, I believe thee not. But, truth or lies,
Never again appear before mine eyes.

(*To* PHENICE) Do not desert me in this strait. I try
My hardest to deceive myself.

[*Exeunt* BERENICE *and* PHENICE.

ANTIOCHUS.

Can I
Really trust mine own ears? Heard I aright?
She bids me never come within her sight
Again. Indeed I never shall. And was
I not about to go, but stayed because
Titus detained me here against my will?
Surely I should go. Let us do so still,
Arsaces. She intends to hurt me, now.
Instead, her hate does me a kindness. Thou
Sawest me bewildered and much torn of late,
Departing love-lorn, jealous, desperate;
And now, when I have had such recompense,
I can perhaps go with indifference.

ARSACES.

Now less than ever shouldst thou go, my lord.

ANTIOCHUS.

I? Shall I stay to see myself abhorred?
For Titus' cold heart shall I bear the blame?
When he is guilty, must she think I am,
And punish me? Unjustly, shamefully,

She to my face charged me with perfidy.
Titus, she says, loves her, and I have been
A traitor to her! The ungrateful queen!
To accuse me of so infamous a crime!
And at what moment? At the very time
When of my rival's tears I spoke to her,
And I, to comfort her, made him appear
Loving and true more than perchance he is!

ARSACES.

Why vex thyself, my lord, with thoughts like this?
Give her grief's angry torrent time to run
Dry. In a week, a month—it matters none—
Naught will be left thereof. Only remain.

ANTIOCHUS.

Nay, I shall leave her, for methinks her pain,
Arsaces, might arouse my sympathy.
My self-respect, my peace admonish me
Alike to go. Come, then, and let us fly
So far from that cruel woman's sight that I
Shall hear none speak of her for a long while.
But of this day a very large part still
Is left. I to my palace shall return
And wait there. Do thou seek at once to learn
How wild her grief is. Hasten! Let me know
At least that she yet lives, before we go.

ACT IV

BERENICE *is discovered, alone.*

BERENICE.

Phenice doth not come? O moments so
Trying, to my impatient soul how slow
Ye seem! Dazed and half fainting, I have paced
Hither and thither in aimless, restless haste.
My strength is gone, yet I cannot be still.
Phenice comes not? Dire forebodings kill
My heart at such delay. Phenice can
Bring me no answer. Titus, that cruel man,
Would not consent to hear her speak. He hath
Now fled; he hideth from my righteous wrath.

[*Enter* PHENICE.

Oh, my Phenice, tell me, didst thou see
The Emperor? What did he say? Will he
Come?

PHENICE.

Yes, I saw him, madam, and before
His eyes I set the picture of thy sore
Distraction. I beheld the tears which he
Would fain have kept back.

BERENICE.

Will he come to me?

PHENICE.

He will come to thee, madam; doubt it not.
But wouldst thou let him find thee thus distraught?
Regain thy self-control. Let me replace
These veils that slipped, the hair that o'er thy face
Hath fallen. Suffer me to wipe away
All traces of thy weeping.

BERENICE.

Leave them, nay,
Leave them, Phenice, so that he may see
His handiwork. Of what avail to me
Were my adornment? If my soul's true faith,
My sighs, tears—tears, say I? my certain death
Which now impends—avail not to recall
Him to me, what would thy vain cares or all
My scant attractions, which can move no more
His heart, accomplish,—tell me, please.

PHENICE.

Wherefore
Makest thou against him these unjust reproaches?
I hear a stir. The Emperor approaches,
Madam. Withdraw, to avoid his courtiers,
To thine apartments, where thou canst converse
In private with him.

[*Exeunt* BERENICE *and* PHENICE. *Enter* TITUS, PAULINUS, *and courtiers.*

TITUS.

Paulinus, pacify
The Queen in her distress. Tell her that I
Will see her soon. I wish to be alone
A little while. Leave me here, every one.

[*Exeunt all the courtiers.*

PAULINUS (*to himself*).

Ah heaven, how I dread this meeting! Great
Gods, save his honour and that, too, of the State!
But I must go unto the Queen.

[*Exit* PAULINUS.

TITUS (*alone*).

           How now,
Titus, what wilt thou do? How rash art thou
Thus to seek Berenice! Art thou prepared
To say farewell? Is thy heart truly hard
Enough? For in the strife awaiting thee
Firmness is not sufficient; thou must be
Ruthless. Can I endure to meet the gaze
Of tender eyes that well know all the ways
Into my soul? Seeing those eyes, that shine
With so much loveliness, fastened on mine
And full of tears, shall I remember still
My sad task, and can I then say: "My will
It is, that I shall see thee never more"?
I come to pierce a heart which I adore,—
Which loves me. But why pierce it? Whose command
Bids me to? None but mine. Hath Rome explained
Her wishes yet? Do we hear cries of hate
Around the palace? Do I see the State
Tottering upon the brink of an abyss?
Can nothing save it but this sacrifice?
All is quiet; I, too quickly disconcerted,
Bring on misfortunes which might be averted.
Who knows if Rome will not say, having seen
All Berenice's virtues, that this queen
Is a true Roman and account her one?
Rome by her choice may justify mine own.
Oh, let us force no issue now, I say.
Let Rome in one scale set its laws and weigh
'Gainst them, in the other scale, such constancy,
Such love, such woe; and Rome herself will be
On our side. . . .

              Titus, open thine eyes. What air

Is this thou breathest? Art thou, then, not where
All, with their mothers' milk, imbibe a hate
Of kings which nothing can eradicate?
Rome passed her sentence on thy queen when she
Drove them out. Hast thou not known her decree
From birth? Hast thou not heard the voice of Fame,
When thou wert in thine army's midst, proclaim
Thy duty to thee? And when Berenice
Followed thee hither, was what Rome thought of this
Not told thee? Canst thou never hear it enough?
Ah, coward! renounce the Empire, and take love!
To the world's farthest bound go, hide amain,
And yield thy place to souls more fit to reign.

Are these the plans for greatness and for glory
Which would enshrine in every heart my story?
I have ruled eight days. In the space thereof
I have done naught for honour, all for love.
Of how I spent such precious time, what can
Be said? Where are those happy days which men
Expected 'neath me? What tears have I dried?
In what glad eyes have I beheld with pride
The fruit of my good deeds? Hath the world seen
Its fortunes change? Do I know what hath been
The time apportioned me by heaven? And how
Many, O miserable man, hast thou
Already lost of those, at best, few days
So long awaited? Now, no more delays!
Let us do that which honour bids me do,
And break the only tie . . .

[Enter BERENICE.

BERENICE (speaking to some one within).

Nay, let me go,

I say. Thou vainly seekest to hold me back.
I needs must see him.
                    Sire, thou'rt here. Alack!
Then it is true. Titus forsakes me. We
Must part. And it is he who wills it—he!

TITUS.

Madam, crush not a hapless ruler so.
We must not melt each other's hearts. A woe
Bewildering enough consumes me now
Without the tears of one so dear as thou
Torturing me further. Reawaken, instead,
That spirit in thy breast which oft hath made
Me hear the voice of duty. 'Tis the hour
To do it. Force thy love to speak no more.
With eyes which honour and reason render clear
Look on my obligations, howsoe'er
Painful they are. Thyself against thy spell
Strengthen my heart. Help me, if possible,
To overcome its weakness and restrain
The tears which ceaselessly I strive in vain
To master; or, if we cannot control
Our tears, let us at least with lofty soul
Endure our griefs and let the whole world see
An emperor and a queen weep blamelessly.
For after all, my princess, we must part.

BERENICE.

Is this a time, thou man without a heart,
To tell me that? What hast thou done? Alas,
I thought myself loved! To the happiness
Of seeing thee, I had grown used, and now
I live no longer save for thee. Didst thou
Not know Rome's laws when I confessed to thee

How great a love thou hadst inspired in me?
Why saidst thou not: "To whom wouldst thou enslave
Thy heart, poor princess? What hope can it have?
Give it not unto one who cannot take
Thy gift." Didst take it but to give it back
When in thy power it was, as it desired
To be? Rome's entire empire oft conspired
Against us. There was time still left thee; why
Didst thou not then forsake me? Then had I
Unnumbered reasons which could make my pain
Less dire. I could have blamed thy father then,
The populace, the Senate, all the land,
All the world, rather than thine own dear hand,
For causing my death. Their hate, long shown to me,
Had long prepared me for calamity.
I would not have received this mortal blow
Just when expecting lifelong bliss, not woe,
When thou couldst have whate'er thy soul found sweet,
When the whole universe was at thy feet,
When Rome was silent and thy father dead,
And when I now had naught but thee to dread.

TITUS.

And it is also I alone who could
Work my undoing! Then I could and would
Live in fond dreams; my thoughts refused to peer
Into the future and discover there
That which might some day part us. Nay, I chose
To hold that there was naught which could oppose
Our love successfully; I would weigh well
Nothing; I hoped for the impossible.
Haply I thought before thine eyes to die
Ere I would ever have to say good-bye.

Obstacles seemed fresh fuel to my love's flame.
The Empire spoke to me; but my fair fame
Had not yet to my heart its claims addressed
In tones it useth in an emperor's breast.
I know what pangs my course will to me give.
I feel that I without thee cannot live.
My soul may soon take flight, so huge its pain;
But life is not what matters; I must reign.

BERENICE.

Well then, reign, cruel man! Have thy "fair fame."
I strive no more. I wished to hear those same
Lips which have sworn a thousand times to me
That love should join our lives eternally—
Those very lips—before mine eyes confess
(So that I might believe it) thy faithlessness,
And bid me never see again thy face.
I wished myself to hear thee, in this place.
Farewell for ever! I have heard enough!
  "For ever"! Ah, my lord, when one doth love,
How terrible is that dire word! Hast thou
Thought of this? In a month—a year—from now,
My lord, how shall we bear it when a sea
So wide between us sundereth me from thee,—
When each day dawneth and each night doth fall
Without thy seeing Berenice at all
And without my once seeing Titus in
That whole day? But how foolish I have been
To waste time with such thoughts! Will any man
Who is so false, and ere I leave here can
Find consolation, care to count the days
One after one when I have gone my ways?
So long to me, they will seem short to him.

TITUS.

Madam, I need but briefly count the time.
I hope that soon sad tidings will compel
Thee to admit that Titus loved thee well.
He cannot, thou wilt see, do aught but die . . .

BERENICE.

Ah, sire, if this be true, why part us? I
Speak not of happy marriage still to thee.
Hath Rome condemned me never even to see
Thee more? Why grudge to me the air which thou
Breathest?

TITUS.

      Ah, I cannot resist thee now,
Madam. Thy power is too great over me.
Stay, then. But well I know my frailty.
Always must I resist thy spell and fear thee—
Vigilant to restrain my steps, that near thee
Seek to come always, by thy charms attracted.
Yes, at this very time, my heart, distracted,
Forgetteth all save that it loves thee still.

BERENICE.

Well, well, my lord, from this can come what ill?
Thinkest thou the Romans ready to revolt?

TITUS.

Who knows how they will bear what doth insult
Their feelings? If they with ever louder voice
Clamour, must blood at last confirm my choice?
If they in silence let me break their laws,
To what dost thou expose me? I, because
Of that, must basely yield some day to their

Will, to repay them. What might they not dare
To ask me to consent to on that day?
Can I enforce laws I cannot obey?

BERENICE.

Thou countest as naught the tears of Berenice.

TITUS.

Count them as naught? Oh, how unjust is this!

BERENICE.

For unjust laws, then, which thou canst undo,
Thou plungest thyself into eternal woe?
Rome hath her rights, sire; but hast thou not thine?
Are hers more sacred than thy own and mine?
Come, speak!

TITUS.

Thou tearest my heart unto its deepest
Core.

BERENICE.

Thou art emperor, sire, and yet thou weepest!

TITUS.

Yes, madam, it is true: I weep; I groan;
I tremble. But in giving the Empire's throne
To me, Rome made me promise to uphold
Her laws. I must uphold them. From of old,
Rome oft put to the test the constancy
Of men who were my like. Ah, thou wouldst see,
If thou shouldst look back to her earliest days,
They were obedient to her in all ways—
See one such, jealous for her honour, go,
To die by tortures, back unto the foe;
Another cut off his victorious son's

Head; and another, dry-eyed and not once
Seeming moved, see his two sons put to death
By his own orders. Grievous was their path;
But ever have their country's good and glory
Come first with Romans, throughout all her story.
I know that none e'er made a sacrifice
As great as mine in leaving Berenice,—
That none e'er did a thing so hard to do;
But dost thou think I lack the manhood to
Leave an example to posterity
Which nowise can be rivaled easily?

BERENICE.

I think that to thy cruel soul nothing can
Be hard. I think thee capable, false man,
Of causing my death. Thy nature is made clear
To me. I say no more of staying here.
Could I have wished to bear, in my disgrace,
Ridicule from a hostile populace?
I wished thee to refuse me even this boon.
'Tis done. Thou wilt no longer fear me, soon.
Deem not I shall heap insults now on thee
Or call on heaven to punish perjury.
Nay, if my tears move heaven, I pray to it
In dying that it will those tears forget.
If I to any prayer 'gainst thee give breath,—
If hapless Berenice would leave, in death,
Avengers of her, ingrate that thou art,—
I need but seek them deep within thy heart.
I know that such love cannot be effaced,—
That my grief now, my fondness in the past,
Yes, and my blood which here I mean to shed,
Alike will torture thee when I am dead.

I tried hard to persuade thee, feel no shame
Thereat, and leave all vengeance unto them.
Farewell.

[*Exit* BERENICE. *Enter* PAULINUS.

PAULINUS.

      What was her purpose, sire, when she
Left thee? Hath she decided finally
To go away?

TITUS.

      Paulinus, I am undone.
I cannot live and bear it. She hath gone
To kill herself. Come, we must follow her,—
Must fly to save her.

PAULINUS.

      Nay, but didst thou, sir,
Not just give orders that she was to be
Watched everywhere she went? Continually
Around her as they are, her women ought
Soon to be able to make her less distraught.
No, no! fear nothing, sire. The worst is now
Over. Do thou but persevere, and thou
Hast won the victory. Thou couldst not hear her
And not feel pity. I myself, when near her,
Felt it. But take a wider, longer view.
Think, midst this woe, what glory will ensue
After a moment's sorrow, what applause
The world is to accord thee for this cause,
What future rank.

TITUS.

      Nay, nay, I am a beast.
I hate myself. Nero, whom all detest

The memory of, was not as cruel as I.
I will not permit Berenice to die.
Come, let us go; let Rome say what she will.

PAULINUS.

How now, my lord!

TITUS.

Paulinus, I know but ill
What words I utter. Too much grief doth drown
All reason.

PAULINUS.

Do not sully thy renown.
Already hath the news that ye have parted
Spread widely. Rome exults, that was down-hearted.
In every temple fumes of incense rise
For thy sake. Thou art lauded to the skies,
And all thy statues are with laurels crowned.

TITUS.

Rome! Berenice! Ah prince, whom woes confound,
Why art thou emperor? why art thou a lover?
[*Enter* ANTIOCHUS *and* ARSACES.

ANTIOCHUS.

What hast thou done, my lord? Death hovers over
Berenice. In Phenice's arms she lies
And, deaf to all our tears and counsels, cries
Aloud for poison or a dagger. Sire,
Thou alone canst take from her that desire.
Thy name, when spoken, calls her back to life.
Ever towards thine apartments turned, as if
She ever begged to see thee, is her gaze.
The sight is more than I can bear to face.

'Twas killing me. Wherefore delayest thou?
Go, show thyself to her. Do not allow
Such beauty, grace, and virtue thus to die,
Or else renounce, sire, all humanity.
Speak but one word.

TITUS.

Alas! what can I say
To her? Do I myself, in my dismay,
Know even if I still am living?

[*Enter* RUTILUS.

RUTILUS.

Sire,
The tribunes and the consuls and the entire
Senate have come to seek thee in the name
Of all the State. A large throng followed them,
Who now in thine apartments wait for thee
Impatiently.

TITUS.

Great gods, in this I see
Your will. Ye wish to reassure a heart
Which from the right path would, ye know, depart.

PAULINUS.

Let us go into the adjoining room,
My lord, and see the Senate there.

ANTIOCHUS.

Oh, come
Quickly unto the Queen!

PAULINUS.

Sire, can it be
That thou wouldst show such great discourtesy

Unto the Empire, trampling 'neath thy feet
Its majesty? Rome . . .

TITUS.

Enough! Let us meet

With them, Paulinus.

(*To* ANTIOCHUS) Prince, I must do this.
It is my duty. See thou to Berenice.
Go, go! When I return, I hope to prove
To her that she no more need doubt my love.

ACT V

Enter ARSACES.

ARSACES (*to himself*).

Where might I find this all too faithful king?
Heaven, assist my loyal care, and bring
Me to him. Let me now announce to him
A happiness of which he dares not dream.

[*Enter* ANTIOCHUS.

Ah, what good fortune sends thee hither, sire?

ANTIOCHUS.

If my return accords with thy desire,
Arsaces, thank but my despair for it.

ARSACES.

The Queen goes hence, sire.

ANTIOCHUS.

She goes hence?

ARSACES.

To-night.

Her orders have been given. It was wrong
For Titus to have left her for so long
Unto her tears, she feels; and now she hath
Proud indignation after her first wrath.
Berenice hath renounced the Emperor
And Rome, and she would fain be gone before
Rome learns and sees her woe, or at her flight
Can e'er rejoice. To Caesar she will write.

ANTIOCHUS.

Who, O ye heavens, would have believed it! What
Of Titus?

ARSACES.

Titus hath before her not
Appeared. The populace in transports stay
His steps and press around him. Loudly they
Applaud the titles given to him by
The Senate; and these titles and this high
Regard and their applause to Titus seem
Links of a chain, in honour binding him
In spite of all his sighs and the Queen's tears,
So that his wavering heart perforce adheres
To duty now. The whole affair is o'er,
And he perhaps will see her never more.

ANTIOCHUS.

Thou givest me, I confess, good grounds for joy;
But Fate so oft hath made of me her toy
And I so oft have seen my hopes betrayed
That I in trembling heard what thou hast said;
And, smitten by foreboding fears, I wait,
Thinking that even to hope may anger Fate.
But what do I behold? Titus this way
Bendeth his steps. What purpose hath he?

TITUS (*in the doorway on the left, speaking
to his retinue behind him within*).

Stay.
Let no one follow me any farther.
(*To* ANTIOCHUS) I
Come here to keep my promise finally,
Prince. All my mind with thoughts of Berenice
Is occupied and tortured without cease.
I come, with heart wrung by her tears and thine,
To soothe an anguish not so dire as mine.

Come, Prince. I fain would have thee see for this
Last time if I indeed love Berenice.

[Exit TITUS *into* BERENICE'S *apartments.*

ANTIOCHUS (*to* ARSACES).

Thus ends the hope which thou hadst given me.
What triumph awaits me thou thyself dost see.
Berenice in just wrath would quit this place.
Titus had left her, ne'er to view her face
Again. What have I done, great gods, that ye
To such a hapless life have destined me?
From fear to hope, from hope to frenzy, I
Pass endlessly; and yet I do not die.
But Berenice—with Titus, too—appears.
Cruel gods, ye shall no more laugh at my tears.

[He rushes out, followed by ARSACES. *Enter* BERENICE,
TITUS, *and* PHENICE.

BERENICE.

Nay, I will hear nothing. My mind is quite
Made up. I mean to go. Before my sight
Why hast thou come? Was it to make my plaint
More bitter still? Art thou not yet content?
I do not wish to see thee any more.

TITUS.

But listen, please.

BERENICE.

The time for that is o'er.

TITUS.

Madam, one word!

BERENICE.

No.

TITUS.

How she doth derange
My soul! Dear princess, why this sudden change?

BERENICE.

All now is o'er. Thou wishedst me to go hence
To-morrow, and it was *my* preference
To go at once; and I am going.

TITUS.

Stay.

BERENICE.

Thou false man! Bid me stay? Why? That I may
Hear my misfortune made in every place
The talk of an insulting populace?
Have their cruel shouts of joy not reached thine ears,
The while I, all alone, was bathed in tears?
What fault is mine, alas, to make them feel
Thus? My sole crime was loving thee too well.

TITUS.

Heedest thou so a mob's insensate cries?

BERENICE.

I see naught here not painful to mine eyes.
All this apartment, by thy care prepared,
Which long beheld my love and which appeared
To give me an eternal pledge of thine,—
These walls' adornments, where our names entwine,
That my sad gaze encounters everywhere,—
Are mockeries which I can no longer bear.
    Phenice, let us go.

TITUS.

Gods! how unjust
Thou art!

BERENICE.

Return, return to that august
Senate, which so applauds thy cruelty.
Well, hast thou heard its praises joyfully?
Art thou quite satisfied with thy fair fame?
Sworest thou to forget my very name?
But that would be too small atonement for
Thy love. Sworest thou to hate me ever more?

TITUS.

Nay, I have sworn naught. I, to hate thee? I?
E'er lose of Berenice the memory?
Good heavens! at what a time thy bitterness
Unjustly doth with such cruel thoughts distress
My soul! Ah, know me better, and recall
In the last five years all the hours and all
The whole days when with sighs and ardent fires
Of love I told thee of my heart's desires.
This day surpasseth all. Ne'er, I protest,
Have love and longing for thee so possessed
My bosom; ne'er . . .

BERENICE.

Thou lovest me, thou maintainest;
And yet I must depart—which thou ordainest!
Is my despair so sweet for thee to view?
Fearest thou that mine eyes shed tears too few?
What serves it me, this vain return now of
Thy heart? For pity's sake, show me less love,
Cruel man! Do not recall fond thoughts to me.

Nay, let me go convinced that, secretly
Banished already from thy soul, I quit
A wretch who gives me up without regret.
          [TITUS *reads a letter which he took from her.*
I had just written what thou tookest from me.
All that I wish from *thy* love, thou canst see
There. Read, thou ingrate, read, and let me go.
[*She starts to leave the room.* TITUS, *who has read the letter,*
     stops her.

TITUS.

Thou shalt not! I cannot consent to it. So,
Then, thy departure was but a cruel ruse?
Thou meanest to die? And thus I am to lose
All that I love save memories, sad though dear!
     (*To* PHENICE) Go, find Antiochus. Have him come here.
               [*Exit* PHENICE. BERENICE *sinks into a chair.*
     Madam, the truth must needs at last be said.
When in my mind I faced this moment dread,—
In which, impelled by duty's stern decree,
I should be forced to look my last on thee,—
Seeing at hand our sad farewell, my fears,
My heart's strife, thy reproaches, and thy tears,
I armed my soul against all griefs which ill
Fortune, however great, could make me feel.
But whatsoe'er I feared, I must confess,
I had foreseen not half of my distress.
I thought my courage was less prone to fail.
I am ashamed to find myself so frail.
Before me gathered, I beheld all Rome;
The Senate spoke to me; but I, o'ercome,
Heard without comprehending and responded
With icy silence to their joy unbounded.

Rome knows not what awaits thee, even yet;
And I myself at times almost forget
That I am Emperor and a Roman, too.
I have come here, not sure what I shall do.
Love drew me hither, but perhaps I came
To seek my own soul and learn what I am.
What do I find?—death pictured in thy face.
Only in search of it thou leavest this place.
Ah, 'tis too much: my grief, at this sad sight,
Hath finally attained its utmost height.
I feel now all the anguish that I can.
But I perceive how to escape my pain.
Yet hope not that, worn out with many cares,
In happy wedlock I will dry thy tears.
Whate'er the straits to which thou dost reduce me,
Honour's inexorable voice pursues me
Always, compels my stricken soul to see
That I cannot both reign and marry thee,
And, after all that I have done and said,
I less than ever ought with thee to wed.

    Yes, madam, and I ought still less to say
That I am ready now to put away
The Empire for thy sake, and follow thee,—
To go, thy willing captive, tenderly
To bide with thee on earth's remotest shores.
Thou wouldst thyself blush at my craven course.
Thou wouldst with sorrow see me following swift
Thy footsteps, an unworthy emperor, reft
Of realm and courtiers, an example base—
To the eyes of mortals—of love's weaknesses.

    To end the pangs of which I am the prey,
There is, thou knowest well, a nobler way.
Madam, that path has unto me been shown

By more than one hero and more than one
Roman. When too long woe sapped their resistance
Finally, they all have taken the persistence
With which Fate hounded them to be a sure,
Secret command for them to bear no more.
If I must always see thee weep,—if I
Must always find thee thus resolved to die,—
If I must needs at every moment fear
Thou'lt cut thy life short,—if thou dost not swear
To cherish it,—thou soon wilt have the right
To shed yet other tears; for in the plight
In which I am, I will not stop at aught,
Nor will I promise thee that I shall not
Before thine eyes, and with mine own hand, seal
In blood our last and piteous farewell.

BERENICE.

Alas!

TITUS.

No, there is nothing that I may
Not do. Thou seest that my life to-day
Is in thy hands. Think well; if I am dear . . .

[Enter ANTIOCHUS.

Come, Prince. I sent to bid thee to come here.
Be witness now of all my weakness. See
Whether I do not love most ardently.
Judge thou.

ANTIOCHUS.

I doubt it not. Well do I know
You both. But know in thy turn how great woe
Is mine. Sire, thou hast honoured me with thy
Esteem; and I, for my part, truthfully

Can swear to thee I tried to be as good
A friend as e'er thou hadst, and shed my blood
In the attempt. Ye both, in spite of me,
Told me—the Queen about her love for thee,
And thou, sire, about thine for her. The Queen,
Who hears me, is my witness: she hath seen
Me, quick to praise thee, always justify
Thy trust in me by my concern for thy
Interests. Thou owest me thanks, thou dost conceive;
But in this fatal hour couldst thou believe
A friend so faithful was thy rival?

TITUS.

Thou,

My rival?

ANTIOCHUS.

I must tell the whole truth, now.

Yes, sire, I always have loved Berenice.
Times without number I have tried to cease
To love her. I could not forget her spell,
But I at least could say naught and conceal
My love. The signs I saw of change in thee
Beguiled me with some hope of what might be.
The Queen's tears quenched that hope. All bathed in
          them,
She begged that she might see thee; and I came
Myself to summon thee. Thou art here. Thou
Lovest her and art loved by her. Ye now
Are reconciled; of that there is no doubt.
Hence for one last time I have taken thought,
And of my courage have made the final test.
Reason resumes its sway within my breast.
My love was never greater or more fond.

New means are needed to break such a bond.
Only by death can I escape it; so
I rush thereto: this I would have you know.
　　Madam, I have recalled him to thee—what
I tried to do—and I repent it not.
May heaven shower upon you, now made one,
A thousand blessings through the years to come;
Or, if it hath for you some anger still,
I pray the gods to pour forth every ill
Which could afflict such precious lives on this
Poor life, which for your sake I sacrifice.

BERENICE (rising).

Stay, stay! Most high-souled princes, to what pass
Do ye twain bring me! Whether 'tis thy face
Or his that meets mine eyes, I everywhere
Look on the very picture of despair.
I see but tears, hear only talk of woe,
Of horrors, and of blood about to flow.
　　(To TITUS) Thou knowest my heart, sire. I can say
　　　　that none
Hath ever seen me sigh for empire's throne.
Rome's grandeur or her Caesars' purple has
In no wise, as thou knowest, charmed my gaze.
I loved thee, sire,—loved thee and wished to be
Loved in return. I will confess to thee
That I to-day was frightened. I believed
Thy love for me was dead. I have perceived
My error, now. Thy love is of the sort
That never changes. Sorely is thy heart
Torn; I have seen thee weeping. Berenice,
My lord, is not worth such dismay as this.
Nor should mankind have the unhappy fate—

Just at the time when it doth concentrate
Its hopes on Titus and doth taste, o'erjoyed,
His virtuous reign's first fruits—of seeing destroyed,
Through his love, in one instant, "the Delight
Of the Human Race." I think that I have quite
Convinced thee, for five years, that mine own love
For thee is great. But that is not enough.
I wish, at this dread moment, by a last
Display of it, to outdo all the rest.
I will live on—will do what thou hast told me.
Farewell, sire. Reign. Thou shalt no more behold me.
  (*To* ANTIOCHUS) Prince, after such leave-taking,
   judge if I
Would e'er consent, when I have said good-bye
To him I love, to go afar from Rome
To hearken to others' vows. Live, and o'ercome
Thy feelings by a noble effort. Do
Like Titus and like me; our course pursue.
He loves me and renounces me, and I
Love him and flee his sight. Bring nowhere nigh
To me thy grief, enthralled. Let us all three
Unto the whole world an example be
Of the tenderest and the most unhappy love
That it can treasure the sad history of.
  All is made ready, and my retinue
E'en now is waiting for me. Prince, adieu.
Follow me not, nor see again my face.
  (*To* TITUS) For the last time, farewell, my lord.

ANTIOCHUS.

Alas!

BAJAZET

INTRODUCTION

NO single formula can wholly account for the work of a writer of genius. The most significant light is shed on Racine's by an envisagement of the conflict between the prevailing pseudo-classicism and his own Hellenistic inclinations in drama; but other factors, too, were of importance. Rivalry with Corneille, as Michaut (and Lemaître earlier) pointed out, influenced him; and it doubtless even determined his selection of the subjects of *Britannicus* and *Mithridate*, as well as that of *Bérénice*, and was responsible for some features of his handling of *Iphigénie*. Delatour was no less clearly right in his suggestion that almost every new play of Racine's was affected by the criticisms made of his last preceding play; this is obviously true of *Bajazet*.

Bérénice lacks the substance of tragedy, insisted Saint-Evrimond and the rest of the hostile faction. Accordingly, in his next drama, Racine sought blood and passion.

He found them in an almost contemporaneous theme—the only one he ever treated—supplied by actual events in Constantinople; these he dramatized with some alterations. Geographical remoteness, he felt, has much the same effect as remoteness of time in lending dignity to the characters of a play, separating them from the commonplace and trivial details of life familiar to the audience, and showing them in not their accidental but their essential human qualities. That such should be done in all tragedies was part of the regnant literary theory of his day, though in practice what all the dramatists of that period really did to a large extent was to impose grotesquely their own artificial, transient fashions of speech and feeling and conduct upon the people of every country and age represented in their plays! Such unwitting grotesquery, however, is not nearly so apparent with Oriental as with ancient classical subject-matter; for though seventeenth-century France probably knew even less about the manners and customs of the Orient than about those of classical antiquity, most of us to-day have made a much greater advance in our knowledge of classical antiquity than in our knowledge of the East.

Racine was not the first to write a play dealing with recent Turkish history. A notable instance of its exploitation earlier was *la Mort de Grand Osman* by Tristan l'Hermite. In 1670, only two years before *Bajazet*, Molière had introduced Turkish scenes into his comedy, *le Bourgeois Gentilhomme*. Political events were especially directing public attention to the Ottoman Empire. *Bajazet*, therefore, was well precedented and timely.

With less striving after "local colour" than Tristan, Racine achieved the atmosphere of the seraglio by a few deft touches[1]—an absolute minimum of effort necessary for that purpose. He well knew that costumes and stage properties could add whatever more the taste of an audience might at any time require.

Stated in its barest outlines, without details, the action of *Bajazet* appears eminently suitable for a "harem tragedy." The Sultan Amurath, while leading his army on a campaign, has left his favourite, Roxana, in power in the seraglio, where he holds in prison his younger brother, Bajazet, before putting him to death—as Sultans usually put to death their near relatives who might overthrow them. Roxana, however, conceives a passion for Bajazet which she is led to be-

---

[1] Allusions to viziers, janissaries, slaves, mutes, expounders of the Moslem law, execution by strangling, the standard of the Prophet, the sacred gate, the secret exit opening on the Bosphorus, Solyman and his beloved Roxelana, etc.

lieve he reciprocates. She conspires with the discredited vizier Achmet to seize the throne for the young prince, with whom she expects to share it; but when she finds that a secret love exists between him and his cousin Atalide, their intermediary, and that these two have been hoodwinking her all the while for their own ends, she has him executed. She herself is killed by an emissary of Amurath, and Atalide commits suicide.

Such a story is not only appropriate to the setting; in essence it is dramatic and piteous. It is made all the more so by certain details in Racine's treatment of it: Bajazet and Atalide have been childhood playmates whose love is but the ripening of long and tender attachment; one item of the bargain arranged by Roxana and Achmet is that Atalide shall be the bride of the aging vizier; and the really tragic turn given to the situation is caused by Roxana's unexpected, eleventh-hour demand to be made not merely the favourite but the wedded wife of Bajazet if she saves him and helps him to the throne. Under such circumstances, it would be only natural that the lovers should wish both to give and to receive—mutually—frequent comfort, encouragement, and reassurances; natural that they should sometimes be imprudent in communicating with each other, and that their secret should hence be suspected and presently discovered. It would not have been difficult to devise a dramatic action in which this course of events could be very sympathetically portrayed.

But Racine just prior to this time had passed through a crisis and made a decision. After *Britannicus* had met with only a tardily achieved success, he had chosen to return in his next drama to some such degree of compromise with pseudo-classicism as had proved so popular in *Andromaque*; and the facile triumph of *Bérénice* was the result. Now, whatever might be the best way to develop the situation in *Bajazet*

and to conduct the love of its hero and Atalide to exposure
and disaster, undoubtedly the *easiest* way was to introduce
into their difficult situation a factor eternally recurrent in
pseudo-classical drama : jealousy. And Racine took the easiest
way.

It permitted him, since jealousy if once born is hard to
extirpate and awakens to renewed life again and again, the
sort of "pendulum-plot," as it has been called, that had gripped
the audiences of *Andromaque.* Just as, in that play, Andromache by her indecision swings the intentions of all the
dramatis personae—and therewith the prospective course of
events—first in one direction and then in its opposite like a
gigantic pendulum, so too in *Bajazet* Atalide's jealousy now
masters her, now is overcome, and now masters her again,
with consequent pendulum-like oscillations in the behaviour
of every one else. No audiences in that day would lose sympathy with Atalide, however unreasonable and extreme her
feelings. What people of later times and other countries, who
had not been brought up on the *Astrée* or *Clélie* nor under-
gone the influence of the Hôtel de Rambouillet, might think
of her did not enter into Racine's calculations.

Since the love of Bajazet and Atalide had grown out of
their affection for each other as children, it had doubtless
been tacitly understood between them rather than passionately
avowed. In consequence, there is nothing surprising or cen-
surable in Atalide's anxiety, at a time before the opening of
the play, lest Roxana's great services to the Prince, combined with so much beauty and ardent love for him, might
win his heart away from her. But Bajazet, so she tells her
confidante, at length dispelled her fears; evidently he swore
to her that he loved her and would love no other. When she
learns of Roxana's resolve to exact marriage of him as the
price of his life and to let him die if he refuses to agree to it,

Atalide at first is sure that he will indeed refuse. She wishes that she could see him before his interview with the Sultana, and persuade him not to defy one in whose power he is. Then abruptly all her jealous distrust and self-depreciation revive.

If I could even have prepared his face!
But, Zaïre, I can wait for him to pass.
I with one word, one glance, can give him aid.
Sooner than he should perish, let them wed.
His fate lies in Roxana's hands. I say
He will destroy himself! . . . Atalide, stay.
Leave, without fear, thy lover to his faith.
Thinkest thou that one for *thy* sake will choose death?
Bajazet well may meet thy wish to save him,
More careful of his life than thou wouldst have him.

She thereupon gives up all idea of trying to assist him in the mortal peril in which she herself says that he stands unless the hypothesis created by her jealousy be true. She says that it only "may" be true, but she at once entertains it and acts as though it were a certainty. Such is her behaviour, when the life of one who loves her is at stake! How petty and despicable her feelings are is shown by the very manner of their expression.

Bajazet does recoil from the proposal which Roxana makes to him and does incur her deadly wrath. Atalide, again in terror for him, persuades him to placate the enraged woman at any cost—to tell her whatever may be necessary to avert his death. It is not easy to conquer his pride and scruples, which make such a course repugnant to him; she prevails on him only by declaring that otherwise she will confess her love for him and her part in deceiving the Sultana, and so will die with him. Then, as soon as he has obeyed her and accomplished what she has bidden him to accomplish, jealousy

again torments her and she reveals to Zaïre that she intends
to kill herself.

But it was solely by making Bajazet think that his dis-
sembling would save her life—by urging precisely this consideration—that she has prevailed on him to do violence to
his instincts and conscience. No wonder she does not trust
the faithfulness of his vows to her, being herself capable of
such bad faith! To her perfidy towards the man who most
deserves fair dealing from her, she adds a readiness to believe
the worst of him, accepting at face value the vizier's statements about the joy of Bajazet and Roxana in their recon-
ciliation—though the slightest use of her intelligence at this
time would have reminded her that her informant, knowing
nothing of the true state of affairs, would not distinguish between a pretended feeling on the part of the Prince, such as
she herself had enjoined on him, and the real ecstasy of the
Sultana. She turns to Zaïre as soon as Achmet has left them:

Come; let us hence. Let us not mar their bliss.

. . . .

Thou seest that all is o'er: they are to wed.
Roxana is content; he vows his love
To her. But I do not complain thereof.
I myself wished it. Yet wouldst thou have thought,
When to be true to me just now he sought
To sacrifice himself with heart suffused
With love—yes, when for my sake he refused
To the Sultana a mere promise—when
I tried to stay him with my tears in vain
And yet was pleased they had so little might—
Wouldst thou have thought, I say, that now, in spite
Of all this show of tenderness, he could e'er
Find so much eloquence in wooing her?

Ah, perhaps after all 'twas not too hard
To make his feelings and his words accord.
Perhaps the more he looked on her, the more
He saw new charms and yielded to their power.

. . . .

When I recalled him to Roxana, I
Had no intention he should not comply.
But after the farewells I lately heard
And the sweet grief wherewith his heart was stirred,
Surely he need not have shown openly
Such rapture as was just described to me.

Here we see her indulging in the same unworthy fancies
about her devoted lover, with complete disregard of all that
has been said between them. When he himself enters, she
reproaches him tearfully. Thus she destroys both him and
herself. He tries to assure her that he has given no promise
of any kind to Roxana, who with eager credulity has taken
all for granted on his first efforts to propitiate her; but Atalide remains deaf to his protestations, and Bajazet says he
will no longer continue the odious deceit which he has practised for her sake. But—and this is a vital defect in the play—
their tragedy does not proceed inevitably from what has taken
place in this scene. Atalide might again have come to her
senses and brought him to his—and after that, since he was going immediately to head the insurrection, any further emo-
tional veerings on her part would not have mattered—but *by
sheer chance* it is exactly at this moment, before she can utter
a word of remonstrance to him, that Roxana enters and is so
rebuffed by his coldness that her fatal suspicions are aroused.
These are presently confirmed by the hackneyed stage device
of the discovery of a letter from Bajazet to Atalide, but even
then the outcome is decided by a purely fortuitous time-se-

quence; for Achmet, learning of the situation, forms a rescue-party which breaks into the seraglio, and it is mere chance that they reach Bajazet just after instead of just before his death. True, suspense is in this way maintained to the end, but it is the suspense not of genuine tragedy but of melodrama.[2]

But this play was already seriously marred beyond mending, in any case. Sympathy for some of the characters, as we have observed in our consideration of *Bérénice*, is an essential in tragedy of the best type, and no one who is not under the spell of the French-classical tradition can sympathize with an Atalide or feel any real concern about what happens to her. Her monologue of self-condemnation before taking her own life cannot have the pathetic effect on us that Racine intended. And his Bajazet, no Turk save in name but rather a French gallant, who can love this Atalide and is weak enough to react as he does to her moods regardless of the consequences to himself or to her or to those who have espoused his cause —he, too, forfeits our sympathy.[3] In these characters Racine

[2] In this denouement the usual pseudo-classical stereotypes of conduct are not absent. Bajazet must defend himself against his executioners and display his prowess, like other pseudo-classical "heroes," before being killed. Atalide must commit suicide after an appropriate speech, like other pseudo-classical "heroines"—and, really, there was not much else that she could decently do as a sequel to her previous behaviour and its results. Zaïre wishes to die with her mistress, and Osmin has expressed a similar wish to die with Achmet when he supposed Achmet would die, like other pseudo-classical confidants. Racine's invention was here strictly in the romanesque groove.

[3] Even in modern times, many critics and scholars who write of French seventeenth-century drama fall into the habit of accepting its ethical code, in which jealousy was looked upon with indulgence and sympathy. Some therefore would have us see Atalide as innocent and dove-like—wholly piteous, commendable, and lovable! It is hard to believe they would view her with the same tenderness if she were a figure in any literature save that of France in this period, in which they have immersed themselves. Sarcey, not thus immersed but a practical dramatic critic, voiced in his *Quarante Ans de Théâtre* the natural feelings of even a French audience

appears to have gone too far even for the taste of the century following his own, if we can judge by so staunch a French-classicist as La Harpe, who wrote of the crucial dialogue between this precious pair:

"It is in this scene that one realizes more clearly than ever how weak and false is the motivation of the plot, which the author has based upon the jealousy of Atalide and the faint-heartedness of her lover. It is inconceivable that the conclusive details into which Bajazet has just gone should make so slight an impression on Atalide that he would think himself obliged to risk everything and lose everything. The very just confidence in him which she has shown in the second act makes it impossible that in the third she should doubt his veracity, in the face of every appearance of truthfulness. This is the first fault.

"The second, which is much more serious, is the puerile despair (not to mince words) that costs Bajazet his life. He ought to have said to her: 'In the crisis we are in, it is a question not of persuading you, but of saving your life as well as my own. Thank heaven, I have promised nothing, and I am on the point of accomplishing everything. Another moment, and I shall have it in my power to repay Roxana in the manner that I choose, and to crown Atalide, and this without being either ungrateful to the one or unfaithful to the other.'

---

in the nineteenth century—and presumably in the twentieth century also —when witnessing this play:
"You cannot imagine the impatience of the public in the third act, when all is supposed to be settled, when Bajazet has given for the second or third time his word to Roxana and to his minister Achmet, and then suddenly, because he has just heard the plaints of that little blockhead (*pécore*) of an Atalide, he changes his mind and leaves everybody in consternation. . . . How do you expect me to be interested in this exalted ninny (*majestueux dadais*) and his whining sweetheart (*plaignarde de maîtresse*)?"

"If he talked thus, he would talk like a man. When one considers that nothing less is at stake than the life of such a friend as Achmet, than the fate of Atalide, of Bajazet himself, and of the empire, one is obliged to admit that refinements of delicacy and insane compliance are alike the exact reverse of tragedy, because they are the reverse of good sense. . . . A prince who in this situation sacrifices everything to such attenuated scruples of love is not only no hero and still less a Turkish hero, but in no way deserves to have any one die to serve him."

What interest the play does possess is to be found in the figures of Achmet and Roxana, which are among Racine's greatest creations. And this is no small interest, though of a lower, less moving kind than that in which sympathy is involved; it is the interest that any superb portrait excites, and the interest—combined with quasi-admiration—stirred by the spectacle of a cool, capable intellect at work or of volcanic, unleashed passions. For such excellence as can be attained where sympathy is lacking, *Bajazet* is comparable among tragedies to *The Alchemist* among comedies—the finest Elizabethan play by any one but Shakespeare, and a play which misses greatness only by that lack—though sympathy with some one is not so important in comedy as in tragedy.

Achmet is one of Racine's few really striking male characters; Roxana is an achievement surpassed only by Phaedra, Hermione, and perhaps Athaliah among his women. Both have been adequately discussed by a number of critics; an understanding of neither presents any serious difficulty. Here, at last, are genuine Orientals.

The vizier is adroit, resourceful, indefatigable, untroubled by scruples and impervious to the influence of any emotion

except pride—which has been sorely wounded when the
Sultan deposed him from his command of the army and,
heading it himself, took the field without him. It is this mortal offence and his knowledge that it merely preludes his
"liquidation" that impel Achmet to plan a revolt which
would seat Bajazet on the throne. Seeing that Roxana is the
key to the situation, he contrives to arouse first interest and
then love in her for the helpless prince, and offers himself as
their instrument for success, with the hand of Atalide to be
his reward—purely with an eye to self-preservation in the
future, as he scornfully tells his friend Osmin, who asks him
if he loves her. He himself attends to everything, overlooks
nothing that might be to advantage:

> I have already contrived secretly,
> By intrigue, to bring over to our side
> The expounders of our sacred law. To guide
> The credulous throng, I know religion's power.

All is so well devised—only he does not foresee in others the
possibility of those insurgent feelings of which he himself is
devoid. At least, when these wreck the whole edifice of his
carefully laid plans, he does not lose his head or waste any
time in futile anger. He knows he has gone too far to be
able to turn back now, stakes all on one desperate but coolly
calculated effort to retrieve the situation, and when it fails
by the narrowest of margins, has a ship ready for his escape
from the death which overtakes the others.[4]

Love—the rank sort of love to be expected in the in-
mate of a harem—together with ambition rules Roxana,
and she is determined to gratify both of these passions at

---

[4] He saves with him those who have compromised themselves by their
loyalty to him (his pride makes them his chief concern; for his own life
he cares little, amid the ruin of his fortunes) and would save Atalide, too,
if she would let him. His consideration for her, even now, is noteworthy.

once. Her infatuation makes her easily believe her love is returned; but Bajazet must give her the one thing that Amurath has withheld, the name of wife, or she will let him perish. When she unexpectedly meets with a refusal, which is little softened by the practical considerations which he urges, the conflict within her bosom between her first fury and her heart's cravings for the Prince finds eloquent utterance in a tempestuous scene of great dramatic power; and when she finally learns the whole deception that has been practised on her, her savage, almost incoherent frenzy of rage is truly awesome. Even yet, however, she will spare Bajazet if she can possess him, and in confident reliance on the power of her physical charms if these are habitually encountered, she makes him a last proposal:

> My rival is here. Follow me instantly
> And see her die by the mutes' hands. Set free,
> Then, from a love fatal to glory's quest,
> Plight me thy troth. Time will do all the rest.

—upon his rejection of which, she utters the terrible "Begone!" ("*Sortez!*") that sends him to his death.

Yet the man who created her gave his leading actress the part, not of this fierce and passionate creature, this magnificent human animal, but of the miserable Atalide. *She*, evidently, was in his opinion the more important, the more effective role!

CHARACTERS IN THE PLAY

BAJAZET, *brother of the Sultan Amurath.*

ROXANA, *the Sultana, favourite of Amurath.*

ATALIDE, *a young girl of the royal Ottoman blood, niece of the father of Bajazet and Amurath.*

ACHMET, *the Grand Vizier.*

OSMIN, *confidant of Achmet.*

ZATIMA, *slave of Roxana.*

ZAÏRE, *slave of Atalide.*

The scene represents a room in the seraglio of the Sultan at Constantinople (called Byzantium throughout the play).

The names "Atalide" and "Zaïre" are pronounced as in French, with the final "e" silent, in this translation. They rhyme, respectively, with "need" and "fear."

BAJAZET

ACT I

Enter ACHMET *and* OSMIN.

ACHMET.

Follow me. The Sultana will come hither.
In the meantime, thou and I can talk together.

OSMIN.

How long, my lord, hast thou had entrance here,
Wherein none ever is even allowed to peer?
Such boldness formerly would have incurred
The speediest death.

ACHMET.

   Osmin, when thou hast heard
Of all that now hath happened, thou wilt be
Surprised no longer that I should have free
Entrance into this place. But let us turn
From idle speech. How long seemed thy return
To my impatient soul! How gladly do
I see thee in Byzantium anew!
What secrets hath a journey taken for me
Alone, and of such length, disclosed to thee?
Tell me what thou hast witnessed, and distort
Nothing. Remember that on thy report
Depend the Ottoman Empire's fortunes. How
Fareth the army, how the Sultan, now?

OSMIN.

Babylon, faithful to her prince, beheld
Our hosts about her walls, and never quailed.

The Persians, marching to her aid, each day
Drew somewhat nearer to the place where lay
The camp of Amurath. He, weary of
The long and fruitless siege, seemed glad enough
To leave the city undisturbed and, making
No further futile efforts toward its taking,
To await the Persians, ready for the fray.
But, as thou knowest, though I made haste, the way
Unto Byzantium from the camp is long,
And by more obstacles delayed than tongue
Can tell, I am in total ignorance
Of all that hath occurred since I came thence.

ACHMET.

But what did our brave janissaries do?
Unto the Sultan are they indeed true?
Couldst thou not read their hearts, though they were
        mute?
Is Amurath's power o'er them absolute?

OSMIN.

He is content, if one may take his word.
Of victory he appeareth well assured.
But his demeanour cannot blind our eyes.
He feigns a calmness that is nowise his.
Vainly doth he his wonted fears suppress
And grant the janissaries free access
To him. He knows how, at no long past date,
He wished, because he felt for them such hate,
To cut to half its strength that gallant corps
When he would fain, to establish his new power,
Escape their tutelage, so he averred.
Oft have they said, as I myself have heard,
How without cease he fears them, they fear him.
Blandishments have not made their memories dim.

They murmur at thine absence; they regret
The time, to their courageous hearts so sweet,
When under thee, sure of success, they fought.

ACHMET.

What! thou thinkest that they have not forgot
My former glory, that it still doth fire
Their spirits, Osmin, and that they still desire
To follow me, and would know their vizier's voice?

OSMIN.

The battle's outcome will decide their choice
Of conduct: they will see the victory
Or flight of Amurath. Though reluctantly
They march 'neath his command, they would maintain
The fame their deeds have won them, and not stain
The honour so long theirs. The combat's end,
However, upon Fate must needs depend.
If Amurath, thanks to their might, anon
Is victor on the plains of Babylon,
Thou'lt see them in Byzantium, in that case,
Set the example of a blind and base
Obedience. But if Fortune in that fray
Shames with defeat, being more strong than they,
His budding empire, and he flees, doubt not
That, made unruly by his adverse lot,
They soon will to their hatred add abuse
And will explain, my lord, the battle's loss
As heaven's judgment upon Amurath.
Meanwhile, if rumour doth not lie, he hath
Sent from the host three months ago a slave
Charged with some secret mission. Therefore have
All of the soldiers trembled, sick with fright,
For Bajazet. They feared the Sultan might
Have sent an order for his brother's head.

ACHMET.

And so he did. The slave came here indeed
And showed that order—but naught did he obtain.

OSMIN.

What! Shall the Sultan, sir, see him again
With empty hands and learn thou wouldst not do
His bidding?

ACHMET.

That slave is now no more. A new
Order, which *I* gave, had him secretly
Drowned in the waters of the Euxine Sea.

OSMIN.

But soon for his long absence Amurath
Will seek the cause—then seek revenge in wrath.
How wilt thou answer him?

ACHMET.

Perhaps I can
Busy him with more weighty cares ere then.
Well do I know that Amurath has sworn
My ruin. I know what greeting his return
Will bring to me. That he may drive me now
Out of his soldiers' hearts, thou seest how
He seeks without me siege and battle. He
Himself commands the army; as for me,
He leaves me in a city, where I wield
A futile power. What task is this, what field,
Osmin, for me, me, a vizier! But I
Have used my leisure not unworthily.
Vigils have I prepared for him, and fears,
And soon the news thereof will reach his ears.

OSMIN.

What hast thou done?

ACHMET.

I hope that Bajazet
This very day will claim the throne and seat
Roxana by his side there.

OSMIN.

What, my lord!
Roxana? she whom Amurath preferred
To all the other fair ones he had brought
From Europe and from Asia to his Court,
Stripping all lands of them? On her alone,
'Tis said, his love is centred; and though no son
She yet hath borne him, he would have Roxana
Even assume the title of Sultana.

ACHMET.

He did still more for her, my Osmin: he
Hath given her complete authority
Here in his absence. Thou art well aware
Of the cruel customs of our Sultans. Rare
It is that they will let their brothers long
Enjoy the dangerous honour of having sprung
From the same stock and being to them too near
Akin. The idiot Ibrahim need fear
Naught from his birth. Exempt from peril, he
Draggeth out a perpetual infancy,
Left to the hands that tendance to him give,
Unworthy equally to die or live.
The other brother well deserves the dread
And jealousy because of which his head
Is threatened without cease by Amurath;

For Bajazet indeed at all times hath
Despised the slothful ease in which the sons
Of Sultans bide. His childhood o'er, at once
He sought the wars; and it was under me
He gained experience in them, gallantly.
Thou hast thyself seen him in combats grim
Charge, taking every soldier's heart with him,
And, bleeding, taste the glory and delight
Youth finds in its first victory. But despite
All his misgivings the cruel Amurath
Did not dare sacrifice unto his wrath
This brother till he had, himself, a son
Who could reign after him; otherwise, none
Might be left presently of the royal race.
    Thus, then, the Sultan, being for a space
Disarmed, left Bajazet a prisoner here.
He went forth, having made sole arbiter
As to his brother's life, to serve his hate,
Roxana, whom he charged to immolate
Him on the slightest rumour, on the least
Suspicion, with no reason else professed.
I, who remained alone here, as I was
Justly incensed, espoused that brother's cause.
I talked with the Sultana, and without
Showing my aims, gave her good grounds to doubt
That Amurath would return, told her of how
The army murmured and how none could foreknow
War's fortunes. Then I spoke of the sad fate
Of Bajazet and told her of his great
Attractiveness, concealed so jealously
From her that, although very near him, she
Had never seen his face. Need more be said?

Roxana soon was so ensnared she had
No wish but to behold him in some wise.

OSMIN.

But could they cheat so many watchful eyes,
Which seemed to set a barrier none might scale
'Twixt them?

ACHMET.

    Thou mayest recall how a false tale
Was widely noised that Amurath was dead.
Roxana, feigning to be sore dismayed,
Won credence for it by her cries of grief.
Her tears compelled her trembling slaves' belief.
The guards of Bajazet were much perplexed;
Gifts did the rest; their vigilance was relaxed,
And those they watched could talk in consequence.
  Roxana, when she saw him, told the Prince
Of the charge entrusted solely to her care.
Winsome is Bajazet, and when aware
That safety lay in pleasing her, he soon
Pleased her. Everything aided him: her own
Concern and efforts for him and her declaring
Her secret to him and the bond of sharing
Its knowledge, sighs the sweeter for the fact
They must be hidden, that both of them were wracked
By nowise daring to speak, their having the same
Rashness, dangers, and fears common to them—
All bound their hearts and fortunes to each other
For ever. Those whose task was to discover
This, having turned from duty, never durst
Return to it.

Osmin.

What! Roxana from the first,
Sayest thou, laid bare her inmost heart to them,
Before their eyes revealing her love's flame?

Achmet.

None yet knows aught of that; for Atalide
Hath lent her name to all Roxana did.
She is the niece of Amurath's father; she
Shared with his sons his heart,—from infancy
Was reared beside them in the royal house.
She seemed to hearken now to the Prince's vows
Yet heard them but to bear them to Roxana,
Thus serving gladly him and the Sultana;
And both of these, to gain my aid, agreed
That I, dear Osmin, shall wed Atalide.

Osmin.

What! *Thou* lov'st *her*?

Achmet.

Wouldst thou that at my age
I should submit to love's vile tutelage,
Or that a heart long years of toil made hard
Should blindly seek vain joys as its reward?
She charms my gaze because of other things;
I love in her the stock from which she springs.
Bajazet binds me to himself through her
And thus assures me of a succourer
Against him. Ever doth a vizier irk
The souls of Sultans. They mistrust their work
As soon as they have chosen him. They deem
His fall a thing desirable for them,
And their displeasure never lets us see

A ripe age. Bajazet now honours me
And courts me. Every day the risks he runs
Rekindle his affection. But when once
Firm on the throne, then may this Bajazet
Think me a friend whom he would fain forget.
For my part, if my aid and loyalty
Restrain him not,—if he dares ask of me
My head some day . . . Osmin, I leave the rest
Unsaid. But I intend that he at least
Will have to ask it a long time. I know
How to serve Sultans faithfully, but to
The common herd I leave the worshipping
Of their caprices, and I will not bring
Myself to such a senseless fealty
As to give thanks when doomed by them to die.
　　This, then, is how I have gained entrance here,
And why Roxana would herself appear
Before mine eyes. Invisible at first,
She only heard my voice and nowise durst
Break the seraglio's rigid laws; but she
Overcame finally the timidity
Which was for us so inconvenient,
Imposing on our converse such constraint.
She herself chose this unfrequented place
Where hearts can speak with freedom face to face.
A slave conducts me hither secretly,
And . . . But some one is coming. It is she
And her dear Atalide. Stay with us here.
Be ready to confirm the news I bear.
　　　　　[*Enter* Roxana, Atalide, Zatima, *and* Zaïre.
　　Rumour and truth, madam, are in accord.
Osmin hath seen our army and its lord.
Ever is Amurath with fears beset;

Ever do hearts incline to Bajazet,
And all, with one voice, call him to the throne.
Meanwhile, the Persians march on Babylon,
And soon must the two hosts beneath its wall
In battle learn to whom shall victory fall.
Our fates, 'tis said, all hang upon this fight—
E'en now decided (if I count aright
The days of Osmin's journey) as it may please
Heaven; and the Sultan triumphs e'en now or flees.

Let us break silence, madam, and declare
Ourselves, Byzantium's gates against him bar,
Nor for the tidings of the combat wait—
His flight or triumph—but anticipate
That news. If he hath fled, what fearest thou?
If he hath triumphed, 'tis needful to act now.
When all prepare to welcome him within
The city's walls, 'twill be too late to win
Away from him the people's fealty.

I have already contrived secretly,
By intrigue, to bring over to our side
The expounders of our sacred law. To guide
The credulous throng, I know religion's power.

Vouchsafe forthwith that Bajazet once more
May look at last upon the light of day
And leave the palace confines. Now display
That fateful standard in his name, whereby
Do we proclaim a great emergency.
The populace are well disposed toward him,
Knowing his virtues are his only crime.
Moreover, a vague rumour, carefully
Fostered by me, hath made our citizenry
Believe most luckily that Amurath
Disdains them, and that he the intention hath

Soon to remove his person and his throne
Far from Byzantium. Let us, then, make known
To them his brother's danger, telling of
The cruel command imposed on thee. Above
All else, let Bajazet assert his claim
Unto the crown and show himself to them
That they may see how 'twould become his brow.

ROXANA.

All that I promised, I will do. Go now,
Good Achmet. Gather all thy friends and learn
Their sentiments; immediately return
With thy report thereof to me, and I
Will then have ready for thee my reply.
I will see Bajazet. I can say naught
Until assured his heart is one in thought
With mine. Go, and come back.

[*Exeunt* ACHMET *and* OSMIN.

Fair Atalide,
The time hath come when Bajazet must decide
Our destinies. For the last time shall I
Confer with him. I shall know certainly
Whether he loves me.

ATALIDE.

Is this the time for doubt
As to that, madam? Hasten to carry out
Thy plans. Thou heardest that which the vizier
Hath told thee. Bajazet is very dear
To thee. How knowest thou if his fate will be
To-morrow subject still to thy decree?
Perchance this very moment Amurath
Cometh, to cut short his fair life in wrath.
Why art thou dubious of his heart to-day?

Roxana.

Wilt thou assure me of it, who dost essay
To speak for him?

Atalide.

What, madam! all the care
That he hath taken to please thee, all that ere
This thou hast done, all that thou yet mayest do,
His peril, his homage, and thy beauty, too—
Cannot these things assurance to thee give?
Doubt not thy favours in his memory live.

Roxana.

Alas! why cannot I for mine own peace
Believe it? Why, to bring my heart some ease,
Cannot this ingrate at least speak to me
As thou hast said he speaks *of* me to thee?
Relying on thy words, how oft have I
Tasted the joys anticipatively
Of seeing his heart's confusion—in my thought—
And had him secretly before me brought,
Wishing myself to prove his love for me.
Mine for him may be such I cannot be
Easily satisfied, but—to spare thine ear
A lengthy story—there did not appear
In him that agitation and keen love
Which thy too sweet reports have told me of.
If I am to accord him life and throne,
I must have surer grounds to build upon.

Atalide.

What test, then, of his love wilt thou essay?

Roxana.

That he must wed me now, this very day.

ATALIDE.

Wed thee? Good heavens! Canst thou expect him to?

ROXANA.

I know that 'tis not thus our Sultans do.
I know that in their pride they have no mind
To seal their troth with nuptial ties that bind.
From those fair women who for their preference strive
They deign to choose a favorite, ne'er a wife;
And she is still a slave, who in her arms
Receives her master, and who with all her charms
Feels no security, and cannot shake
The yoke off, which their laws impose, nor take
The title of Sultana till she bear'th
A son to him. Fonder is Amurath
Of me, and he desireth, as did none
Before him, to bestow for love alone
This honour. I have had from him the power
It carries, with the title; at any hour
I can his brother's death or life decree.
But even Amurath never promised me
That marriage would some day his kindness crown;
And I, who have aspired unto this one
Thing only, have now lost the memory
Of everything he did for me. But why
Seek to excuse myself?
      'Tis Bajazet,
Really, that maketh me all else forget.
In spite of his misfortunes he hath been
More fortunate than his brother was: to win
My heart—without intending so to do,
Perhaps. My maids, the guards, the vizier too—
I have corrupted all of them. Thou seest,

In short, what I have done for him. The best
Uses have I made of the power supreme
Which Amurath granted to me over him.
Bajazet to the Sultan's throne draws nigh.
One step remains. But it is there that I
Await him. Despite all my love, if now
He will not bind me his by wedlock's vow,—
If he dares quote an odious law to me,—
When I do everything for him, if he
Will not do everything for me,—straightway
Without considering whether I love him (yea,
Or whether I destroy myself) I shall
Cast off the ungrateful wretch and let him fall
Back into that sad plight I drew him from.
Hereon must he declare himself. His doom
Or safety hangs on what he now will say.
    I nowise ask thee to attempt to-day
To serve with him as my interpreter;
I wish him to reveal before me here,
By his own mouth and face, his heart without
Leaving me even the shadow of a doubt.
I wish him to be brought here secretly
And unexpectedly encounter me.
When we have had this interview, thou shalt hear
And know all from my lips. Farewell.

        [*Exeunt* ROXANA *and* ZATIMA.

ATALIDE.

        Zaïre,
This is the end. Atalide is undone.

ZAÏRE.

Thou?

ATALIDE.

I foresee already what will come
To pass. My only hope is my despair.

ZAÏRE.

But, madam, wherefore?

ATALIDE.

Didst thou not just hear
Roxana tell us what she had in mind—
What fatal vows she would impose to bind
Bajazet unto her? The Prince must wed
With her this day or else be slain, she said.
What will become of me in my grief supreme
If he submits? What will become of him
If he does not?

ZAÏRE.

I understand thy woe;
But, to be frank, thy love ought long ago
To have foreseen this.

ATALIDE.

Ah, Zaïre, hath love
Ever such foresight? All things, 'twould seem, strove
To further our desires, with one accord.
Roxana relied wholly on my word,
Felt certain that the heart of Bajazet
Was hers, and left all matters that relate
To him unto my care, beheld him through
My eyes, and spoke to him through my mouth. Unto
That happy moment I had now come, I
Believed, when I could crown my lover by
Her hands. Of all this, heaven will have none.

And yet, Zaïre, what ought I to have done?
Not have allowed Roxana thus to err?
Have destroyed him I love, to enlighten her?
Before her love for him was ever born
I loved him, and I knew that he in turn
Loved me. From infancy, thou wilt remember,
Our bond of kindred blood was by more tender
Ties reinforced. Nursed at his mother's breast
With him and Amurath, I loved him best.
She by our fondness was much gratified,
And we, though we were parted when she died,
In absence still desired each other's love
Through all the years, while ne'er we spoke thereof.
    Roxana, who suspected naught, hath since
Beheld and loved perforce this hero-prince,
And wished to associate me with her plans.
She eagerly stretched to him helping hands;
And Bajazet, surprised, showed thankfulness
And high regard for her—could he do less?
How prone is love to think what fain it would!
Roxana, by the least similitude
Of fondness satisfied, enlisted us
Both, in her own credulity, to abuse
Her trust. Zaïre, I must confess that I
Could then not keep from feeling jealousy.
My rival, doing so much for Bajazet,
Against my poor charms could a kingdom set.
Countless boons kept her ever in his thought.
She held a dazzling prize before him. What
Could I on my part give him? Nothing. I
Could only heave an oft-repeated sigh.
Heaven alone knoweth how many tears
I shed. But he at length dispelled my fears.

Ashamed, I wept no more, and to this day
Urged him to feign and said what he should say
For him.
                    Alas, now all is o'er and done!
Roxana, scorned, will learn her error soon.
For Bajazet cannot hide what he thinks
And feels. I know his noble nature shrinks
From falsehood. Ever in the past have I,
Trembling, had to be ready to supply
Words for him tenderer than he would employ.
Bajazet now is certain to destroy
Himself. If as my rival formerly
Did, she would only let him speak through me!
If I could even have prepared his face!
But, Zaïre, I can wait for him to pass.
I with one word, one glance, can give him aid.
Sooner than he should perish, let them wed.
His fate lies in Roxana's hands. I say
He will destroy himself! . . . Atalide, stay.
Leave, without fear, thy lover to his faith.
Thinkest thou that one for *thy* sake will choose death?
Bajazet well may meet thy wish to save him,
More careful of his life than thou wouldst have him.

ZAÏRE.

Ah, in what woe, madam, wouldst thou immerse
Thyself, for ever torturing worse and worse
Thy heart ere aught of evil comes to pass!
Thou knowest that Bajazet in any case
Adores thee. Curb, then, or at least conceal
Thy anguish. Do not by thy tears reveal
The love between you twain. The hand that hath
Saved him till now will save him still from scathe

If to the end Roxana know not of
Her rival and still deem she hath his love.
Come, and hide somewhere else thy fears until
Thou hearest the outcome of their meeting.

ATALIDE.

Well,

Then, let us go; and if for the deceit
Of two young lovers punishment seems meet,
Just heaven, and if our love seems wrong to thee,
I am the guiltier, punish only me!

[*Exeunt.*

ACT II

BAJAZET and ROXANA are discovered.

ROXANA.

The fateful hour, Prince, hath finally
Come in which heaven again would set thee free.
Nothing restrains me longer; and I can
Bring to fruition on this day the plan
My love conceived. I do not have the power
To assure thee of an easy triumph or
Place in thy grasp a sceptre giving thee
Over a tranquil realm the sovereignty.
But all I can, keeping my promises,
I do. I arm against thine enemies
Thy valiant hand and from a manifest
Peril deliver thee. Thou wilt achieve the rest.
Osmin hath seen the army; it, at heart,
Is thine. The masters of our law take part
In our conspiracy. Achmet the vizier
Will answer to thee for Byzantium, sir;
And well thou knowest, my least word, as suits
My will, the numerous officers, slaves, mutes,
And others in these palace walls controls.
To gain my favour have these abject souls
Given me their silence and their lives, long since.
Now do thy part. That great career, my prince,
Which I have opened unto thee, begin.
  The course thou art to run involves no sin.
Thus only canst thou 'scape the murderer's hand.
Many have done the same before thee, and
Our Sultans at all times have not been loath

To take this road to power. But let us both,
For the best start thereon, hasten to seal
At once my happiness and thine as well.
Show by thy now binding thyself to me
That I but served my husband, serving thee;
And by the sacred ties of marriage prove
Me justified in giving thee my love.

BAJAZET.

Ah! what is this which thou wouldst have me do?

ROXANA.

How now! what obstacle is there unto
Our happiness?

BAJAZET.

Canst thou be unaware
That the throne's dignity . . . Wilt thou not spare
To me the pain of saying it?

ROXANA.

I know
That ever since a Sultan, long ago,
When captured by a savage conqueror,
Beheld his wife bound to the victor's car
And through all Asia dragged along behind,
Those who succeeded him, having no mind
To see their Ottoman honour risk such shame
Thereafter, rarely deigned to take the name
Of husband. But love laughs at rules like this;
And, not to mention humbler instances
Solyman (nor of any hast thou heard,
Among thy sires whose swords the whole world feared,
That raised the Turkish power to such a height)—

Yes, Solyman, found pleasing in his sight
His Roxelana, and for all his pride
This haughty monarch placed her at his side,
To share his throne with him and royal bed,
Although to such estate no claim she had
Save some small beauty and much clever charm.

BAJAZET.

'Tis true. But think how feeble is my arm,
What Solyman was, and what I am to-day.
Solyman ruled with undisputed sway.
Egypt regained by him, Rhodes—that grim rock
Whereon the tide of Turkish conquest broke—
Become the tomb of all its garrison,
The Danube's lands ravaged and seized upon,
The expanse of Persia's empire made less broad,
The burning climes of Africa subdued
Silenced all opposition to his will.
How is it with *me*? My only fame is still
The tale of my misfortunes. All my hopes
Depend upon the people and the troops.
Wretched, proscribed, and doubtful yet of reigning,
Ought I to alienate instead of gaining
Adherents? If men see our ecstasies,
Will they feel pity for our miseries?
Will they believe my danger or thy tears
Genuine? Flatter, then, no more mine ears
With talk of Solyman, that mighty prince.
Instead, recall the murder not long since
Of hapless Othman. When they mutinied,
The leaders of the janissaries tried
To excuse the bloody schemes they had devised.
They thought that these were fully authorized

By reason of the fatal marriage he
Had made—like that which thou proposest to me.
    What shall I tell thee, then? In time I may
Reign o'er their hearts and dare more than to-day.
Let us not be too hasty; but commence
By giving me the power to recompense
Thine aid to me.

ROXANA.

        I understand thee, sir.
I see my rashness, see that naught can blur
The keenness of thy foresight, careful of
The slightest peril that my impatient love
Might bring on thee. Thou fearest what harm may come
To thee, or to thy honour, sir, therefrom;
And I believe thee, since thou sayest 'tis so.
But hast thou thought of the worse perils, though,
Which, if thou dost not wed me, thou'lt be in,—
Of how 'tis I whose favour thou must win
Above all else,—how if I aid thee not,
All will be hard for thee? Hast thou forgot
That it is I who hold the palace gates?
That I can open them for thee, thy fate's
Mistress, or keep them closed for evermore?
That I have o'er thy life absolute power?
That thou still breathest only because I
Love thee, and that without this love which thy
Refusal of me doth offend, thou'dst be
Dead even now?

BAJAZET.

        Yes, I owe all to thee;
And I had deemed thou'dst find thy glory sweet
Enough in seeing the whole realm at my feet
And hearing me avow that I do owe

All to thee. I indeed shall fail not so
To testify. This shall my lips confess,
My deference confirm it without cease.
My life itself thou givest me. But dost thou
Wish verily . . .

ROXANA.

Nay, I wish nothing now.
Vex me no more with logic drawn so fine.
I see how distant are thy hopes from mine.
No longer will I urge thee, thankless man,
To grant my wish. Back to the night again
From which I drew thee forth! . . .

(*To herself*) For what, indeed,
Stays me? What further proof do I still need
Of his indifference? Doth my ardour move
The ingrate? In his reasonings can love
Be found at all? . . .

(*Again to* BAJAZET) Oh, I perceive thy thought!
Thou deemest mine own peril, no matter what
I do, assures thy pardon,—that I am tied
To thee with bonds too strong to dare divide
Thy interests from mine. But I am still
Certain thy brother holds me in good will.
Thou knowest he loves me; and, despite his wrath,
Thy false blood can atone for all, thy death
Suffice to exculpate me. Do not doubt
This very moment 'twill be brought about!

Bajazet, hear me! I find that all too well
I love thee. Thou art destroying thyself. Still, still
The way lies open to repent. Take care
Thou lettest me not go hence, nor to despair
Drivest a woman mad with love. If one
Word leaves my lips, thy life is o'er and done.

BAJAZET.

Thou canst deprive me of it. 'Tis in thy hands.
Perhaps my death will further best thy plans,—
Will from triumphant Amurath win grace
And give thee in his heart thy former place.

ROXANA.

In *his* heart? Dost thou dream, though he should fain
Have me, that if I lose the hope to reign
In thine, when I so long have cherished that dear
Delusion, I a different thought could bear
Henceforth, or live unless I lived for thee?
I have given thee, cruel man, weapons against me
Too surely, and I should have yielded less.
Thou wilt o'ersway my weakness. I confess
I feigned before thee a false pride. On thee
Depends my joy and my felicity.
My bloody death will follow hard on thine.
And to preserve thy life, what toil was mine!
    Thou sighest at last and seemest sore distraught.
Go on. Speak.

BAJAZET.

Oh, if I but *could* speak out!

ROXANA.

How now! What sayest thou? What did I hear?
Thou hast, then, secrets that I may not share?
Thy feelings cannot be revealed to me?

BAJAZET.

Madam, I repeat, 'tis now for thee
To make thy choice. Open for me a way
That I may take unto the throne, or slay
Thy victim. I can bear the worst. Decide.

ROXANA.

This is too much. Thou shalt be satisfied.
Ho, guards! come hither!

[*Enter* ACHMET.

Achmet, all is o'er.
Thou mayst go. I have naught to tell thee more.
I bow to Amurath's authority.
Nay, go! Let the seraglio henceforth be
Shut fast, and all be as in former days.

[*Exit* ROXANA.

ACHMET.

Sir, what have I just heard—with what amaze?
What will become of thee? What will become
Of me? Whence did this change take place, and whom
Ought I to blame for it? O heavens above!

BAJAZET.

There is no reason I should not tell thee of
What hath occurred. Roxana is offended
And will have vengeance. Our accord is ended,
Encountering a hopeless obstacle.
Vizier, shift for thyself, I warn thee well.
Act as seems best, counting no more on me.

ACHMET.

What!

BAJAZET.

Find some safe place, unto which to flee,
Thou and thy fellows. I know the perils brought
Upon you by my friendship. I had thought
To give you, some day, better recompense.
That dream is over with, believe me; hence
We must no longer think of it.

ACHMET.

But tell
Me what, sir, is this hopeless obstacle.
Just now I left all peaceful here within
These walls. What madness seized her soul and thine?

BAJAZET.

She wishes me to marry her.

ACHMET.

She does?
The custom of our Sultans doth oppose
Her wish. But is that rule so strict that thou
Must at thy life's expense observe it now?
Of all laws, the most sacred is to save
One's life,—to snatch, sir, from the waiting grave
Thyself, the last in whom the royal blood
Of the Ottomans flows.

BAJAZET.

That life so ill-starred would
Be bought too dearly if the price it cost
Were any act of cowardice.

ACHMET.

Why dost
Thou deem the price blackened with infamy?
Does Solyman's marriage stain his memory?
Yet Solyman was threatened by no dread
Perils like those which hang above *thy* head.

BAJAZET.

And in those very perils and that base
Concern about my life lies the disgrace
Of this vile marriage. Solyman's was quite

Different. His slave found favour in his sight
And therefore he, though not at all constrained
To wed her, gave her both his heart and hand.

ACHMET.

Thou lovest Roxana.

BAJAZET.

Achmet, say no more.
Less than thou wouldst suppose do I deplore
My fate. Death is not to my mind the worst
Of evils. Following thy steps I durst
Seek it while yet a youth; and when I lay
In prison, I beheld it day by day
Close at hand always, till it was a wonted
Sight unto me. Oft have I been confronted
With it by Amurath. I end by it
A troubled life. Alas, if I now quit
That life with some regret . . . Forgive me! cause
Enough, Achmet, have I to pity those
Whom I have ill repaid for love which sought
To serve my interests with its every thought.

ACHMET.

Ah, if we die, my lord, the blame must fall
On thee. Speak but one word, and save us all.
Whatever janissaries are left here,
The guardians of our faith, whom all revere,
Those citizens the Byzantine populace
Respect the most, and whose example sways
Their suffrage—all are ready and now wait
To be thy escort to the sacred gate
Through which new Sultans first their entrance make.

BAJAZET.

Well then, good Achmet, let them straight betake
Themselves here, if they love me so indeed.
Force the seraglio's doors if this ye need
To do, and pluck me from Roxana's hands.
Enter accompanied by those valiant bands.
Sooner would I go forth covered with blood
Than be compelled to be, whether I would
Or not, her husband. In the confusion, I
Shall with the courage of despair rely
On mine own arm to save me, and perchance
Can fight on till thou comest to my defence.

ACHMET.

Ah, would my utmost haste not be too slow
To thwart Roxana's vengeance—one swift blow?
Then what will such impetuous zeal have done?—
Incriminated us, with gain to none!
Promise her all; escape this threatened death,
And later see what weight thy promise hath.

BAJAZET.

I?

ACHMET.

Blush not. None of Ottoman blood should have
To keep his pledges like a common slave.
Take counsel of those heroes whom the right
Of conquest set, victorious in their might,
O'er earth's remotest lands, and whom the sword
Made masters—and not bondmen—of their word.
State policy prescribed their course, alone;
And half this sacred empire rests upon
Promises which they rarely would fulfil.
Pardon my warmth, my lord.

BAJAZET.

Yes, I know well,
Achmet, how far they went for the State's good.
But these same heroes gave their veins' last blood.
'Twas not their lives they bought with perfidy.

ACHMET.

O dauntless courage! too steadfast probity,
Which, though it brings me death, I must admire!
Shall o'er-nice scruples at this time require . . .
But what blest fate now sends us Atalide?

[*Enter* ATALIDE.

Oh, madam, join thy voice with mine to plead!
He is destroying himself.

ATALIDE.

'Tis why I came
To talk with him. Leave us. Roxana's aim
Being his death, she means to shut and bar
The palace doors. But, Achmet, go not far
Away. Thou mayst be called back speedily.

[*Exit* ACHMET.

BAJAZET.

The time has come to say farewell to thee.
Heaven punishes my deceit, undoes
Thy clever plans. Against its latest blows
Naught could protect me. Nothing was in store
For me but death or being thine no more.
What hath it served us that I stooped to feign?
I die less soon—that is our only gain!
I told thee 'twould be thus; but thou wert bound
To have me take this course. I have postponed
Thy grief as long as I could do so. Hence,

Now, in return for my obedience
To thee, fair Atalide, I beg thee, flee
Roxana's presence. By thy tears would she
Perceive thy secret. Hide them from her eye;
And risk no lingering here, saying good-bye.

ATALIDE.

Nay, sir, thy kindness to a hapless maid
Hath striven enough for that which Fate forbade.
'Twould cost thee far too much to spare me pain.
Thou needs must strive no more. Leave me, and reign.

BAJAZET.

Leave thee?

ATALIDE.

I wish it. I have taken thought.
Till now, with countless jealous pangs distraught,
'Tis true, I was not able to conceive
Without dismay that Bajazet could live
And be no longer mine; and whensoe'er
I pictured in my mind, with grievous cheer,
My happy rival's triumph, even thy death
(Forgive a loving woman's frenzy!) hath
Not seemed for me the worst of miseries.
But then that was not shown to my sad eyes
In all its horror—and when 'twould come, and how.
I did not see thee, as I see thee now,
Bidding me, for the last time, farewell.
I know, indeed, with what unshakable
Courage thou'lt go to meet death face to face.
I know that proving thus thy faithfulness
To me will give thy heart some joy amid
Thy life's last breaths. But pity Atalide.
Thy dauntless spirit, alas, she doth not share.

Limit thy ill fate to what she can bear.
Do not expose me to the keenest grief
That e'er drained dry the eyes of maid or wife.

BAJAZET.

What will thy future be, if I to-day
Before thy face contract this marriage?

ATALIDE.

                         Nay,
Inquire not what my future, sir, will be.
Perhaps I shall accept my destiny.
How do I know? I shall seek charms to heal
My pain. I shall perhaps remember still,
Mid my tears, that thou wert resolved to die
For me, and that thou livest, and 'twas I
Who willed it thus.

BAJAZET.

              Nay, thou shalt never see
Those cruel rites. The more thou biddest me
Now to be false to thee, the more 'tis plain
How truly thou deservest not to obtain
That which thou askest. Shall this tender love,
Born in our childhood, which in silence throve
And grew as we grew, until I alone
Could comfort thee in thy distress, my own
Repeated vows ever to cleave to thee—
Shall all these end in foulest treachery?
     I then should wed—whom, if the truth be told?
A slave, who is in everything controlled
By thoughts of self,—who sets before my face
The sight of death awaiting me, and says
That I must marry her or surely die—

While thou dost view my peril with anxious eye,
And, worthy of that blood which thou art of,
Wouldst sacrifice for me thine own heart's love!
Ah, let my head be to the Sultan brought,
Ere at such price its safety should be bought!

ATALIDE.

Sir, thou couldst live and not be false to me.

BAJAZET.

How? If I can, I will—most willingly.

ATALIDE.

Despite her anger, the Sultana loves thee;
And if, sir, thou wouldst take, as it behooves thee
To do, more pains to please her,—if thou wouldst let
A show of fondness make her hopeful that
Some day . . .

BAJAZET.

　　　　　I understand thee. But what thou
Wishest, I cannot do. Ne'er think that now
A craven self-distrust hath so dismayed
My soul that cares of State make me afraid
To mount an offered throne and I prefer
To shun them by a speedy death. I hear
Rash counsels perhaps all too readily.
I cherished the hope, having in memory
Ever the many great names of my race,
To flee ignoble ease and win a place
Among those heroes. But however hot
Ambition's flame or love's is, I cannot
Longer deceive a doting woman's heart.
Vain would my promise be, to play this part,
Even to save my life; for mine own eyes

And lips, to falsehood natural enemies,
When I would seek most to beguile her, might
In my confusion do the opposite,
And by my coldness she with rage would see
I spoke not from my soul, too obviously.

Ah heaven! how often would I have disclosed
The truth to her, if I could have exposed
No life but mine unto her hate thereby,—
If I had not feared that her jealous eye
Might with suspicion fix on thee its glance!

And I should cozen her with a false pretence,
Perjure myself, and by this baseness . . . ? Oh,
Were not thy heart so full of love, I know,
Far from bidding me practise this deceit,
Thou'dst be the very first to blush at it!

To save thee from unrighteous prayers, good-bye.
I go at once to find Roxana. I
Will leave thee, now.

ATALIDE.

And *I* will not leave *thee*!
Come, come; thou shalt be led to her by *me*.
'Tis I will tell our secret to her ears.
Since my distracted lover scorns my tears
And finds his joy in dying before my sight,
Roxana shall in spite of thee unite
Us to each other. She will thirst more for *my*
Blood than for thine; and I shall give to *thy*
Affrighted eyes as dread a spectacle
As thou wouldst make mine view, hadst thou thy will.

BAJAZET.

Ye heavens! Couldst thou do this?

ATALIDE.

                      Couldst thou believe,
Thou cruel man, that I am less sensitive
To honour's claims than thou? Canst thou in sooth
Believe that when I put words in thy mouth,
My blushes were not ready to betray me
A hundred times? But I then saw, to sway me,
Death threatening thee. How, ingrate, can it be
When mine is certain, thou darest not do for me
What I durst do for thee? One word and glance
Which seem more tender may suffice. Perchance
Roxana in her heart forgives thee. Thou
Seest, thyself, how much time she doth allow
Thee for repentance. Hath she, when she went
From thee, made Achmet go hence? Hath she sent
Guards to arrest thee here before my face?
Truly, when even in her wrath she prays
Mine aid, do not her tears reveal her love?
She may but wait for some vague hope, enough
To cause all weapons from her hands to fall.
Go, sir, and save thy life, and mine withal.

BAJAZET.

Well, be it so. But what am I to say
To her?

ATALIDE.

      Oh, do not ask me that! Some way
The occasion's need and heaven will teach thee what
Are the right words to speak. Go. I must not
Be at your meeting. Thy confusion then,
Or mine, would needs unmask us. Go. I again
Tell thee I dare not be there. Say to her
All that is necessary to save thee, sir.

ACT III

ATALIDE and ZAÏRE are discovered.

ATALIDE.

He is forgiven? Zaïre, is that true?

ZAÏRE.

So have I told thee, madam. A slave flew
To carry out Roxana's will and let
The vizier enter at the palace gate.
To me they spoke not, but the exultant look
On Achmet's face, better than words, bespoke
The blessed change that hath recalled him hither
Where he hath come to seal a peace for ever.
Roxana chose the kindlier course, 'tis clear.

ATALIDE.

Thus now do joy and gladness disappear
Everywhere from my life and go with them.
I have done all I had to do, and am
Not sorry.

ZAÏRE.

       How now, madam! What new alarm
Is thine?

ATALIDE.

       Hath no one told thee by what charm
Or rather by what compact Bajazet
Hath wrought a change so sudden? To dissipate
Roxana's anger seemed impossible.
Hath she some pledge that binds him all too well
To her? Speak. Will he wed her?

ZAÏRE.

Nay, I know
Nothing of that. But if he only so
Could escape death,—if he hath done as thou
Thyself hast bidden him do, and if he now
Weds her, in short . . .

ATALIDE.

Weds her, thou sayest!

ZAÏRE.

What!

Dost thou regret thy generous words, which sought
To enjoin him to preserve his precious blood?

ATALIDE.

No, no! He will do only what he should.
Too jealous instincts, ye must needs be still.
Bajazet, wedding her, obeys my will.
Respect the good in me that treads you down,
Nor with its noble counsels mix your own.
Far from depicting him in her embrace,
Let me conceive him, without bitterness,
Enthroned where 'twas my love that made him climb.
I am myself again and for all time.
I wanted him to love me, and he does.
Now I at least find solace, feeling thus,
That I shall die worthy and proud of him.

ZAÏRE.

What sayest thou? Die? Is thine intent so grim?

ATALIDE.

I have given him up, and doth the rest surprise
Thy heart? Dost reckon among calamities,

Zaïre, a death that cheats so many a woe?
Enough that *he* lives. I have wished it so;
And still I wish it, cost me what it can.
'Tis not a question of my joy or pain.
I love him well enough to say good-bye;
But he can judge—ah, justly—that if I
Would make for him so great a sacrifice,
A soul that guards his life with care like this
Loves him too well to see him wed to-day.
Let us go learn . . .

ZAÏRE.

              Control thyself, I pray.
Some one is coming. All will soon be known.
'Tis the vizier.

[Enter ACHMET.

ACHMET.

           Our lovers are at one
Finally. A calm hath fallen; its gentle breath
Brings us to harbour. The Sultana's wrath
Has been disarmed, her latest will declared
Unto me. Bajazet will be prepared
Ere long to follow me; and while she displays
Forthwith unto the city's startled gaze
The Prophet's dreadful standard, I shall tell
All men the reason 'tis unfurled, instill
Due fear into the hearts of all of them,
And the new sovereign publicly proclaim.

    In the meantime, let me recall unto thee,
Madam, what rich reward was promised me.
Do not expect from me such rapturous sighs
As I from those two lovers' hearts heard rise;
But if by means more suited to my age,

Profound respect and lifelong vassalage
Such as we owe to one of royal blood,
I can . . .

ATALIDE.

With time all these things can be showed
To me; and time can make thee know me, too.
But tell me of those transports thou didst view.

ACHMET.

Canst thou not guess how great the ardour is
Of two young lovers in their ecstasies?

ATALIDE.

Yes, but this miracle amazes me
Truly. Hath it been said at what price he
Was pardoned by Roxana? Is he now
To wed her?

ACHMET.

Madam, I believe so. Thou
Shalt hear all I with mine own eyes have seen.
Stunned, I confess, by their mad quarrel and spleen,
Exclaiming against lovers, love, and Fate,
I left this palace in despair, and straight
Storing the remnant of my wealth aboard
A ship which at the quay I had kept moored,
Already planned flight to some foreign shore.
From this sad purpose being called once more
To the palace, full of joy and hope anew,
I ran; my feet had wings; then open flew
The doors of the seraglio at my voice.
A female slave appeared. Not the least noise
She made, but led me to a chamber where

Roxana listened with attentive ear
Unto her lover. All those near them held
Their peace. I, too, my own impatience quelled,
And to respect their secret converse stood
Aloof, and marked their manner and their mood
For a long time. At last, with eyes which said
Plainly all that was in her heart, she laid
Her hand in his to pledge to him her love;
And he, with glances that were eloquent of
His passion, assured her of his heart's flame.

ATALIDE (aside).

Alas!

ACHMET.

They finally saw me, both of them.
"Behold," she said to me, "our prince and thine.
Him to thy hands, brave Achmet, I consign.
Go, and prepare for him fit regal state.
Let a submissive, loyal people wait
For him, to pay him homage in the temple.
Soon will the palace set you its example."
Then at the feet of Bajazet I fell,
And the next moment I was gone. Right well
Pleased am I to bring to thee, on my way
Thence, the good news that now indeed are they
Reconciled, and my due respect to accord
To thee. I go to crown him, I pledge my word.

[Exit ACHMET.

ATALIDE.

Come; let us hence. Let us not mar their bliss.

ZAÏRE.

Ah, think . . .

ATALIDE.

What wouldst thou have me think of this?
What! Shall I go to view a sight so dread?
Thou seest that all is o'er: they are to wed.
Roxana is content; he vows his love
To her. But I do not complain thereof.
I myself wished it. Yet wouldst thou have thought,
When to be true to me just now he sought
To sacrifice himself with heart suffused
With love—yea, when for my sake he refused
To the Sultana a mere promise—when
I tried to stay him with my tears in vain
And yet was pleased they had so little might—
Wouldst thou have thought, I say, that now, in spite
Of all this show of tenderness, he could e'er
Find so much eloquence in wooing her?
  Ah, perhaps after all 'twas not too hard
To make his feelings and his words accord.
Perhaps the more he looked on her, the more
He saw new charms and yielded to their power.
She will have poured her plaints into his ears.
She loves him; a throne beckons through her tears.
Such love cannot but touch a generous heart.
Alas! how all against me takes her part!

ZAÏRE.

But the result is still uncertain. Wait.

ATALIDE.

Nay, 'twould be futile to deny it yet.
I see no joy in adding to my woe.
To save his life, I know what he must do.
When I recalled him to Roxana, I
Had no intention he should not comply.

But after the farewells I lately heard
And the sweet grief wherewith his heart was stirred,
Surely he need not have shown openly
Such rapture as was just described to me.
    Be thou the judge if I am self-deluded.
Why from these plans was I alone excluded?
Am I concerned so little in the fate
Of Bajazet? To seek me, would he wait
So long unless his own heart's just reproach
Made him perhaps unwilling to approach
My presence? But no, I wish to spare him this.
He shall no more behold me.

ZAÏRE.

Here he is.—

[*Enter* BAJAZET.

BAJAZET.

'Tis done. I spoke. Thy will hath been obeyed.
Thou needest no longer, madam, be afraid
For me. I would be happy if my sense
Of honour did not censure the pretense
By which I won good fortune quite amiss,—
If mine own heart, whose secret lack of peace
Condemns me, could as quickly pardon me
As did Roxana. But I at last am free,
My hand is armed, and I can now contend
With my cruel brother, not having to depend
On silence aided by thy cleverness
To win his mistress' favour in this place,
But myself seeking him 'neath alien skies
And in fair fight, where manly danger lies,
Vying for the people's and the soldiers' hearts,
The outcome to depend on our deserts.
    What do I see? What ails thee? Why that tear?

ATALIDE.

Nay, I begrudge not thy good fortune, sir.
Heaven, just heaven, owed thee this miracle.
Thou knowest if e'er I raised an obstacle
Against it. While I breathed, as thou'rt aware,
Thy perils have engrossed my every care;
And since they end but with my life alone,
It is without regret I lay that down.
     'Tis true, if heaven had to my prayers lent ear,
It could have made my death much happier.
Thou wouldst have wed my rival e'en as now,
And proven faithful to thy marriage vow;
Yet thou wouldst not have, with thy nuptial faith,
Given her those proofs of love which now she hath.
Roxana would have felt herself repaid,
And I in death would this sweet thought have had,
That, having myself moved thee to this design,
I sent thee to her with a heart all mine,—
That, bearing thy love among the dead with me,
Not as her lover do I leave her thee.

BAJAZET.

Why talkest thou thus of marriage and of love?
What grounds hast thou for such words? Heavens above!
Whose false report can so have made thee err?
I, I, could love Roxana?—live for her?
Oh, far from having such an idea, how could
I even have forced myself to say I would?
I neither thought nor said it. There was no need
To do so. The Sultana was misled
As easily as before, and whether she
At once conceived my seeking her to be
Absolute proof I loved her, or she deemed

Time was so precious that it now beseemed
Her not to offer long resistance, I
Had scarce begun to speak, when with a cry
And flood of tears she cut short words that she
Had hardly heard. She gave her destiny,
Her life, into my keeping, with a blind
Trust in my gratitude, and in her mind
Had not a doubt that we ere long would wed.
    Such utter love, so little merited
By me,—such faith misplaced,—filled me with shame;
And while she to the heat of my heart's flame
Ascribed still the confusion which my face
Displayed, I felt myself wrong, cruel, and base.
Believe me, in that moment I had need
To think of all my love for Atalide
That I might keep unbroken to the end
A silence so perfidious. But when I bend
Hither my steps after that task—none worse—
Seeking some help to stifle my remorse,
I find thee charging me with lack of faith
To thee, and blaming thine expected death
Upon my harassed conscience! I can see,
See plainly, that all this I say to thee
E'en now is little heeded. Let us have done,
Madam, with what leaves peace to neither one
Of us; and vainly torture both, I pray,
No more. Roxana is not far away.
Let us act honourably. I shall be
Far better satisfied with myself and thee
To go and tell her that I have constrained
My soul to abuse her love for me with feigned
Affection, than I ever went to play
The hypocrite. Here she is.

ATALIDE.

Just heaven! Nay!
What will he bring upon himself?
(*To* BAJAZET) If thou
Lovest me, do not undeceive her now!

[*Enter* ROXANA.

ROXANA.

Come, come, sir. It is time for thee to show
Thyself and let the palace see and know
Who is its master. All the many folk
Who dwell within its walls, together flock
At my command—to hear my will expressed.
These my slaves, whose example all the rest
Will follow, are the first my love will give
To thee as subjects.
(*To* ATALIDE) Madam, couldst thou believe
That such a sudden change as this e'er hath
Made so much love follow such frenzied wrath?
Just now, resolved on vengeance, come what might,
I swore he should not see to-morrow's light.
Scarcely one word Bajazet then hath spoken
To me; love took that oath, by love 'tis broken.
I deem he loves me, seeing him so stirred.
I have forgiven him, and I trust his word.

BAJAZET.

Yes, I have promised thee, and sworn solemnly,
Ne'er to forget all that I owe to thee—
Sworn that my care and my solicitude
Shall ever prove to thee my gratitude.
If thy good offices I hence can claim,
I go to wait for the results of them.

[*Exit* BAJAZET.

ROXANA.

What shock, O heaven, so stuns me and appals?
Is this a dream? Have mine eyes played me false?
Such dour response, these frigid words I heard,
Which seem to cancel all that hath occurred
Between us—oh, what mean they? For what cause
Doth he suppose I yielded and he was
Restored to favour which he had spurned away?
I thought he vowed that till his dying day
His love would make me sovereign o'er his fate.
Does he regret appeasing me of late,
Already? But was I myself just now
Deluded? Ah! . . .

     (*To* ATALIDE) But ye twain—he and thou—
Were talking, madam. What did he then say?

ATALIDE.

To me? He loves thee always.

ROXANA.

                      He will pay,
Unless I think so, with his life—naught less!
But when he hath such grounds for happiness,
Tell me, please, how dost thou explain the gloom
Which filled him—visibly—when he left this room?

ATALIDE.

Madam, I saw not any gloom in him.
He spoke about thy goodness a long time
To me. His heart was full of it when he came
And met me here. He seemed to me the same
When he went out. But couldst thou feel surprise
If Bajazet, when this great enterprise
Impends, should after all be ill at ease,

Madam, and let some signs escape of these
Many cares which must occupy his mind?

ROXANA.

Great is thy skill, excusing him. I find
Thou speakest for him better than he does
Himself.

ATALIDE.

And is there any other cause . . .

ROXANA.

Enough! I comprehend, much more than thou
Thinkest, thy reasonings, madam. Leave me, now.
I wish to be a little while alone.
This day has given me troubles of my own.
Like Bajazet, I am vexed and full of care,
Whereof I fain would ponder, with none near.
                    [*Exeunt* ATALIDE *and* ZAÏRE.
    Ah, how must I construe all I have seen?
Is there some understanding, then, between
Those two, to cozen me? Wherefore this change,
These words, and this abrupt departure strange?
Did I not even see a glance that flashed
From one to the other? Bajazet's spirits dashed
And Atalide aghast! Am I condemned
By them, great heavens above, thus to be shamed?
Is this the fruit that my blind love must reap?
So many grievous days, nights without sleep,
Plots, and intrigues, and treason risking death—
And by all this a rival profiteth?
    Yet I may torture myself too readily
And note a transient cloud with anxious eye,
Too prone to judge by his mere mood his love.

Would he not carry deceit far enough
When on the point of seeing his wiles succeed?
Could he not feign one moment more, at need?
No, no; let us take courage. I am afraid
Because I love to excess. Why should I dread
Atalide in his heart. Yes, what would be
The reason for his loving her? What has she
Done for him? Which of us crowns him to-day? . . .
    But do we not know love's resistless sway?
Alas, what matters it that he owes his throne
And life to me, if Atalide by her own
Charms doth attract him? Are there boons that can
Outweigh love in one's heart? When this false man,
To look no further, won mine, did I show
More gratitude for his brother's favours? Oh,
If he had had no other ties, would he
Have shrunk so from the thought of marrying me?
Would he not gladly have shown deference
To *my* will? Would he, at his life's expense
Even, have flouted it? What good grounds . . . Who now
Comes here to speak with me? . . . What seekest thou?

[Enter Z<small>ATIMA</small>.

Z<small>ATIMA</small>.

Forgive me, madam, if I thus presume
To intrude. A slave hath from the army come;
And though the gate was shut facing the sea,
The guards without delay, on bended knee,
Opened it at the Sultan's orders, sent
To thee. But much to my astonishment
'Tis Orcan brings them.

R<small>OXANA</small>.

Orcan!

ZATIMA.

Yes, of all
Minions the Sultan hath to serve, at call,
His will, the one on whom he most relies—
Blackest of those who 'neath the burning skies
Of Africa were born. He asks for thee,
Madam, impatiently. But it seemed to me
That I should warn thee first; and since my fears
Were greatest that he might take thee unawares,
I have in thine apartments kept him close.

ROXANA.

Upon me fall what unexpected blows!
What are these orders? How shall I reply?
The Sultan, much perturbed, doth doubtlessly
The death of Bajazet once more command.
Without my sanction none can lift a hand
(For all obey me here) to do him scathe.
But should I save him now? Is Amurath
Or Bajazet my sovereign? To the one
I have been faithless; the other may have done
As ill by me. Time presses. How decide
With such dread doubts? But they can never hide
The truth. The most discreet love will reveal
Its secret by some sign. Let us use well
The moments left us. I shall carefully
Watch Bajazet, and Atalide shall I
Confound—to crown my lover if he does
Prove true, or slay him if perfidious.

ACT IV

Atalide and Zaïre are discovered.

ATALIDE.

Knowest thou my affright?—that I saw here
Fierce Orcan's hideous face? Oh, how I fear
His presence at this crisis of our fate!
How I fear . . . But hast thou seen Bajazet?
Tell me! What says he? Will he now give heed
To my good counsel, and to Roxana speed
And rid her of all vestige of suspicion?

ZAÏRE.

He cannot see her without her permission.
Such are Roxana's orders; 'tis her will
That he should wait. She doubtless would conceal
Him from that dread slave. When I found him I
Pretended not to have sought him, covertly
Gave him thy letter, and now have brought thee his
Reply. Thou shalt see, madam, what it is.

ATALIDE (*reading the letter*).
        "After all thy needless pangs
And changes, wouldst thou have me still pretend?
        But I, too, would my life defend
        Since thou sayst thine upon it hangs.
I shall to the Sultana go, and by
Deference and new-shown gratitude will try
        To appease her wrath if this may be.
Require naught more; not death nor thou, to move her,
Will ever make me tell her that I love her,
        Since I shall ever love but thee."

Alas! Why tell me that? Does he believe
I know it not? Do I not, then, perceive
Sufficiently that he loves, adores me? Is
It only thus that he can heed my pleas?
He has Roxana, not me, to persuade.
He leaves me still how desperately afraid!
O fatal blindness! Faithless jealousy!
False tale, why did I heed thee? Doubts which I
Could not o'ercome, why let you be expressed?
All was done. My good fortune far surpassed
My fond hopes. I was loved, I should have been
Happy; Roxana was content, serene.
Zaïre, go back to him, if thou canst, apace.
Let him indeed "appease her." What he says,
Is not enough for me. Let his lips, his eyes,
Assure her that he loves her, in such wise
That she must needs believe it. Would that I
Might with my tears make him more ardently
Woo her, and put into his words to her
All the love *I* feel for *him*. But I fear
I would make worse his plight, instead of better.

ZAÏRE.

Here is Roxana.

ATALIDE.

Oh, let us hide this letter.
[*She thrusts it hastily into her bosom. Enter* ROXANA *and*
ZATIMA.

ROXANA (*to* ZATIMA).

Come. I received this mandate. Needs must I
O'erwhelm her with it.

ATALIDE (*to* ZAÏRE).

Go, make haste; and try
Hard to persuade him.

[*Exit* ZAÏRE.

ROXANA (*approaching* ATALIDE).

Madam, I have now
Had letters from the army. Knowest thou
Aught of all that which lately hath occurred?

ATALIDE.

A slave hath come here from the camp, I heard.
Nothing was told me of the news he brings.

ROXANA.

Amurath triumphs. Fortune finally swings
To *his* side. Babylon obeys his will.

ATALIDE.

What! Really, madam? Osmin . . .

ROXANA.

He was ill
Informed, and his departure was before
This slave set out. 'Tis o'er. The war is o'er.

ATALIDE.

What a dire blow to us!

ROXANA.

And now, to crown
Our woes, the Sultan, who dispatched him, on
His heels at once hath followed.

ATALIDE.

The hosts, then,
Of Persia stay him not?

ROXANA.

No; he again
Is nearing us, post-haste.

ATALIDE.

Ah, madam, how
I pity thee! This very instant thou
Must do what thou wouldst do.

ROXANA.

It is too late
To seek to oppose the conqueror.

ATALIDE.

Oh, great

Heavens!

ROXANA.

Time hath not made his severity
Grow less. This is the order telling me
His sovereign will supreme.

ATALIDE.

What does he bid
Thee now to do?

ROXANA.

See for thyself. Here, read!
[*She gives the letter to* ATALIDE.
Thou knowest the handwriting and the seal.

ATALIDE.

They are cruel Amurath's. I know them well.
(*She reads*) "I sent thee positive commands before
Babylon put my power to the test.
I fancy Bajazet now lives no more.

I fain would think thou hast obeyed my hest.
Beneath my sway hath Babylon been brought;
Leaving there, I reiterate those commands.
Come not before me, if thou carest aught
For life, save with his head borne in thy hands."

ROXANA.

Well?

ATALIDE (*to herself*).

Hide thy tears, unhappy Atalide.

ROXANA.

How seems it to thee?

ATALIDE.

He still has, indeed,
His fratricidal purpose. But he believes
That he proscribes a prince to whom none gives
Support. He knows not of the love that speaks
To thee in Bajazet's behalf and makes
Of him and thee one soul,—that thou wouldst die,
Rather, if necessary . . .

ROXANA.

I, madam? I

Would gladly save him; truly, I cannot
Hate him; but . . .

ATALIDE.

Then "but" what? Thou wilt do
what?

ROXANA.

Obey.

ATALIDE.

Obey!

ROXANA.

What else is to be done
In this dire strait? I must.

ATALIDE.

　　　　　　This dear prince . . . one
Who loves thee—shall he see the life which he
Hath pledged unto thee end?

ROXANA.

　　　　　　　So must it be.
My orders are already given.

ATALIDE (*swooning*).

I

Am dying!

ZATIMA.

　　　She falls! . . .
(*After bending over* ATALIDE) She seemeth truly nigh
To death.

ROXANA.

　　　Go; take her to the neighbouring
Chamber. Note well her looks, words, everything
That will afford proof of their perfidy.

　　　　　[*Exit* ZATIMA, *supporting* ATALIDE.

(*Alone*) My rival at last reveals herself to me.
This, then, is she on whom I have relied!
For six whole months I thought her watchful-eyed
And zealous night and day to serve my love—
And it was I who was the abettor of
Hers all too well, who watched for her, it seems,
Those six months, and who would, myself, find means
To expedite their secret converse sweet,
Anticipate her wish for them to meet,
And speed the happiest moments she e'er knew!

This is not all: I must discover, too,
In what degree her treachery hath succeeded,—
Must . . . But what information more is needed?
Is not my woe writ plainly in her face?
Can I not see, through all her sore distress,
She is assured her lover's heart is hers?
Free from my own tormenting doubts, she fears
Now only for his life. No matter! We
Will learn the truth. Perhaps she trusts, like me,
False promises. To have him make all plain,
Let us devise a trap. But what a vain,
Vile task I set myself! Forsooth, shall I
Employ the greatest ingenuity
For mine own torture, to cause him to display
His scorn for me before mine eyes? He may
Himself perceive my purpose and outwit me.
　　Vizier and slave and mandate all beset me,
And I must choose my course without delay.
To everything that I have seen to-day
'Twere better I should close mine eyes, refrain
From searching out their love—to mine own pain.
Let us proceed with this ungrateful man,
And try our fortune: find out if he can
Betray, when I have raised him to the throne,
My love that saved him,—if, as with his own,
He will make free with what I gave him, and
Will crown my rival with a dastard's hand.
Truly, it will be always in my power
To punish her and him. I shall watch o'er
The traitor in my righteous wrath. I need
But to surprise him with his Atalide,
And I in death will join them, with the same
Dagger stab them and myself after them.

That, surely, is the part I should assume.
I wish to know naught.

[Enter ZATIMA.

Oh, what hast thou come

To tell me, Zatima? Is Bajazet
In love with her? From her words, seemeth it
That both of them have one desire and will?

ZATIMA.

She hath not spoken at all. Unconscious still,
She gives no sign that some life yet is hers
Except long sighs and moans which, it appears,
At any moment may also with them heave
Her very heart out. Anxious to relieve
Her suffering, thy ladies bared her breast
To ease her breathing. I flew to aid the rest
Of them and chanced this letter to discover
Hid in her bosom. 'Tis from the Prince, thy lover.
I recognized his hand. In loyalty,
I thought that I should bring it unto thee.

ROXANA.

Give it me. . . . Why do I shudder? Why should it make
My blood run cold, my hand that holds it shake?
He can have written it and yet wronged me not,—
Can even . . . Let us read, and learn his thought.
(Reading) ". . . . . . . Not death nor thou, to move her,
Will ever make me tell her that I love her,
Since I shall ever love but thee."
Ah! this, then, shows me their whole treachery.
I see the way they have deluded me.
'Tis thus, base wretch, that thou repayest my love.
The life I saved thou art not worthy of!
Oh, now I breathe again! What joy I taste!

The traitor hath betrayed himself at last.
Free from the cruel doubts that racked me, I
With soul untroubled can to vengeance fly.
Yes, vengeance! He shall die. Seize him forthwith!
Have the mutes make arrangements for his death.
Bid them to bring the bowstring, whose grim noose
Cuts short such lives as his, ready for use.
Fly, Zatima! Be swift to serve my hate.

ZATIMA.

Oh, madam!

ROXANA.

Well, what?

ZATIMA.

If without too great
Offence to thee, in the just wrath with which
I see thee filled, madam, I may beseech
Thee timidly to hear me and give heed:
Bajazet well deserves to die, indeed,—
To be consigned unto those ruthless hands.
But though he is an ingrate, as now stands
The case, is not the one who should be feared
Amurath? He may—who can tell?—have heard
Of thy new love from some disloyal tongue
Already. Hearts like his, if any wrong
Is done them, cannot, as thou amply know'st
Ever again be softened; and the most
Immediate death, in that dread hour, will prove
To be the dearest token of their love.

ROXANA (*who has not listened to* ZATIMA).
How cruelly and how insultingly
They both made sport of my credulity!

I was so glad, so ready, to believe!
No mighty deed, false wretch, didst thou achieve
In cozening this heart already yielded,
Which feared to lose the dream that it had builded.
I first, from that high place which made me proud,
Myself have sought thee, 'neath misfortune bowed—
To link my days, quiet and with blessings crowned,
To perils wherewith thine were girt around—
And after favours, care, and love so free,
Thy tongue can never say thou lovest me!
  But midst what memories doth my fancy stray?
Thou weepest, unhappy woman? Ah, that day
Shouldst thou have wept when foolish impulses
First bred thy fatal wish to see his face!
Thou weepest? and he, resolved on perfidy,
Prepares the words with which to hoodwink thee.
He fain would live, such being thy rival's will!
Oh, thou shalt die, thou traitor!—
      (*To* Zatima) What! here still?
Go.—
  But ourself, let us go, let us fly.
Me shall he see, most fain for him to die,
Show him both what his brother ordereth
And this too certain proof of his bad faith.
  Do thou, Zatima, keep my rival here.
No last farewell shall reach his dying ear
Except her screams. But take care of her. Give
The best of tendance to her. She must live.
My hate requires it. Ah, if she can be
Moved for her lover's sake so easily
That fear of his death almost caused her own,
What added vengeance and new sweetness soon
To show him to her lying pale and dead,

See her eyes fixed upon him, and be paid
Thus for the raptures which they had through me!
    Go, keep her here. Say naught, especially.
I—But who comes now, my revenge to stay?
[Enter ACHMET and OSMIN.

ACHMET.

What art thou doing, madam? Why this delay,
Wasting such precious moments? My endeavor
Hath gathered all Byzantium's folk together,
Who, frightened and confused, interrogate
Their leaders; and with them my friends await
The signal thou didst promise me, to announce
All to them. Why, vouchsafing no response
To their impatience, does the seraglio still
Maintain a gloomy silence all this while?
Madam, declare thyself; no more postpone . . .

ROXANA.

Thou shalt be satisfied. It shall be done.

ACHMET.

Why does thy look—does thy harsh voice—despite
Thy words, assure me of their opposite?
What! hath thy love, by obstacles dismayed . . .

ROXANA.

Bajazet is a traitor, and has had
Only too long a life.
ACHMET.
A traitor? he?

ROXANA.

To me, to thee, perfidious equally.
He played us both false.

ACHMET.

How?

ROXANA.

That Atalide,
Who was no adequate reward, indeed,
For all that thou attemptedst for his sake . . .

ACHMET.

Well?

ROXANA (*handing him* BAJAZET's *letter*).

Read this; judge if we should undertake,
After such treatment, that false man's defence.
Let us, instead, act in obedience
To the most just, however stern, command
Of Amurath, who now is near at hand,
Coming in triumph home. Without regret,
Let us make sacrifice of Bajazet,
Our base accomplice; for the Sultan still
We may appease by promptly doing his will.

ACHMET (*giving the letter back to her*).

Yes, since the ingrate dares to wrong me thus,
I myself will avenge thee, avenge us,
Madam. Let me remove the taint of crime
By which his life endangers thine and mine.
Set me the course, and I will run it.

ROXANA.

Nay.
Leave *me* the joy of seeing his dismay
When I confound the wretch—of seeing his shame.
With too swift vengeance I would miss my aim.

I go to make all ready. And do thou
Go and disperse thy friends assembled now.

[*Exeunt* ROXANA *and* ZATIMA.

ACHMET (*to* OSMIN, *who turns to depart*).
Wait, Osmin; 'tis not yet the time to go.

OSMIN.

What, sir! does jealousy transport thee so?
Hast thou not carried revenge far enough?
His death, besides, wouldst thou be witness of?

ACHMET.

What wouldst thou say? Art thou so credulous
As to suspect me of ridiculous
Anger? I, jealous? Would that the perfidy
Of the rash Bajazet angered only me!

OSMIN.

Then why, instead of words in his defence . . .

ACHMET.

Is she now one whom reasoning would convince?
Didst thou not see, when I was going to try
To find him, 'twas to save him or else die?
O luckless fate of plans so well designed!
Love-blinded prince—or rather all-too-blind
Minister! It becomes thee now, forsooth,
To have entrusted to the hands of youth
All thy great projects, when thou art laden with years
And honours, and permitted a vizier's
Uncertain fortunes to depend upon
Mad lovers' conduct!

OSMIN.

Let their frenzy run
Its course among themselves. Bajazet fain
Would perish. Look to thine own safety, then.
Who can disclose thy secret schemes, my lord,
Except some friends whom thou canst be assured
Will speak not? Thou wilt see the Sultan's wrath
Greatly mollified by his brother's death.

ACHMET.

Roxana in her rage may reason thus;
But I, who can see further, who by long use
Have had in monarchs' codes my tutelage,—
Who, serving 'neath three Sultans to old age,
Have seen my fellows' fearsome downfalls,—I
Know, without flattering myself, that by
Boldness alone can one like me make shift,
And that a bloody death is the sole gift
A slave can look for from his master's hate.

OSMIN.

Fly, then.

ACHMET.

I would have said the same, of late.
My enterprise had not progressed so far.
'Tis harder to give up, as things now are.
My failure must be such a signal one
And leave such wreckage that, when I have gone,
My foes' pursuit of me will be delayed.
Bajazet still lives. Why are we dismayed?
Achmet has rescued him from a worse plight
Earlier. Let us, in his own despite,
Save him from this great peril, for our own sake,
Our friends', and even Roxana's. Didst thou take

Note of how, anxious to protect him, she
Stayed mine arm, which it seemed would speedily
Avenge her? Little do I know of love;
But nowise death does she ('tis plain enough)
Who would confound and shame him now decree him.
Some time is left us. Roxana means to see him,
Osmin. She loves him still, howe'er despairing.

OSMIN.

And even so, what fills thee with such daring?
If she so orders, we must leave this place.
'Tis wholly filled . . .

ACHMET.

            With slaves, nameless and base,
Untrained to arms, reared in this sheltered spot;
But thou, whom Amurath neglects,—whose lot
Is linked by common grievances with mine,—
Wouldst thou support my desperate design
To the very end?

OSMIN.

         My lord, thou wrongest me.
If *thou* diest, then I, too, will die, with thee.

ACHMET.

A valiant band of friends and soldiers waits
For us to issue from the palace gates.
Besides, Roxana thinks my words sincere.
I was brought up in this seraglio, where
Well do I know the windings of its maze.
I know, too, Bajazet's usual lodging-place.
Let us delay no longer, but go try
Our fate; and if I must die, let us die—
Me as beseemeth a vizier, and thee
As should the favourite of a man like me.

ACT V

Enter ATALIDE.

ATALIDE.

Alas! I search in vain. Naught do I see.
How, how could I have lost it? Wretched me!
Heaven, hast thou let me in one day expose
So oft my lover and, to crown our woes,
This fatal letter reach my rival's eyes?
'Twas here I was when taken by surprise
By the Sultana's sudden entrance; and
I hastily thrust it with a trembling hand
Into my bosom. Her presence was too sore
A trial for my distracted soul. Before
Her threats, her tones, the order given, I quailed.
I felt my strength ebb, and my senses failed.
When I revived, her women were around me.
They have all vanished, and this, too, doth confound me.
Oh, cruel hands that succoured me! I paid
Too dearly for your help, for ye conveyed
That letter to Roxana. Unto what
Fell purposes doth she now turn her thought?
On whom, first, will her vengeance fall? What blood
Will ever satisfy her savage mood?
Ah, Bajazet is dead, or being killed
E'en now—while I a prisoner here am held!
    But the door opens. I shall learn his fate.

             [*Enter* ROXANA, ZATIMA, *and guards.*

ROXANA (*to* ATALIDE).

Withdraw.

ATALIDE.

Oh, pardon my unfortunate . . .

ROXANA.

Withdraw, I say; and answer not a word.
Guards, keep her out.

[*Exeunt* ATALIDE *and guards.*
Yes, all is ready—cord
And mutes and Orcan, all await their prey.
His life is still, though, in my hands. I may,
I can, yet save him. But if hence he goes,
Zatima, 'tis to death. Comes he?

ZATIMA.

He does.
Behind me a slave brings him, and so far
Is he from dreaming what disasters are
Soon to befall him that he seemed to me
To leave his own apartments eagerly
To seek thy presence.

ROXANA (*to herself*).

O base soul, canst thou
(Only too worthy to be deceived) allow
This wretch to appear before thee? Dost thou deem
That words of thine can move, can conquer, him?
Canst thou forgive him, even if he should submit?
What! shouldst thou not have vengeance even yet?
Dost thou still think that not enough thou art
Wronged? Waste no efforts more on that hard heart.
Wherefore should I not let him die? . . . But here
He is.

[*Enter* BAJAZET. *Exit* ZATIMA.

(*To* BAJAZET) I will reproach thee not. Too dear
The time could cost, to spend it futilely
In talk. Thou knowest what I have done for thee.
It comes to this: thy very life thou owest
To me; nor would I tell thee things thou knowest.
In spite of all my love, if I could not
Win thine, nowise do I complain of aught—
Though, to hide nothing from thee, this same love
And these same boons perhaps should have enough
Enhanced my few charms. But I am indeed
Amazed that thou, in gratitude and as meed
For so great love, for so great trust in thee,
Hast so long, by such vile shifts, feigned for me
A love thou didst not feel.

BAJAZET.

Who, madam? I?

ROXANA.

Yes, thou. Wouldst thou not still wish to deny
The scorn for me thou thinkest I know not of?
Wouldst thou not still seek to disguise that love,
'Neath false appearances, which bindeth thee
Unto another and still swear to me
With thy perfidious tongue all, in thy need,
That thou feelest only for thine Atalide?

BAJAZET.

Atalide, madam! Heavens! Who hath told
Thee such a . . .

ROXANA.

Stop, thou faithless man! Behold
Thy written words, and give the lie to them.

BAJAZET.

I say no more. This letter doth proclaim
Frankly a hapless love, concealed till now.
Thou knowest a secret that I wished to avow
A thousand times and almost did impart
To thee. I love, indeed, and ere thy heart,
Clashing with what I hoped, revealed to me
Its love's flame, my own heart, filled utterly
With a love born in childhood, had no room
For any except that. Then thou didst come,
Offering me life and power. If I may dare
To tell thee this, thou, being well aware
Of all the kindnesses which in thy love
Thou didst me, thoughtest that they were enough
To reassure thee of my feelings, too.
I saw thy error. But what was I to do?
'Twas one with which thou wouldst be loath to part.
How much a throne tempts an ambitious heart!
A gift so noble opened mine eyes wide
To see how matters stood. I prized, I tried
To seize, without further delay, the good
Chance given me to escape from servitude,—
All the more since I had to do it or die,
All the more since thyself didst ardently
Urge me thereto and fearedst most to be
Refused, and since that would imperil thee;
For after having dared to see and speak
With me, 'twas dangerous for thee to turn back.
     Yet—be thine own complaints my witnesses—
Have I beguiled thee with false promises?
Think of how often thou hast blamed me so
For silence, caused by my soul's strife and woe.

The nearer glory, owed to thee, approached me,
The more mine own distracted heart reproached me.
That heaven which heard it, knows I never meant
To be with hollow vows to thee content;
And if the outcome had fulfilled my hope,
Allowing to my gratitude free scope,
I with such honours would have satified
My debt to thee and gratified thy pride
That thou thyself, perhaps . . .

ROXANA.

What couldst thou do?
How couldst thou please me without giving, too,
Thy heart to me? What care I for the vain
Fruit of thy "vows"? Dost thou no longer, then,
Remember who and what I am? Lo, I—
Mistress of the seraglio, and of thy
Life and the realm itself (full power whereo'er
Amurath gave me), Sultana, and yet more,
That which I wrongly thought I was to thee,
Queen of a heart that loveth none but me—
I on this pinnacle of glory stand.
What paltry honours for me hadst thou planned?
Was I to drag out here a wretched fate,
Spurned by the man I crowned, from my estate
Fallen to a rank that countless others have,
Or even to be my rival's foremost slave?
Vex me no more. Let us now end these vain
Words. For the last time: wouldst thou live and reign?
Here is the Sultan's order; but I can still
Save thee. Decide at once.

BAJAZET.

Tell me thy will.

ROXANA.

My rival is here. Follow me instantly
And see her die by the mutes' hands. Set free,
Then, from a love fatal to glory's quest,
Plight me thy troth. Time will do all the rest.
Thus, if thou wishest, thou canst thy pardon buy.

BAJAZET.

If I were to consent, 'twould be that I
Might wreak revenge upon thee and make plain
To the whole world the horror and disdain
With which this offer fills me! . . .
                              But I let
Rage carry me away. Shall I thus whet
Thine anger 'gainst poor Atalide? She had
No part whatever in that transport mad,
Nor in my love or my ingratitude.
Far from trying to keep me hers, she would
Oft urge me to be thine, whate'er she felt.
Do not confuse her innocence with my guilt.
Give rein, if need be, to thy righteous wrath.
Carry out the commands of Amurath.
But let me, at least, die without hating thee.
He did not condemn her along with me.
Spare one whose life hath ever been so sad.
To all thy favours to me, madam, add
This one, and if I e'er was dear to thee . . .

ROXANA.

Begone!
                              [*Exit* BAJAZET.
       Thou nevermore shalt look on me.
Thou goest to the death that is thy due.
                              [*Enter* ZATIMA.

ZATIMA.

Atalide wishes to be listened to
One moment, madam. She begs thee to permit
Her now to do obeisance at thy feet
And truthfully impart unto thy ear
A secret which concerns thee more than her.

ROXANA.

Yes, let her enter. And do thou straightway
Follow Bajazet, who just left here. Stay
Till all is o'er, and tell me of it then.

[*Exit* ZATIMA. *Enter* ATALIDE.

ATALIDE.

Madam, no more do I intend to feign
Or to abuse thy goodness, as of late.
I blush at having so deserved thy hate,
And lay my heart before thee, and my crime.
      Yes, madam, it is true: for a long time
I have deceived thee. With no other thought
Than my love's interests, I was in naught
Loyal to thee. At sight of Bajazet,
I tried in all my words only to get
The better of thee. I loved him ever since
Our childhood, and have striven with diligence
To have his love. The future being hid,
His mother, the Sultana, hoped we would wed.
Alas, that hope wrought mischief to him. Later,
Thou lovedst him. For both 'twould have been better
If thou hadst known my heart or concealed thine
From me—thou, in thy love, suspecting mine.
I do not, to excuse him, take the blame
Wrongly; I swear by heaven, that sees my shame,

By those great Ottoman sovereigns whose own seed
He and I are. They kneel with me and plead
To thee for the last pure blood left them yet.
　　Sooner or later needs would Bajazet,
Seeing how much thou didst for him, have lost
His heart to beauty such as thou canst boast.
But in my jealousy I would ever make
Use of anything that might hold him back.
Complaints, tears, anger—naught did I neglect.
Sometimes I even adjured him to respect
The wish of his dead mother. On this day
Itself, of days most luckless, did I lay
Upon his head the blame that I would die,
Reproaching him for giving thee hope; and I
Stayed not my importunity till he
Against his will pledged his faith unto me,
Undoing thus himself and me as well.
　　Why shouldst thou tire of aiding him, or dwell
Upon his coldness in the past? 'Twas I
Who drove him to it. When I am dead, each tie
That I have broken will soon be closely knit
Again. Whatever punishment doth befit
My crime, though, do not thou thyself decree me
That doom. Let his distracted gaze not see thee
Bathed in my blood, which thine own hands did spill.
Spare that shock to his heart, too tender still.
Thou canst leave *me* the mistress of my fate.
My death will not be less immediate;
Enjoy a happiness it assures thee of.
Crown now a hero whom thou canst so much love.
My death be *my* concern, his life *thy* care.
Go, madam, go. Ere thou returnest, I swear
Thou'lt have no rival to offend thine eyes.

ROXANA.

I am not worth so great a sacrifice.
I know myself, madam, and my desert.
To-day, far from compelling you to part,
I shall with everlasting bonds unite
You twain. Thou soon shalt feast upon his sight.
Now rise.
            But what is it that so dismays
Zatima?

[*Enter* ZATIMA, *hastily.*

ZATIMA.

            Oh, come quick and show thy face,
Madam, or Achmet will be master here.
Not reverencing these sacred precincts, where
Our Sultans have their home, his wicked friends
Have forced the doors and entered. None defends
The place, and of thy trembling slaves full half,
At least, have fled. They know not if he hath
Rebelled or acts by thine authority.

ROXANA.

The traitors! I shall go and instantly
Confound him. Thou, guard well my prisoner
And know thou'lt answer with thy life for her.

[ROXANA *rushes out.*

ATALIDE.

Alas! for which ought I to pray? I do
Not know the aims of either of the two.
If any pity for my countless woes
Moves thee, I beg thee—nay, not to disclose
Roxana's secrets—but to tell me how
It fares with Bajazet, only that! Hast thou
Seen him? Need I not yet fear for his life?

ZATIMA.

Madam, I can but grieve at thy heart's grief.

ATALIDE.

What! hath she said already he must die?

ZATIMA.

I am above all bound to secrecy.

ATALIDE.

Nay, tell me only if he still draws breath.

ZATIMA.

I cannot tell thee aught. 'Twould mean my death.

ATALIDE.

This is too much, cruel woman! Make an end,
And give her surer proof, with thine own hand,
Of loyalty. Thy silence kills my heart.
Pierce it, merciless slave, then, that thou art,
Of a most savage slave! Cut short the days
That she would rob me of, and show apace
That thou art worthy to serve her, if one can
Be that! Thou seekest to keep me here in vain;
For in this very hour needs must I
See Bajazet, or else I needs must die.

[*Enter* ACHMET.

ACHMET.

Where is he? Where can I find Bajazet,
Madam? Is there time left to save him yet?
I have scoured all the palace. At the gate
Thereof did my brave comrades separate
Into two bands. One in the footsteps trod
Of gallant Osmin, and by another road

The others followed me. We ran throughout
Our course, yet I have seen naught but a rout
Of frightened slaves and fleeing women.

ATALIDE.

Oh,
I know less of his fate than thou dost know.
This slave knows all.

ACHMET (*to* ZATIMA).

Answer me, wretch, or fear
My righteous anger.

[*Enter* ZAÏRE.

ZAÏRE.

Madam!

ATALIDE.

Speak, Zaïre.
What is it?

ZAÏRE.

Thy foe is dead, thy danger o'er.

ATALIDE.

Roxana dead?

ZAÏRE.

What will surprise thee more,
Orcan, Orcan himself, just slew her.

ATALIDE.

What!
He?

ZAÏRE.

Having failed to kill the man he sought,
In disappointed rage he doubtless craved
This victim.

ATALIDE.

O just heaven, thine aid hath saved
Innocence. Bajazet still lives. Vizier,
Fly to him.

ZAÏRE.

Osmin saw it all. Thou'lt hear
The whole truth from his lips.

[*Enter* OSMIN *and followers.*

ACHMET (*to* OSMIN).

Her eyes misled
Her not? Roxana, then, is really dead?

OSMIN.

Yes; I have seen her slayer from her side
Draw out his dagger, with her lifeblood dyed.
Orcan, who from the first had meditated
This brutal deed, only anticipated
Thus her resolve to take her own life. He
Was bidden by the Sultan secretly
To put to death her lover and her, too.
He himself, when he saw us come in view
Of him, some little distance from him still,
Said to us: "Reverence your master's will.
Recognize here his seal—its imprint plain—
Traitors, and quit this palace ye profane."
Thereon he left Roxana where she lay
Dying, and came to meet us and display,
Unfolded to our sight with reeking hand,
The order which bore Amurath's command
That this fiend should commit a twofold crime.
But we, my lord, would give him no more time
For words. Made mad alike by rage and grief,

We with impatient hands cut short his life
And thus avenged the death, upon his head,
Of Bajazet.

ATALIDE.

Bajazet!

ACHMET.

What!

OSMIN.

Yes, he is dead.

Did ye not know it?

ATALIDE.

Gracious heaven!

OSMIN.

She
Who loved him, wholly frenzied, fearing that he
Would otherwise be rescued by thee, sir,
Consigned him, in a place not far from here,
Unto the fatal bow-string. Mine own eyes
Have seen the saddest sight beneath the skies,
And I have vainly tried to find in him
Some spark of life. The Prince was dead. A grim
Circle of dead and dying round him lay
Of those whom he compelled, when brought to bay,
To go with him among the shades, and so
Heroically avenged himself, although
Finally o'ercome by numbers. Now that we
Have failed, sir, let us save ourselves.

ACHMET.

Ah me!
To what hast thou reduced me, hostile Fate!
Madam, I know thy loss in Bajazet.

I know too well that in thy grief it ill
Becometh me to offer in good will
To thee the aid of some few wretches who
Themselves had put all their hopes in him, too.
His death has overwhelmed me with despair,
But comrades in misfortune claim my care.
Though naught I value *my* life, to the end
Those lives they staked with me will I defend.
As to thy going with us to other lands,
Trusting thy sacred person to my hands,
Consult thy wishes, madam. Masters here,
My faithful friends will wait till these are clear
To thee—while I shall go, that I may waste
No precious time, whither my presence best
Will serve our interests; and where the sea
Washes the palace walls, my ships will be
Awaiting thee ere long, ready to sail.

                [*Exeunt all but* ATALIDE *and* ZAÏRE.

        ATALIDE (*to herself*).

And so the end has come. What doth avail
All my deceit? Because of my unjust
Caprices and my fatal lack of trust,
I now have reached this hour of agony
When through my fault I see my lover die.
Cruel destiny, was it not, then, enough
That I was doomed to outlive him I love?
Must I, to crown the horror, know that he
Died for no reason but my mad jealousy?
Belovèd, it was I who wrought thy death.
'Twas not Roxana, 'twas not Amurath.
I, I alone, fashioned that fatal cord
Whereof thy throat hath felt the noose abhorred.

And I can still live and endure that thought—
I, who when danger threatened thee could not
Prevent myself from swooning, recently?
Oh, have I loved thee but to murder thee?
Nay, I can bear it not. My hand forthwith
Must punish me, take vengeance for thy death.

    Ye whose rest I did vex, whose honour stain,
Heroes who should in him have lived again,
Unhappy mother, who long ere we grew up
Gave me his heart with a far different hope,
Luckless vizier, his friends now desperate,
Roxana—come ye all, banded in hate,
To torture a distracted woman's heart!

                              [She stabs herself.

Take your revenge: that is her just desert.

ZAÏRE.

Ah, madam! . . . She is dead. Oh, would that I,
Grief-stricken as I am, with her might die!

MITHRIDATE
(MITHRIDATES)

INTRODUCTION

AFTER *Bajazet*, Racine's position as the leading tragic dramatist in France was assured. He had decidedly bested Corneille in the duel of "the two *Bérénices*." He had triumphed with *Bajazet* while Corneille was failing with *Pulchérie*. He was soon to be received into the French Academy. But he was not yet entirely satisfied. In the eyes of the public, especially of older people who had worshipped Corneille in his prime and who clung to him with dogged devotion in his later, less happy days, Racine was still only the writer of tragedies of love, who was incapable of treating historical subjects concerned with war and politics, the special province of their aging favourite. The success of *Britannicus* had been slow in coming, and was therefore of questionable impressiveness. Its author wanted to prove, beyond dispute, that he too could write a historical drama; he wanted to write one which would be generally recognized as equal or superior to any of Corneille's.

In some degree he would write it in his own fashion, as he did *Britannicus*. Let Corneille try to capture the spirit and circumstances of a given moment of history and show it, above all, in its political aspects, taking the greatest liberties with important historical figures as best suited his purpose. It was precisely these noted figures in whom Racine found his chief interest, and whom he was at pains to portray—to the extent that he could under the dramatic conventions to which he was subject—as he conceived them really to have been. Accordingly, he did not select, as Corneille usually did, personages who were not well known and who could therefore be distorted without a shock to his audience. In *Britannicus* he had painted portraits of Nero and Agrippina; and now in his new play, to compete with Corneille at his very best in historical drama—that is, with *Nicomède*—he chose no unfamiliar Prusias or Nicomedes for his central character in a play dealing with the resistance of the Near East to Roman aggression, but the great and terrible Mithridates.

Of the death of this famous king of Pontus, history tells that when he attempted to renew his war with Rome after being routed and becoming a fugitive, he met with treachery at the hands of his own son, Pharnaces, in consequence of which he killed himself. Here were proper elements of drama ready to hand. But the unfilial conduct of Pharnaces had to be motivated, and it was not enough that he should merely be in sympathy with that conquering nation which was the object of his father's lifelong hate. Moreover, in addition to the external conflict resulting from their opposite attitudes towards Rome, there had to be provided, to secure the most potent dramatic effects, some struggle within the breast of Mithridates himself.

"To explain and excuse the odious treason of Pharnaces as being caused by a rivalry in love," says N. M. Bernardin, "must have been the first idea that occurred to Racine." Certainly. It could not have failed to be the first idea to occur to him, for it was the absolutely stereotyped sort of motivation that all romanesque dramatists were employing. And that would have been the best of reasons for rejecting it. But Racine sought no further; he adopted it. He was still largely taking "the easiest way." After all, the invariable formula of French "classical" tragedy called for a love-element, in which nearly always the protagonist himself was involved. Corneille had more than once depicted an elderly man in love, not intending him to be a grotesque, ridiculous figure as such a one traditionally is in comedy, but dignified and "sympathetic"— thus Marcian in *Pulchérie* only the year before, to say nothing of Sertorius earlier. In contrast, Racine would show how fearsome a thing the love of an aging man can be when the man is Mithridates—its sensitiveness, its suspiciousness, its ferocious jealousy.

The object of that stark passion could not love Pharnaces and remain, herself, a "sympathetic" character; his perfidy is too infamous. So Racine had to supply Mithridates with another son, Xiphares, for his heroine, Monime, to love; and in order that their mutual affection might be subject to no possible blame, she and Xiphares are depicted as each having secretly loved the other before Mithridates ever saw her.

Thus did the dramatist's material take shape—in a decidedly conventional mould (mingling love and affairs of State, and having all the prominent male characters, regardless of their age, in love with the same woman) yet with great opportunities for powerful scenes and for the arousing of strong sympathies in any audience. Unfortunately, with the work of his rival so much in his mind—work which it was his first aim to parallel and to surpass—there was bound to be a larger element of artificiality in what he produced than when he was wholly intent on the "convincing" dramatization of his subject. A greater-than-usual remove from the lifelike invariably results when authors imitate other plays rather than life. We have already observed the increase of conventionality in *Bérénice*, where Racine was primarily competing with Corneille. In *Mithridate* he again and again sacrifices truth-to-life for convenience in plot-development or to secure a momentary stage effect or to have opportunities for "dramatic" speeches—as a brief review of this tragedy will disclose.

At the opening of the play the half-brothers Pharnaces and Xiphares, on the report of their father's defeat and death, have come to Nymphaeum in Tauris (the Crimea), where

Mithridates had sent Monime, his affianced bride, for her safety during the war whose outbreak prevented their nuptials. Declaring that Pharnaces is the most odious of men to her and that she would kill herself rather than marry him, she begs Xiphares to protect her against him; he assures her that he will do so, and then undertakes to make known to her his own love. In view of her helplessness, her fears, and her dependence upon him, the situation is a delicate one, requiring great tact in his avowal, as he is well aware. But this is how he begins:

XIPHARES.

Madam, of my obedience have no doubt.
Here thy authority is absolute.
To make himself feared, Pharnaces may go
Elsewhere. But thou still knowest not all thy woe.

MONIME.

Alas, what new woe can afflict Monime,
Sir?

XIPHARES.

If to love thee is so great a crime,
Not Pharnaces alone is guilty now.
I am far guiltier than *he* is.

MONIME.

Thou?

XIPHARES.

Of thy misfortunes, reckon this the worst.
Invoke the gods against a race accurst,
Destined to bring unhappiness to thee,
Ever inspired—the father formerly,
And now the sons—to do thee some ill turn.

He could hardly have found an approach more certain to alarm and dismay her, even if he had tried; and no one, except in a play, could have failed to realize this. But his ineptness causes tension and suspense, and therefore Racine represents him as being thus unbelievably inept.

The stupidity which this alert, capable, and usually far-from-stupid young man is made to display on this occasion is as nothing, however, beside that which the dramatist ascribes to him later. Though Monime, on his confession of his love, does not tell him that she returns it, she does tell him that he may continue to see her—a significant concession for a heroine of French "classical" tragedy to make under such circumstances. She reiterates to Pharnaces, in Xiphares' presence, her inflexible determination to wed no friend of Rome; and Pharnaces makes obvious insinuations as to her real reason for refusing him. Then the supposedly dead Mithridates appears. He thinks that it is only Pharnaces, not Xiphares, who loves Monime; he concludes from her coldness to himself that she loves this recreant son of his, and complains to Xiphares that she does. And Xiphares more than half believes him! Xiphares, who has seen and heard so much with his own eyes and ears, and who knows how fatal it would be for Monime to reveal to the despot her true feelings, promptly entertains the idea—on Mithridates' mere assertion that it is a fact—that she loves Pharnaces, after all! And when she protests to him, in horror, that she does not, he still fails to suspect—in spite of all that he has seen and heard—that it is himself whom she loves; and when she confesses that it is, he can hardly credit his ears. Had ever man so little sense, outside of a play? A "dramatic" scene, however, is thus obtained.

At length the King discovers, by trickery, who is the real object of Monime's affections; and Xiphares is warned by his

friend Arbates that his father knows all and that he must
fly. He hastens to Monime to inform her of this and take
a hurried last farewell. Some hidden foe, he tells her, has betrayed their secret—who, he cannot imagine. Whereupon:

MONIME.

Dost thou not know,
Then, even yet, who is thy secret foe?

XIPHARES.

To crown my grief, madam, I know him not.
How gladly would I pierce, before I got
My death, that false and treacherous heart of his!

MONIME.

Well then, sir, I must tell thee who it is.
Seek not elsewhere the foe that did such harm
To thee. Strike. No respect should stay thine arm.
I am the traitor. Thou shouldst punish me.

Great surprise of Xiphares! Effective climax, well worked
up. Yet in real life he would be bound to guess who has revealed his secret. For he knows that only two or at most
three people besides himself knew it: Arbates and Monime,
and Monime's confidante, Phaedima. Pharnaces divined it
and accused him before Mithridates; but evidently some one
has now confirmed the charges of Pharnaces against him and
Monime, which the King hitherto had refused to credit. This
could only have been one of those two or three people; and
Arbates has warned him of his danger, and he well knows
Monime's guilelessness and his father's infernal cunning. But
it is theatrically effective for him to be amazed, and for Monime to offer her breast to his vengeance and say "Strike!"
though she must have realized that Xiphares would not want

to strike *her* in any case—even if her betrayal of him had not
been wholly innocent, as it was.

Her own ingenuousness, however, and her incapacity for
dissimulating are represented as too extreme; such over-sim-
plification of a character belongs rather to melodrama than
to tragedy. Common report could not have left her ignorant
of Mithridates' possessive, suspicious, vengeful nature, unrestrained in its savagery by any human ties. She knows it
would mean ruin for Xiphares as well as for herself if she
should arouse the jealousy of this passionate tyrant and he
should guess whom she loves. Yet when he seeks hungrily
for some evidence of concern for him in her breast, she makes
no effort to represent herself as anything but the unresisting
victim of his will. She might at least have said then, quite
truthfully, what she does say later when defending herself
against his recriminations in the fourth act: that she was glad
to be able to give happiness to so great a man. But she will
not say even this when it would be helpful. Again, when
Mithridates perpetrates his cruel fraud to discover her heart's
secret (pretending that he now wishes her to wed Xiphares
instead of himself, but that he believes she loves the infamous
Pharnaces, with whom he will therefore join her in marriage)
and she is finally convinced of his sincerity, it is altogether
too much that she forthwith confesses all her feelings—that
she stakes everything on not being deceived, without any
reticence as a precaution against the possibility that she is.
Instead, it would be sufficient for her to assure him that
she detests Pharnaces and that she would much prefer Xiphares if she must marry one of the two. Here once more we
have a conventional ineptness which serves the ends of drama
—or rather of melodrama—but which would be almost un-
believable in real life.

It is also a convention of French "classical" tragedies to

magnify the prowess of their heroes; and in doing so, this play falls, near its end, into sheer absurdity: we are told that when Mithridates, brought to bay by overwhelming numbers and determined to die fighting, showed himself at the gates of the palace, the Romans all recoiled a short distance on beholding their redoubtable foe, and some of them in panic even fled back to their ships. Racine probably had in mind the great passage in the *Iliad*, when the Trojans recoiled at the mere sight of Achilles across the trench, unarmed though he was; but in *Mithridate* it is not Trojans but the veteran legionaries of all-conquering Rome who we are asked to believe were thus dismayed when confronted by a man whom they had beaten again and again!

Yet this drama, though conventionally plotted and though marred by false touches, has excellences which go far towards redeeming it. Its "story" is a good one—sure to appeal, as we have already observed, to an audience, and especially to people who are not too critical. In witness of this fact is the testimony of a teacher in an American college, that *Mithridate* "is by far the best play with which to begin the study of Racine," he having found, over a period of twenty-five years, that it "enlists, in higher degree than *Andromaque, Britannicus, Iphigénie, Phèdre,* or *Athalie*," the interest of his classes.[1] Its Xiphares, despite his occasional lapses of intelligence, is a rather attractive, if conventional, figure—as none of Racine's other young-men-in-love is. And the play has two very notable pieces of characterization in Mithridates himself and—aside from the one flaw in her portrayal discussed above—Monime.

Mithridates, with his sanguinary greatness and violent passions, more nearly accords with the conception of a "tragic

[1] L. B. Lewis, in his edition of *Mithridate*, New York, 1921, p. v.

hero" held by Shakespeare and his fellow Elizabethans than
does any other protagonist of Racine. He answers well, in
many respects, to our conception of the Mithridates of history—however much more concerned with love, to satisfy
the requirements of French-classical tragedy. Menace lurks in
his smoothest words, as in the first that we hear him utter,
on his arrival, to his sons:

> Princes, whatever reasons ye profess,
> Duty could ne'er have brought you to this place
> Nor made you quit, when issues bulked so large,
> Thou Pontus, Colchis thou, left in your charge.
> But 'tis a loving sire who judges you.
> Ye thought the rumours which I spread were true.
> I deem you guiltless, since ye will have it thus;

and the wild-beast fangs of the savage Oriental ruler are
bared in his admonition regarding Monime:

> My love's indulgence hath enough been tried.
> Let her not drive that very love, defied,
> To how know I what frenzy, which my soul
> Would not repent of till avenged in full.

His indefatigable, undismayed resilience in defeat, his
grandiose plans and overweening hopes of success against
mighty Rome are revealed with a virile eloquence in one of
the most famous monologues (and the longest one) that Racine ever wrote—a supreme effort to surpass Corneille in the
elder dramatist's own field. Yet except for this one speech,
Mithridates is so preoccupied with his fierce love and jealousy
throughout the play that the most frequent criticism made of
it is that we are not prepared for his sparing the young lovers
in the end and consigning them to each other. This criticism,

however, does not seem to me warranted. The motivating reasons for either vengeance or mercy on his part have been clearly shown, and no one could say certainly to which of two such possible alternatives the mind of a dying man would incline. His decision in favour of either was not inevitable, but can be accepted—whichever it is—for that very reason without incredulity; and that is enough.

Monime is generally considered the most attractive of all Racine's heroines. Gentle and innocent though she is, she displays a self-respecting pride, a quiet courage, strength of will, and devotion to duty which make her "Corneillian"—in Racine's own, how different way. The sweet, modest dignity with which she commences her account of herself wins every heart; and her becomingly restrained but fearless defiance of the tyrant King when she is finally pushed to the wall cannot but thrill every heart.

One thing she always longs for in her soul, with almost the keenness of a physical craving, and she recurrently gives wistful expression to that desire: to be free. Free she has never been—to wed as she chooses, to love as she chooses, not even to die as she chooses—and she eagerly receives the poison cup sent her by Mithridates, happy to be thus free at last.

He relents before she can drink of it, and unites her with Xiphares.[2] It is not unnatural, perhaps, that this ever-loyal son should weep for him as he lay dying; for Xiphares, though well aware of his father's ruthlessness, cruelty, and guile, had sincerely loved and admired him. But I cannot believe that Monime, too, would weep then, beseeching Mithri-

[2] This denouement, like that of *Bajazet*, is melodramatic in that it depends on the mere luck of time-sequence. Monime would have died if the intervention of Arbates had been two seconds later than it was.

dates to live, as Racine represents her as doing. Thankful she
might indeed be, that she was spared and was granted her
heart's dream of happiness; but his sins against her and
against the man whom she adored had been too great and
too recent for her to feel any affection for him; he had made
her suffer too much.[3] One does not love a tiger that has been
mangling him—not though the beast, for some reason, should
capriciously refrain at last from tearing out his throat. But
no other conduct on the part of her and Xiphares would have
been acceptable to audiences in the France of Louis XIV; to
them, monarchs were sacred, privileged beings, who must
not only be pardoned for all their past wickedness but loved,
too, as soon as they do one good deed. With such indulgence
for the faults of kings, people in Racine's time doubtless found
Mithridates a more "sympathetic" figure, in his greatness
and his sufferings through jealousy in the hour of his defeat,
than he is for us now. Audiences of the twentieth century will
realize that, however great and however tortured he is, stroke
after stroke of the dramatist's brush has painted him as a
villainous monster—the slayer formerly of other women he
loved and of other sons—and will wish only to see him removed from the path of those whose lives he threatens and
whose happiness he prevents. Obviously, the play is more
effective, more powerful, if he can be sympathized with; and
this goes to show *Mithridate* to be a play of greater value
for the age in which it was written than "for all time."

In that age it enjoyed a success marred by no important
adverse criticism. Racine had achieved his purpose; his long
duel with Corneille was finished at last, and he was com-

[3] The only kind of tears she might really have shed at that time were
tears of relief—in a natural reaction from the strain of her ordeal just
ended.

pletely victorious. Now he could finally turn to his own preferred field of endeavour, the world of Greek tragedy he so
much loved, from which that duel had kept him so long. He
never thereafter wrote any play—nor is said to have considered writing any—except in that field, redepicting that world,
until, late in life, he sought instead to apply the methods of
Greek drama, fundamentally a religious drama, to themes
connected with the religion of his own land.

CHARACTERS IN THE PLAY

MITHRIDATES, *King of Pontus and of many other realms.*

MONIME, *betrothed to Mithridates and already declared Queen.*

PHARNACES, *eldest son of Mithridates.*

XIPHARES, *younger son of Mithridates, by a different mother.*

ARBATES, *Mithridates' governor of Nymphaeum.*

PHAEDIMA, *female attendant of Monime.*

ARCAS, *servant of Mithridates.*

Guards.

The scene represents a room in the palace at Nymphaeum, a city in Tauris (the Crimea) on the Cimmerian Bosphorus (the straits between the Sea of Azov and the Black—or Euxine—Sea).

The name "Monime" is pronounced as in French, with the final "e" silent, in this translation. It rhymes with "seem."

MITHRIDATES

ACT I

Xiphares and Arbates are discovered.

Xiphares.

Too true, Arbates, are these tidings dread.
Rome is triumphant, Mithridates dead.
Near the Euphrates, in a night attack,
Her troops surprised my father, though to lack
Care was unlike him. After a long fight
His army, routed, left him in their flight
Among the slain. A soldier, now hath word
Come, placed in Pompey's hands his crown and sword.
Thus he who had for forty years, alone,
Baffled the ablest generals of Rome,
And in the East upheld, through varying
Fortunes, the common cause of every king,
Died, leaving to avenge him by ill chance
Two sons who are at hopeless variance.

Arbates.

What! hath desire to reign made Xiphares
Already, sir, the foe of Pharnaces?

Xiphares.

Nay, good Arbates, never thus would I
The wreckage of this luckless kingdom buy.
I could respect his birth's priority
And, happy in the lands assigned to me,
See fall into his hands without regret
All that he e'er will through Rome's friendship get.

ARBATES.

Rome's friendship? He? The son of Mithridates?
Can it be true, sir?

XIPHARES.

                Doubt it not, Arbates.
Pharnaces, long since Roman to the core,
Expects much from the Roman conqueror;
And I, more loyal now unto my sire
Than ever, cherish towards Rome undying ire;
Yet whom I hate and what his realm will be
Are the least reason for our enmity.

ARBATES.

What other cause sets thee at strife with him?

XIPHARES.

I shall astonish thee. That fair Monime,
Who won the King our father's love, for whom
After his death, Pharnaces here hath come . . .

ARBATES.

Yes, my lord?

XIPHARES.

            I, too, love her, and no more
Will I thereof keep silent, since I for
A rival now have but my brother. Thou
Didst not expect to hear such words, I trow;
But no new secret mine, Arbates, is.
Long hath my love, unspoken, grown ere this.
How can I unto thee the greatness show
Of my first longings or my latest woe?
But when we are reduced to misery

Now, 'tis no time to task my memory
With telling thee the story of my love.
    To justify me, let it be enough
To say that it was I who saw the Queen
First, and who loved her first,—that of Monime
My father had not even heard the name
When in my heart she lit a holy flame.
Later, he saw her. But no marriage he
Offered her, though so beautiful was she,
Nor any suit deserving to be heard.
He thought his fancy, she would deem, conferred
Honour enough on her and she would prove
An easy conquest. Thou knowest how he strove
To tempt her virtue, and how, tired at length
Of this vain effort, and with his passion's strength
Still undiminished though she was far away,
Through thee did he a crown before her lay.
Judge of my grief when tidings to me came
Of the King's love and purpose, and by them
I learned Monime, chosen to be his bride,
Was journeying to Nymphaeum, by thy side.
    Alas, 'twas in that bitter hour and drear
My mother to Rome's overtures lent ear,
And to avenge the troth this marriage would break
Or to win Pompey's favour for my sake,
False to my father, she to Rome betrayed
The fortress and the treasures which he had
Entrusted to her care, to guard for him.
How changed I was on hearing of her crime!
He was no more my rival in mine eyes.
I thought not of my love, thwarted by his—
Only of the wrong done him. I attacked
The Romans; and my mother, at this act

Aghast, saw me retake the stronghold she
Had given to them, and, trying by death to free
Myself from all taint of her treason, expose
My body to a thousand mortal blows.
The Euxine hath, since then, belonged to us.
From Pontus even to this Bosphorus
All owned my father's sway. His vessels have
For enemies had only wind and wave.
I hoped to do yet more : I planned, Arbates,
Myself to march, to aid him, to the Euphrates.
News of his death came as a stunning blow ;
But even amid my tears, I must avow,
Monime, left by my father in thy care,
And all her loveliness beyond compare,
Arose before me in my mind. Nay, more,
I trembled for her life in that sad hour,
Dreading the cruelty of the King's love.
Thou knowest how often jealousy would move
His heart to assure himself of any one
He loved, by slaying her. I thereupon
Sped to Nymphaeum and found, to my dismay,
Pharnaces 'neath its ramparts. I straightway
From this foreboded evil, be it confessed.
Thou didst receive us both and knowest the rest.
      Pharnaces, by nature violent,
Concealed not his presumptuous intent,
Related to the Queen my father's fall,
Told her that he was dead, and therewithal
Offered himself to her, to take his place.
He means, Arbates, everything he says.
But now I, in my turn, intend to act.
Just as my love treated with due respect
A sire to whom I was from infancy

Devoted, so now, feeling itself free
To speak at last, it challenges the claims
Of this new rival. Either to its flames
Monime herself must be averse and say
Nay to my suit to her or, come what may
Of harm to me as Fortune may contrive,
She shall not be another's while I live.

These are the things I felt I should disclose
To thee. Thou must decide whose cause to espouse,—
Which of us seems to thee the worthier one,
The slave of Rome or thy king's loyal son.
Proud of Rome's friendship, Pharnaces may try
To lord it in Nymphaeum and speak as my
Master; but here no rights will I resign.
His heritage is Pontus, Colchis mine;
And always any one who o'er Colchis reigns
Hath had this Bosphorus in his domains.

ARBATES.

Thine is it to command me. 'Twixt you two
My choice is made already; I will do
My duty, if some power I still possess.
With the same courage, the same faithfulness,
That served thy sire, holding against thy brother
And thee this fortress, I against all other
Men will serve thee, now that the King is dead.
Do I not know that but for thee my head
Would surely have fallen as soon as Pharnaces
Had entered here? Do I not know that these
Walls I defended 'gainst him would have been
Stained with my blood by him? As to the Queen,
Learn for thyself her feelings and her choice.
Regarding all the rest, unless my voice

No more hath here any authority
Pharnaces, leaving this Bosphorus to thee,
Will go to enjoy Rome's kindnesses elsewhere.

XIPHARES.

How great my debt is to thy zealous care!
But here is some one. Friend, 'tis Monime! Away!

[*Exit* ARBATES. *Enter* MONIME.

MONIME.

Sir, I have come to thee. For where to-day,
If thou forsakest me, can I find aid?
An orphan, friendless, desolate and afraid,
Queen long in name, but really prisoner,
A widow who never had a husband—sir,
These are the smallest portion of my woe.
I fear to name to thee my most dread foe,
And yet I hope that one with heart so great
Will nowise sacrifice the unfortunate
Because of blood-ties which unite you twain.
I speak of Pharnaces, it must be plain
To thee. 'Tis he, sir, he, whose wicked thought
Is, by sheer force, to make me share his lot
With nuptials worse than death to me, by far.
I had my birth under what hostile star?
Decreed an earlier, loveless marriage, I
Have scarce escaped it, and some peace thereby
Have tasted, when I am required to link
Myself to that one from whom most I shrink.
Perchance, more humble in my misery,
I ought at least not to forget that I
Speak to his brother, but whether reason or Fate
Prompts me, or whether it be only hate
That in my mind confounds him with the Rome

Whose help he seeks, no marriage could be a doom
So frightful to me as the one I dread—
Not though with blackest signs accompanied.
And if Monime can move thee by no tear,—
If naught can aid me but mine own despair,—
Before that altar where I am to stand,
Sir, thou wilt see me pierce with mine own hand
This heart which others always would deprive
Of free choice, and which ne'er was mine to give.

XIPHARES.

Madam, of my obedience have no doubt.
Here thy authority is absolute.
To make himself feared, Pharnaces may go
Elsewhere. But thou still knowest not all thy woe.

MONIME.

Alas, what new woe can afflict Monime,
Sir?

XIPHARES.

If to love thee is so great a crime,
Not Pharnaces alone is guilty now.
I am far guiltier than *he* is.

MONIME.
Thou?

XIPHARES.

Of thy misfortunes, reckon this the worst.
Invoke the gods against a race accurst,
Destined to bring unhappiness to thee,
Ever inspired—the father formerly,
And now the sons—to do thee some ill turn.
But with whatever pain thou mightest learn

Of this forbidden love which startles thee,
Never couldst thou have such great misery
As I in trying to hide it. Yet, I pray,
Think not I am like Pharnaces and to-day
Serve thee to take his place here. Fain wouldst thou
Be thine own mistress, and I have made a vow
To see to it that thou art. Thou shalt not be
Dependent upon either him or me.
But when thy wish is fully satisfied,
In what place hast thou chosen to abide?
Will it be far from my domains, or near,
Madam, and may I lead thy footsteps there?
Do crime and innocence seem alike to thee?
Fleeing from my rival, wilt thou flee from me?
For so well furthering thy desires, must I
Resign myself to bidding thee good-bye
For ever?

MONIME.

Ah, what hast thou told me?

XIPHARES.

Nay,

Fair Monime, this, too, I must needs now say.
If there are some rights in priority,
I was the first of all to see thee, I
Resolved to make thee mine, ere anything
My father yet knew of thy burgeoning
Loveliness, which till then had not been shown
Except unto thy mother's eyes alone.
Ah, if my duty forced me to depart
And I could not lay bare to thee my heart,
Dost thou no more remember now, all else
Aside, what grief appeared in my farewells?—

No more recall how, when I left thy beauty,
I railed at my inexorable duty?
'Tis only I who have forgotten naught.
Madam, confess: I speak to thee of what
Had vanished from thy soul. While I was burning—
Far from thee, and without hope of returning—
Still with my hopeless love, thou hadst a mind
Content, to marriage with my sire resigned.
The sorrows of his son scarce troubled thee.

MONIME.

Alas!

XIPHARES.

Thou for a moment pitiest me.

MONIME.

Prince, do not take advantage of my plight.

XIPHARES.

Advantage of it? Gods! I fly to fight
In thy defence, asking naught, hoping naught.
Besides, I promise thee to bring 't about
That thou needest never see me more—that, too!

MONIME.

This is to promise more than thou canst do.

XIPHARES.

What! thou despite mine oath believest that I,
False and abusing my authority,
Intend upon thy freedom to encroach?
    But some one doth approach, e'en now approach,
Madam. Explain thyself. One word, please, please!

Monime.

Protect me from the rage of Pharnaces.
To keep me, sir, from seeing thee no more,
Thou wilt not need to use unrighteous power.

Xiphares.

Ah, madam!

Monime.

Here thy brother is.

[*Enter* Pharnaces.

Pharnaces.

Until
When, madam, wilt thou expect my father still?
Proofs of his death come every hour. They
Leave thee no grounds for doubt or for delay.
Flee, then, the sight of these inclement skies
Which speak but of sad bondage, to thine eyes.
Obedient subjects wait on bended knee
In fairer, fitter climes to welcome thee.
Pontus hath long acknowledged thee her queen.
The proof thou art is on thy brow still seen.
This royal fillet was given thee to wear
As a sure warrant thou wilt be sovereign there.
I, master of that realm, the heritage
My father left me, should fulfill his pledge.
But thou canst bide no longer. We must speed
Our marriage and departure, both: so plead
Our common interests and my heart as well.
My ships await thee, ready to set sail,
And from the altar thou mayest go aboard,
Queen of the seas that bear thee hence.

MONIME.

My lord,
Such graciousness might well embarrass me;
But since time presses and I must answer thee,
May I now put concealment and pretence
Aside and show thee the true sentiments
Thus of my inmost heart?

PHARNACES.

Let them be shown.

MONIME.

I think thou knowest my story. My own home
Is Ephesus, but in mine ancestry
Are kings—or else, sir, heroes whom their high
Deeds, in the eyes of Greece, made greater men
Than kings are. Mithridates saw me. Then
The prosperous empire that he ruled contained
Ephesus and Ionia still. He deigned
To send this token of his troth to me.
It was a mandate to my family
Which had to be obeyed. A crownèd slave,
I went to make the marriage that Fate would have.
The King, awaiting me in his own domains,
Found himself forced to go thence by new plans,
And while war occupied him, out of harm's
Way sent me to this place, far from all storms;
So I came hither, and I still am here.
But meanwhile, sir, my father has paid dear
For the honour done me. First of all to be
Slain, following the Romans' victory,
Was Philopoemen, father of Monime.
It was that title which brought death to him.

'Tis of just this, my lord, that I desired
To speak to thee. However justly fired
With anger, I can nowise against Rome
Array an army. To avenge his doom
I have no sovereign power nor soldiery;
A helpless witness of such crimes am I.
I only have a heart. All I can do
Is to remain to his dear memory true,
Never consenting with his blood to dye
My hands by wedding, in thee, Rome's ally.

PHARNACES.

Of Rome and her alliance speakest thou?
Why all this talk, why these suspicions, now?
Who says I am to be allied with her?

MONIME.

But thou thyself, canst thou deny it, sir?
How couldst thou offer me free entrance, crowned,
Into a land which Roman troops surround,
If secret pacts with Rome had not bestowed
That land on thee and opened wide each road?

PHARNACES.

I might inform thee of my purposes
And the good reasons justifying these
If thou indeed hadst put aside pretence
And told me thy real feelings. But I commence,
After so many windings, to divine
The meaning of these various shifts of thine.
Methinks thy secret I no more need seek.
'Tis not thy father who thus makes thee speak.

XIPHARES.

Whate'er it be that makes the Queen speak thus,
Should thy reply, sir, be ambiguous,
Or for one instant shouldst thou hesitate
Frankly to say thou holdest Rome in hate?
What! we have learned our father is dead, and loath
To avenge him, swift to take his place, we both
Our duty and his blood alike forget?
He is dead; but is he buried even yet?
Who knows but that while thou art fain to feast
On thoughts of wedded bliss, he whom the East,
Which saw his deeds and with their fame still rings,
Can justly call the last of all her kings
Lies without honours midst the slain obscure,
In his own realm deprived of sepulture,
And cries out against heaven which leaves him there
And his unworthy sons, who do not dare
To avenge him? Oh, let us no longer thus
Bide in our haven by this Bosphorus!
If in the whole world any king still free—
Parthian, Sarmatian, Scythian—there be
That loveth liberty, he is our ally.
Let us go thither; let us live or die
True sons of Mithridates. Let us plan,
Whatever love beguiles us, how we can
Save from the yoke ourselves and our domains—
Not constrain hearts that force alone constrains.

PHARNACES.

He knows thy feelings, madam. Was I wrong?
Behold what had o'er thee a power so strong—

That father and those Romans whom thou so
Reproachest me with!

XIPHARES.

                    Nothing at all I know
Of her heart's secret feelings. But if I thought
Like thee I understood them, sir, in naught
Would I presume, but bow to her decrees.

PHARNACES.

Thou wouldst do well. I shall do what I please.
No rule does thy example set for me.

XIPHARES.

Yet here I know of none who must not be
Governed by the example I supply.

PHARNACES.

In Colchis thou couldst speak thus boldly.

XIPHARES.

                                        I
Can do it in Colchis, and I can do it here.

PHARNACES.

Here? It might cost thy life to interfere.

[Enter PHAEDIMA.

PHAEDIMA.

Princes, ships cover all the sea and, giving
The lie to tales he was no longer living,
Soon Mithridates will himself appear.

MONIME.

Mithridates!

XIPHARES.

          My father!

PHARNACES.

    What do I hear!

PHAEDIMA.

Some lighter vessels came, this news to bring.
'Tis he. Arbates, to receive the King
As duty bids him, hath already gone
Out, in a boat, from shore.

XIPHARES.

    What have we done!

MONIME (*aside to* XIPHARES).

Farewell, Prince. Oh, what news!

        [*Exeunt* MONIME *and* PHAEDIMA.

PHARNACES (*to himself*).

        Returned, hath he?

Alas, how cruel Fortune is to me!
My life and love are both in peril. Too late
The Romans will arrive, whom I await.
(*To* XIPHARES) What shall we do? I know thy heart doth
    ache,
Prince; I can guess what parting words she spake
To thee; but more of this some other time.
We now are faced with problems great and grim.
Back Mithridates comes, implacable
Perhaps—the more unfortunate, the more fell.
Much deadlier than thou deemest, our danger is.
We both are guilty: well thou knowest this.
Affection seldom hath disarmed his wrath.
A sterner, crueler judge none ever hath
Than his sons have in him, and two of them
We have beheld him with less reason condemn

To death because of his suspicions. We
Must for the Queen herself, as well as thee
And me, have fear. I pity her the more,
The more our Mithridates loves her; for,
As he is in his love most passionate
But jealous when 'tis not returned, his hate
Always goes farther than his love. Do not
Trust his affection for thee. Still more hot
His jealous rage will burn because of it.
Consider well. The soldiers' favourite
Art thou; I shall have aid I do not need
To name. Wilt heed my counsels? With all speed
Let us assure our pardon: of this place
Make ourselves masters—thee and me—apace,
And force him thus to offer to his sons
Terms they would willingly accept at once.

XIPHARES.

I know what guilt is mine, and I know what
My father is; but I, as thou dost not,
Have weighing on me, too, a mother's crime,
And love cannot so blind me at this time
That when he comes here, I shall not obey
His will.

PHARNACES.

Let us at least, then, not betray
Each other. Thou dost know my secret; I
Have divined thine. The King's capacity
For wiles is limitless, and we can make
His wrath destroy us by the least mistake
Of speech. Thou knowest his way: how with a show
Of fondness he will mask his hate's dire blow.
Come. Since I needs must, I will do like thee.
Let us obey but keep faith mutually.

ACT II

Monime and Phaedima are discovered.

Phaedima.

What! thou art still here when the King doth land
And all, to bid him welcome, throng the strand?
What meaneth this, madam, and what inward thought
Hath stayed thy steps and turned thee back. Do not
Anger a monarch who adoreth thee,
Almost thy husband now . . .

Monime.

          Not yet is he
That, Phaedima; and until he is, I deem
I should receive him here, not go to him.

Phaedima.

But, madam, this no common lover is.
Remember that thy sire pronounced thee his,
That of the love of this great king thou hast
A formal pledge, and at the altar fast
In wedlock ye shall be united when
He will. Be ruled by me; go, greet him, then.

Monime.

See, with what face wouldst thou that I go greet him?
See these cheeks wet with tears. Rather than meet him,
Tell me, O tell me, where to hide my head!

Phaedima.

What! O gods!

MONIME.

He came back! Would I were dead!
Wretch that I am! Oh, how can I stand now
Before him, with his fillet on my brow,
And in my heart's core, Phaedima . . . Thou dost see
My blushes, and thou understandest me.

PHAEDIMA.

Hast thou again the same anxieties
That oft in Greece drowned with thy tears thine eyes?
Must Xiphares for ever make thee grieve?

MONIME.

My woes are crueler than thou wouldst conceive.
Xiphares then before my fancy came
Only as great in manhood, great in fame.
I did not know he was in love with me.
No other mortal loves so ardently.

PHAEDIMA.

He loves thee, madam? This hero, loved so well . . .

MONIME.

Is as unhappy as I am miserable.
He worships me, and that which was the cause
Of my pain, here, tortured him where he was.

PHAEDIMA.

Knows he what thy regard for him now is?
Knows he thou lovest him?

MONIME.

Nay, he knows not this.
The gods have helped me and made strong my heart
To say naught of it—naught, or no large part.

Alas, if thou but knewest how great violence
This sad heart did itself, then, to keep silence!
What battles it hath fought, what stress it bore!
If possible, I will see his face no more.
Try howsoe'er I might, beyond a doubt
When I beheld his grief I would speak out.
He will, despite me, make me own my love.
No matter, his shall have scant joy thereof.
Better would he, so dear that knowledge will
Cost him, remain in ignorance of it still.

PHAEDIMA.

Some one is coming. Madam, thou wouldst do what?

MONIME.

I cannot, will not, be seen thus distraught.
[*Exeunt* MONIME *and* PHAEDIMA. *Enter* MITHRIDATES,
   PHARNACES, XIPHARES, ARBATES, *and guards.*

MITHRIDATES.

Princes, whatever reasons ye profess,
Duty could ne'er have brought you to this place
Nor made you quit, when issues bulked so large,
Thou Pontus, Colchis thou, left in your charge.
But 'tis a loving sire who judges you.
Ye thought the rumours which I spread were true.
I deem you guiltless, since ye will have it thus;
And I thank heaven for here uniting us.
Vanquished and nigh to shipwreck though I be,
I cherish a purpose worthy of me. Ye
Will be informed more fully of it soon.
Go; let me rest a moment.
                [*Exeunt* PHARNACES *and* XIPHARES *and guards.*

So, after one
Whole year, thou seest me here again, Arbates—
No more the fortune-favoured Mithridates,
Who in the balances of destiny
Was weighed with Rome for the world's mastery,
Which long was doubtful. I have met defeat.
    Alert was Pompey, his success complete,
In darkness which for courage left scant room.
Our soldiers were half-clad amid night's gloom,
Their ranks ill formed, ill maintained everywhere,
By their confusion making worse their fear,
Turning their weapons 'gainst each other, cries
Re-echoing from the rocks and from the skies—
With all such horrors of a midnight fray,
What good was valour? Panic held full sway.
Some died, flight saved the rest, and I no doubt
Owed my life solely, in the general rout,
To the report of my own death, which I
Had spread. Unrecognized, eventually
I crossed the Phasis and pressed onward thence
Until I reached the foot of the Caucasus, whence
I soon on ships that in the Euxine waited
Rejoined my army's fragments, separated
Widely in flight, but now there gathered. Thus
Driven by disasters to this Bosphorus,
I find misfortunes here, too, facing me.
Burning with the same love, as thou dost see,
This heart with carnage fed, for war athirst,
Despite its burden of years and Fate's dire worst,
Carries the love with it, where'er it goes,
Which binds it to Monime, nor hath it foes
Worse than the two unnatural sons whom here
I meet.

ARBATES.

"The two," my lord?

MITHRIDATES.

Nay, hearken. Whate'er
My anger, I would fain not fail to see
Xiphares' difference from his brother. He,
Always obedient to my behests,
I surely know, as much as I detests
Our common enemies; and his valour I
Have seen, displayed for my sake, justify
My secret preference for him. I am no less
Aware—yes, well aware—in what distress,
Setting his duty above every other
Claim, he forthwith disowned his traitorous mother
And won new honour from her villainy.
I cannot, dare not, now believe that he,
This loyal son, would wrong me. And yet what
Concern brought either of them to this spot?
Have they alike aspired to wed the Queen?
Towards which doth she in secret seem to lean?
And with what countenance should I greet her? Speak!
Though longing draws me to her, I must seek
True knowledge of their hearts. What happened, then?
What didst thou see? What knowest thou? Why, since when,
And how didst thou yield to their force or pleas?

ARBATES.

Eight days ago, the impetuous Pharnaces,
Sir, was the first to come here. He beneath
These walls confirmed the story of thy death,
And wished to be let in at once. I was
By such a wild report not given pause,

Nor would I e'er have heeded it, had the Prince
His brother not been able to convince
My mind, when he arrived, that thou wert dead—
Less by his words than by the tears he shed.

MITHRIDATES.

What did they do then?

ARBATES.

Pharnaces hath scarce
Entered when to the Queen he flies, declares
His love for her, and offers on her brow
Firmly to fix, by wedding with her now,
The fillet she did from thy hand receive.

MITHRIDATES.

The traitor! giving her no time to heave
Sighs or weep tears she to my ashes owed!
What of his brother?

ARBATES.

He hath never showed,
Down to this very day, the slightest signs
Of love, my lord, in any of his designs.
His heart hath always seemed, like to thine own,
To pant for war and for revenge alone.

MITHRIDATES.

But still, what purpose could have brought him here?

ARBATES.

Sooner or later, sire, that will be clear.

MITHRIDATES.

Nay, I must know all now, without delay.
Speak, I command thee!

ARBATES.

Down to this very day,
Thus hath it seemed: that this prince thought he could
Quite properly, after thy death, include
This land in his domains; yet he could claim
No help here but his courage, and he came
To pit force against force and so protect
His rights.

MITHRIDATES.

'Tis the least prize he should expect
For his reward, if I can yet bequeath
That which is mine! Arbates, I can breathe
Again. My joy is great. I shall confess
That for a son I love, and no whit less
For myself, too, I trembled, being afraid
In equal measure of losing now such aid
As his and having a rival such as he.
If Pharnaces offendeth against me,
In him mine anger finds only a son
Who long hath flouted my displeasure—one
Who hath admired the Romans secretly
All his life, and who never willingly
Hath done aught against them. And if Monime
Proves to have been kindly disposed towards him
And gave a look elsewhere that was my due,
Woe to the wretch who robbed me of her,—who
Is bold to wrong me, but most faint hath been
To serve me. Doth she love him?

ARBATES.

Sire, the Queen
Draws near.

MITHRIDATES.

　　　Gods, who behold my love and hate,
Spare me in my misfortune! Let me wait
Longer to find those I shall seek anon.
Enough, Arbates. Leave me with her, alone.
　　　　　　　[*Exit* ARBATES. *Enter* MONIME.
　　Madam, heaven hath finally brought me back
To thee. It shows at least to my heart's ache
Some kindness, and restores thee unto me
Lovelier than ever. I did not foresee
That I would have to wait so long before
Our wedding-day, nor that when I once more
Came hither, my return would not display
My love, but my misfortune. Yet to-day
It is that love which would not, out of many
Places of refuge, let me go to any
Save where thou art, nor could a misfortune be
So great that it might not seem sweet to me
If unto thee my presence is not one.
I have said enough to make my feelings known
If thou desirest to know them. Long must thou
Have been prepared for this day, and thy brow
Weareth a token, madam, of my troth,
Which tells thee thou art mine. Then let the oath
Of marriage make our tie unbreakable.
My honour calleth me, and thee as well,
Far hence; and we, without a moment lost,
Heeding its summons, by to-morrow must
Depart—but thou to-day shalt be my wife!

MONIME.

Thy will is law, sire. Those who gave me life
Yielded to thee their sovereign power o'er me,

And when thou usest this authority
My sole response is to obey thee.

MITHRIDATES.

So,
Submissive to a grievous yoke, thou'lt go
To the altar as a victim—nothing else!
I, who constrain thee when thy soul rebels,
Even in possessing thee shall owe thee naught.
Ah, madam, how canst thou thus give me what
Will satisfy my heart? Must I aspire
No more to win thy love, and have no higher
Aim with thee henceforth than to be thy master?
Tell me directly: is it my disaster
That makes thee scorn me? Even if I did not see
Roads beckoning me anew to victory,—
If hostile Fate had hurled me down yet lower,
Defeated, hounded, without realm or power,
Wandering from sea to sea, not so much king
As pirate, naught being left me but one thing,
The name of Mithridates,—understand:
With that illustrious name, in every land
In the world I would attract all eyes to me;
There is no monarch that deserves to be
A monarch, who, firm fixed upon his throne,
Would not prefer, mayhap, to all his own
Splendour my glorious downfall, dearly bought,
Which Rome and forty years have scarcely wrought.
Wouldst thou thyself not view me otherwise,
Seeing me through thy Greek forefathers' eyes?
And since thy husband I must be indeed,
Were it not nobler, worthier of their seed,

To let free choice make duty be less hard,
To oppose to Fate's injustice thy regard,
And reassure me, lightening my woes,
'Gainst the distrust that with misfortune goes? . . .
How now! hast thou naught, madam, to reply?
Thou standest mute, and all my ardency
Serves only to confound thee; and, far now
From answering me, despite thy efforts thou
Canst scarce, 'twould seem, hold back thy tears, instead.

MONIME.

I, my lord? Nay, I have no tears to shed.
I shall obey thee. Needest thou know aught
More? Is that not enough?

MITHRIDATES.

                              No, it is not!
I understand thee better as to this
Than thou supposest. I now see it is
The truth that I was told. My jealousy
Is by thy words too well avouched. I see
That a disloyal son, enamoured of
Thy beauty, hath spoken unto thee of love
And thou hast hearkened. I have roused thy fears
For him, but he will in thy faithless tears
Find little joy. If any still obey
My orders, thou hast looked on him to-day
For the last time.
(*To his guards, outside*) Call Xiphares!

MONIME.

                                    Ah, what
Wouldst thou do? Xiphares . . .

MITHRIDATES.
                                    Xiphares hath not
Betrayed his father. Needlessly dost thou
Make haste all wrong with him to disavow.
And with my fond affection for him, I
Am glad that thus it is. My shame and thy
Sin would be less if that son who so well
Is worthy of thy esteem could make thee feel
Some love for him; but that a traitor, brave
Only in angering me, who doth not have
One virtue to redeem his frowardness—
That Pharnaces, in short, should take my place!
That he should be loved, madam, and I be hated!

[*Enter* XIPHARES.

    Come, my son, come; thy father is mistreated.
A recreant son affronts me in my woe,
Crosses me, flouts me, deals me a mortal blow—
Loves the Queen, that is—wins and robs me of
A heart which owes to me alone its love.
But I am happy, with such wrongs as these,
That I can blame no one but Pharnaces,—
That thou art vainly set by thy false mother
A bad example, as by thy headstrong brother.
Yes, my son, I rely on none but thee.
Thee only have I long since chosen to be
The fitting partner in my vast design,
Heir to my crown and this proud name of mine.
Pharnaces and my outraged love cannot
Even now wholly occupy my thought.
The plans and preparations for a great
Project conceived, the vessels that must wait
In readiness to sail, the soldiery
Whose willingness I would test, to follow me,

Demand my presence at the selfsame hour.
Do thou, meanwhile, watch here, to make all sure.
Foil my presumptuous rival's plottings. Ne'er
Leave the Queen's side, and thyself render her,
If possible, less unyielding to a king
Who loves her. Turn her from what needs must bring
Ruin upon her. Thou canst, as a man
Dispassionate, sway her better than I can.
My love's indulgence hath enough been tried.
Let her not drive that very love, defied,
To how know I what frenzy, which my soul
Would not repent of till avenged in full.

[*Exit* MITHRIDATES.

XIPHARES.

What shall I say? How must I understand
These strange, amazing words and this command?
Can it be true that Pharnaces indeed
Is loved by thee, to bring upon his head
This wrath? Is it for him thou feelest such fear?

MONIME.

Pharnaces? Pharnaces? What do I hear?
O gods! Is it not enough that this cruel day
From all I love is tearing me away,
And that I see myself, a hapless slave
Of duty, chained to lifelong grief? I have
Insults now added to my miseries!
It is believed I weep for Pharnaces!
In spite of my aversion, plainly enough
Displayed, 'tis thought that he could win my love!
I pardon the King for this; rage makes him blind,
And he knows not my secret heart and mind.
But thou, my lord, but thou, to treat me so!

XIPHARES.

Madam, forgive a lover mad with woe,
Who is himself caught fast in duty's snare,—
Who is about to lose all, yet can dare
Not even to take vengeance. What must I
Deem of the fury of the King, whose cry
Is that another's love defeateth his?
Who is the miscreant so blest as this?
Who? Speak!

MONIME.

Thou torturest thyself, perverse
Prince. Mourn thy pain; ne'er seek to make it worse.

XIPHARES.

I know too well the torment I prepare
Myself. A misery far less hard to bear
Is that my father shall wed her I love.
It is a pang all other pangs above
To see a rival honoured by thy tears;
Yet mine own breast would I, despairing, pierce.
Tell me, in pity's name: who is this lover,
Madam, of thine? Whom have I to discover?

MONIME.

Is that so hard a thing for thee to guess?
Just now, when I was fleeing from duress
By Pharnaces, to whom have I appealed?
My heart in whose protection sought a shield?
To whose love have I hearkened without displeasure?

XIPHARES.

Ah gods! What! *I* the man beyond all measure
Blest, on whom thou couldst look with favouring glance?
Thy tears could flow for Xiphares?

MONIME.

Yes, Prince.
I can no longer feign. Too violent,
Now, is my grief, to be within me pent.
Duty enjoineth silence upon me,
But I despite its stern laws finally
Must speak out for the first time and the last.
Thou long hast loved me. Long, too, hath my breast
By no less love for thee been touched and torn.
Recall that day of old when love was born
In thee for my ill-fated charms, of worth
Too scant; recall thy hopes that died at birth,
The turmoil which thy father's love for me
Engendered in thy soul, the agony
Of losing me and seeing me his, the strict
Demands of duty, which would needs conflict
With all our dearest wishes—thou canst not
Remember nor recount these things without
Telling my story, sir; and while I heard
Of them this morning, my heart, too, was stirred
By all thou saidst, responding silently.
Futile—nay, rather, fatal—sympathy!
Too perfect union, which the Fates forbade!
Ah, by what cruel care hath heaven made
Two hearts be joined which never could entwine
With one another! For however mine
Is drawn to thee, I tell thee once for all
That I shall hearken to my duty's call
And go, as honour, sir, constraineth me,
To the altar, where I am to swear to thee
An everlasting silence. Yes, I know:
Thou sighest, but such is my full cup of woe.
I to thy father, not to thee, belong.

Thou must thyself now help me to be strong
In this resolve and from my too-weak breast
Banish thee. I expect of thee at least
So much considerateness as to take care
Henceforth to flee my presence everywhere.
I have just said enough to make thee see
That I am right in asking this of thee,
And if thy lofty heart hath ever known
A real love for Monime, from this time on
I shall perceive that love's sincerity
Only by how well thou avoidest me.

XIPHARES.

Just gods! What proof for hapless love to show!
In one same instant how great joy and woe!
From what a height of glory and of bliss
Thou hurlest me down into what dire abyss!
What! I can win a heart like thine? I can?
Thou canst love *me*? And now another man
Is to possess thee, cheating our love's due!
Father unjust and cruel—yet hapless, too! . . .
     Thou'dst have me flee and see thee never again?
But now the King stations me in thy train!
What will he say?

MONIME.

No matter; obey *me*.

Give reasons that will blind his eyes. For thee
Impends the hardest of a hero's tests:
Contrive, contrive, 'gainst thine own interests,
Such stratagems as, for their hearts' content,
The common run of lovers oft invent.
Weak as I know myself, with life at stake,
I now distrust all efforts I could make.

The sight of thee would rouse fond memories
And from my breast draw forth unworthy sighs.
I would behold my heart, in secret cleft
In twain, seeking the joys whereof 'twas reft.
But I know, too, if it depends on thee
To make me cling to thy dear memory,
Thou wilt not hinder me, who once forgot
Honour, from punishing each wrongful thought,
Or, groping for thee in my bosom, thence
Plucking thee to restore its innocence.
But no! in this last moment left us still,
I feel a guilty sweetness sap my will.
The more I speak with thee, the more do I
Weakly prolong the peril from which I fly.
I must, I must constrain myself, not lose
My last, scant fortitude in fond adieus.
I go. Remember, Prince, to shun my sight.
Deserve the tears thou'lt cost me, by thy flight.

                    [*Exit* MONIME, *hastily.*

                    XIPHARES.

Ah, madam . . . She departs, and will not hear.
Unhappy Xiphares, thy path lies where?
She loves thee, and she drives thee from her. Thou
Thyself canst clearly see thy duty, now,
Chimes with her duty. Therefore do thou fly
To end by a swift death thine agony.
Nay, let us wait until her fate is plain,
Rather, and if some rival needs must then
Take her from thee, at least in perishing
Let us not give her up save to the King.

ACT III

MITHRIDATES, PHARNACES, *and* XIPHARES *are discovered.*

MITHRIDATES.

Draw near, my sons. The hour to lay bare
My secret to your eyes at last is here.
All things combine to aid my noble plans;
Only to tell you of them yet remains.
    I have fled. Hostile Fate hath willed it so;
But my life's history too well ye know
To think that I would hide in these wild regions
Long, and await the coming of Rome's legions.
War brings defeats but also victories.
Already, more than once mine enemies,
Deluded by my flight, have ridden through
Their streets in the triumphal car, which drew
The fatuous throng to follow it as it went,
And have inscribed on bronze their transient
Success and borne in chains statues of my
Lands they have conquered—and in the meantime I
Have doubled back; the Bosphorus hath viewed
The sight of me now issuing with renewed
Strength from her marshes, spreading terror, driving
The Romans out of Asia, and contriving
In one day to undo the work at least
Of a whole year!
               New times, new tasks. The East
Can face her foes' increasing might no more.
Vanquished, she sees her plains as ne'er before
Swarming with Romans, unto whom will fall
Our lands' wealth. Tales of it draw hither all

Those greedy plunderers of whoe'er is rich.
They flock in crowds here, vying each with each.
They leave their country, ours to inundate.
I, I alone resist them. A sore weight
My friendship is to all my friends, subdued
Or worn out. There is none of them but would
Rid himself of it. Pompey's great name makes
His triumph sure. Hearing it, Asia quakes;
And far from seeking for him there, my sons,
It is on Rome I mean to march at once.

    This purpose takes you by surprise. Ye may
Think 'tis despair that gives it birth to-day.
I pardon your mistake. Such projects must,
Till they are carried out, meet with distrust.

    Deem not that we are separated here
From Rome by an eternal barrier.
I know the roads to follow, every one;
And if death does not come to thwart me soon,
Within three months—I need no longer time—
We shall be camped beneath the Capitoline.
Cannot the Euxine bear me to the place
At which the Danube empties, in two days?
Will not the pact the Scythians swore with me
Thence into Europe give me entrance free?
Admitted to their ports, joined by their host,
We shall at each step greater numbers boast.
Dacians, Pannonians, Germans—all await
Only a leader 'gainst Rome's tyrant State.
Ye have seen Spain, yes, and still more the Gauls
Urge me to vengeance against those same walls
Which formerly they stormed, and even in Greece
Ambassadors blame me for my slothfulness.
They know this torrent, about to burst on them,

Will, if it sweeps me down, all else o'erwhelm,
And to prevent this they will every one
Guide me to Italy and then follow on.

There shall ye, more than on the route we came,
Find everywhere the horror of Rome's name
And hapless Italy all smoking yet
With fires her dying liberty hath lit.
No, princes, 'tis not earth's remotest folk
That Rome makes feel the full weight of her yoke.
As she inspires near-by the bitterest hate,
Her greatest foes are at her very gate.
Ah, if they once chose for their liberator
Spartacus, a vile slave, a gladiator,
Or followed brigands to avenge their wrongs,
How nobly will they flock in ardent throngs
To the standard of a long-victorious king
Who knoweth his line doth e'en from Cyrus spring!

Nay, picture what will be the state of Rome.
Empty of legions for defence at home
While all attempt to hunt me down and slay me!
How can her women and her children stay me?

Then onward! Let us bear into her breast
The havoc that she spreads from east to west.
Attack these conquerors proud behind their walls;
Make them in their turn fear for hearth and halls.
Great Hannibal said it; trust him: 'tis in Rome
Alone that Rome can e'er be overcome.
Drown her in her own blood, spilled righteously.
Burn down this Capitol, where I was to be
A captive; wreck its trophies and efface
A hundred kings' disgrace and my disgrace—
Yea, torch in hand obliterate each name
That Rome hath blazoned with eternal shame!

'Tis this ambition that has filled my soul.
But think not that in undisturbed control
Of Asia I shall leave the Romans, though
I be so distant from it. Well I know
Where I can find for it defenders stout.
'Tis my intent that Rome, when ringed about
With foes, shall call in vain for Pompey's aid.
The King of Parthia, whom she holds in dread
As she does me, agrees to make his own
My righteous anger. Ready to be one
With me in hate and household, he asks now
Of me a son to wed his daughter. Thou
Shalt have this honour; I have chosen thee,
Pharnaces, for it. Straightway go and be
The happy bridegroom. I without delay
Will set forth, that to-morrow's break of day
Shall find my fleet far from this Bosphorus.
Naught keeps thee here. At once take leave of us,
And by the ardour and alacrity
With which thou actest, deserve my choice of thee.
Contract this marriage; then, crossing the Euphrates,
Let Asia see a second Mithridates
And our oppressors turn pale when to Rome,
Even as to me, news of thy deeds shall come.

PHARNACES.

I cannot, sir, hide from thee my surprise,
Hearing thee broach this mighty enterprise.
I marvel at it. Naught more boldly planned
Ever put arms in a defeated hand.
I, above all, thy tireless spirit admire,
Which seems more resolute as its load is dire.
But if I may with frankness speak to thee:

Art thou reduced to this extremity?
Why on a useless errand go so far
When in thy realm asylums still there are?
Why wish to challenge dangers without end,
More like the leader of an outlaw band
Than a great king who lately with some right
From east to west went trusting in his might,
Built upon thirty States his prosperous throne,
Imposing even in ruins? Thou alone,
Alone, sir, after forty years, canst still
Struggle against the Fates. Implacable
Foe both of Rome and peace, dost thou conceive
Thy soldiers all are heroes? Canst thou believe
That they with hearts shaken by their defeat,
Tired from a long and arduous retreat,
Will court death gladly under foreign skies,
And hardships worse than perils? Before the eyes
Of their own people more than once have they
Been beaten. Will they elsewhere hold at bay
Their raging conqueror? Will he be less grim
And terrible? Will they better vanquish him
In his own city, while his gods look on?
     The Parthian king wooed thee and asked a son
Of thee, to be his son-in-law! Would he,
This monarch who was eager, sir, to be
Our aid when the whole world seemed on our side,
Still wish, when we are weak, to be allied
To us? Shall I, Fate's outcast, go alone
To be received with Parthia's well known
Fickleness, and perhaps expose thy name,
Because of my rash suit, to public shame?
At least, if we must yield and 'gainst our wont
Assume the aspect of a suppliant,

Without dispatching me to embrace the knees
Of the King of Parthia or addressing pleas
Thyself to sovereigns not so great as thou,
Could we not take a surer course and throw
Ourselves into arms opened willingly
To us? Rome, easily appeased by thee . . .

XIPHARES.

Rome, brother? Gods! what darest thou to propose?
Wouldst have the King, abased before his foes,
Belie his whole life in a single day,
Trust Rome, and shamefully accept the sway
'Gainst which he hath defended all earth's kings
For forty years?

    (*Turning to* MITHRIDATES) Fight on, sir! The sole things
That are thy refuge, vanquished though thou be,
Are wars and dangers. Rome pursues in thee
Her mortal enemy, more bound withal
By oaths, more feared by her, than Hannibal.
Drenched in her blood of old, do what thou please,
Thou canst expect from her no better peace
Than Asia had when in one day thy word
Put five score thousand Romans to the sword.

    Yet spare thy sacred head. Do thou not go
Thyself from land to land and, going, show
A broken Mithridates unto them,
Dimming the glory of thy mighty name.
Just is thy vengeance. It must be straightway
Accomplished. Burn the Capitol and lay
Rome in ashes. But 'tis enough for thee
To point us the roads thither and decree
That younger hands shall carry the flame there.
While Pharnaces hath Asia for his sphere,

Grant me the honour of this other task.
Give to us thy commands; let us, I ask
Of thee, prove unto all men that we are
Thy sons indeed, each an executor
Of thy great purposes. Kindle thus the lands
Of sunrise and of sunset, by our hands.
Fill with thy presence the whole world, without
Leaving this Bosphorus; let Rome, ringed about
And hard beset on every side, despair
Of finding thee, yet find thee everywhere.
This very moment order me to start.
Here all things stay thee, all bid me depart;
And if I am not equal to this mission,
Failure at least beseems my sad position.
I shall go, happy to advance the time
That ends my woes . . . to atone my mother's crime,
My lord. Thou seest me, blushing for it, kneel
To thee, ashamed of my scant worth. I feel
That all my blood should wash out this dark stain,
But I desire a death whereby thou'lt gain;
And for a child of Mithridates Rome,
My desperation's goal, is a fit tomb.

MITHRIDATES.

Of thy false mother speak no more, my son.
Thy father is content, thy zeal is known
To him, nor will he let thee anywhere
Face perils his affection doth not share.
Nothing shall part us; thou shalt follow me.
(*To* PHARNACES) Thou, Prince, prepare to obey me in-
    stantly.
The ships are ready. I have made all due
Provision for thy needs and retinue.

Arbates, in whose charge thou art to go,
Will bring thee to thy bride and let me know
What thy behaviour is. Go and uphold
The honour of thine ancestors of old.
Receive in this embrace my fond good-byes.

PHARNACES.

Sire . . .

MITHRIDATES.

To express my will, Prince, should suffice.
Obey. I should not have to speak again.

PHARNACES.

Sire, if to please thee I must needs be slain,
None will meet death more willingly than I.
Fighting before thine eyes, pray, let me die.

MITHRIDATES.

I have commanded thee to set out now;
But after this . . . Thou hearest me, Prince, and thou
Art lost if thou repliest one word more.

PHARNACES.

Hadst thou a thousand deaths for me in store,
I could not woo a girl I ne'er have seen.
My life is in thy hands.

MITHRIDATES.

Ah, it is e'en
As I expected, traitor. Thou "couldst not" go;
And well I understand thee, well I know
Wherefore thou shunnest this marriage. I perceive
Thou hast a quarry here thou'rt loath to leave.
'Tis Monime stays thee. It was thy desire

To carry off the bride of thine own sire.
Neither the ardour wherewith, thou dost know,
I wooed her, nor my fillet on her brow
Already, nor this place of refuge where
I had her guarded, nor my just wrath struck fear
Into thy soul. Thou false wretch, thy base love
For Rome was not to me a black enough
Offence; there also had to burn in thee
Just this perfidious flame ere thou couldst be
The horror and the scourge of all my days.
Repenting naught, thou showest by thy face
That thy distraction springs from rage alone.
Thou longest from my presence to be gone—
Hie thee to ruin me—sell me to Rome—
But I will take, before I go herefrom,
Vengeance. I warned thee.

                    (*Calling*) Guards! What ho, there!

                                        [*Enter guards.*
                                            Seize,

Arrest him! Yes, I mean *him*, Pharnaces.
Take him away, and let him from this hour
Be closely guarded, locked up in the tower.

                    PHARNACES.

Very well, I shall not pretend to be
Innocent. Thou art right in hating me.
What thou wert told about the love I feel,
Is true. But Xiphares did not reveal
All that he could to thee. This is, indeed,
The least important secret there was need
To acquaint thee with. That faithful son of thine
Ought to have let thee know how, even as mine,
His passion long hath burned. He like me, sir,

Loveth the Queen—and he is loved by her.

[*Exeunt* PHARNACES *and guards.*

XIPHARES.

Dost thou believe that such a wicked thought . . .

MITHRIDATES.

Thy brother, I am sure, would stop at naught,
My son. Just gods, grant that I never may
Suspect that thou so cruelly couldst betray
My kindness and that he in whom I found
Always the chief joy of my life could wound
His father's trusting heart. No, I do not
Believe it. Go. Far from imagining aught
Like that, I shall but think of how I can
Avenge us.

[*Exit* XIPHARES.

(*To himself*) Thou dost not believe it? Vain
Thy effort to beguile thyself! Thou dost
Believe it all too thoroughly, O most
Unhappy Mithridates. Xiphares
My rival? Can the Queen's heart, then, be his?
And did she dare to hoodwink me to-day?
Hath every one, turn wheresoe'er I may,
Ceased to be loyal to me? Everywhere
Do all forsake me? Are all treacherous here?
Pharnaces, friends, affianced bride, and thou,
Alas, my son, whose courage hath till now
Been my best comfort in adversity? . . .
But know I not Pharnaces' villainy?
How weak of me to take the word of one
Who, mad with rage and envy, turns upon
His brother, and who would in his despair,

Inventing idle tales, make it appear
That others, too, are guilty, hoping he
Might save himself thus, and confusing me!
No, let us not believe him, but herein
Delve without undue haste. Yet where begin?
What will convince me? who as a witness? what
Evidence? Heaven suggests to me a thought.
(*Calling*) Summon the Queen!

                  (*To himself*) Yes, without further quest
I will hear *her*. She is, of all, the best
Witness to choose. Love credits eagerly
What gives it pleasure. Who better than she
The conqueror of her thankless heart can name?
Let us learn which of my two sons to blame
For winning her love. If such a stratagem
Beseems not *me*, 'tis meet to use 'gainst *them*.
Let us deceive those who are false to us;
For to discover treachery any ruse
Is lawful. . . . But I see her. Let us feign,
And, by a clever lie arousing vain
Hopes in her breast, draw thence the truth.

                              [*Enter* MONIME.
                             Mine eyes

At last are opened, and I recognize
Mine error. 'Twould be no fit offering
Unto thy loveliness if I should bring,
Madam, together with my love to thee
The weight of years and woes that burden me.
My fortunes and my victories heretofore
Hid my grey hairs 'neath thirty crowns. No more
'Tis thus. I was a king; I have become
A fugitive. My age is greater. None
Remaineth of my proud titles; and my brow,

Stripped of these royal honours, showeth now
Too plainly all the ravages of time,
By which 'tis blighted. Countless plans of mine,
Besides, claim my attention. Thou canst hear
The shouts of troops for whom the hour is near
At which they will set forth. 'Twas but to-day
I disembarked, yet I must sail straightway.
How ill consorteth marriage with a flight
So hurried, madam! How could I unite
Thy fate with mine, when I seek only war
And death? But think of Pharnaces no more.
If justice is my aim, it must be thine.
I cannot suffer this vile son of mine,
Whom I to-day have banished from my sight
For ever, to enjoy a love I might
Not have, and even make thee Rome's ally.
My throne was promised thee. Thereof do I
Nowise repent, and I myself will now
Place thee upon it, ere I go, if thou
Art willing to accept the hand of one
Who hath been ever dear to me, of a son
Worthy of his father's love, of Xiphares
In short, and let him thus on Pharnaces
Avenge me, and discharge my debt to thee.

MONIME.

What! Xiphares, my lord?

MITHRIDATES.

          Yes, madam, he.
Why at his name doth such confusion fill
Thy soul? Against a choice so suitable
What maketh thee rebellious? Is it some
Repulsion which thou canst not overcome?

Again I say it: my second self is he,
A son victorious, who loveth me
And whom I love, the enemy of Rome,
The heir of an empire and a name, in whom
That name will be reborn. Whatever thou
Hast cherished the hope of in thy heart, I vow
That unto none but him shalt thou be given
By me.

MONIME.

What! Couldst thou then approve . . . ah heaven!
Why, why, sir, dost thou wish to try me so?
Do not torment a hapless soul. I know
That I was destined to be thine alone;
I know that now, to seal our union,
The victim waits at the altar. Come.

MITHRIDATES.

I too
Plainly can see that, whatsoe'er I do,
Thou wilt have none but Pharnaces. I again
Encounter thy unmerited disdain.
It is transferred now to my luckless son.

MONIME.

I disdain *him*?

MITHRIDATES.

With all this, let us have done,
Madam. Burn with love's shameful flames. While I
Seek with that son at the world's end to die
A glorious death, far from the sight of thee,
Do thou share here his brother's slavery
And to the Romans sell thy father's blood.

Let us go, then. There is no way so good
In which I can requite thee for thy scorn
As to consign thee unto one forsworn.
I shall no more care aught for thy fair fame.
I would forget thee, even thy very name.
Come, madam, come; thou shalt to him be wed.

MONIME.

Rather a thousand times would I be dead!

MITHRIDATES.

Vainly dost thou protest. 'Tis plain to me
Thou only feignest.

MONIME.

        To what extremity,
My lord, am I reduced! But I at last
Believe thee, for I cannot think thou hast
The power to force thyself to play a part
So long. Heaven is my witness that my heart
Sought but thy pleasure, nor murmured at its fate.
But if some weakness still could agitate
And frighten it, so that it had to strive
Hard to defend itself, do not conceive
That 'twould be Pharnaces who could rouse my fears,
Sir, or could ever cost me any tears.
This son victorious, whom thou favorest,
Thy second self, who fills with pride thy breast,
The Romans' foe, the living image of
His sire, this Xiphares thou wouldst have me love . . .

MITHRIDATES.

Thou lovest him?

MONIME.

       Had the Fates not made me thine,
To have him for my husband would have been
My happiness. Ere *thy* love prompted thee
To send to me this token of it, we
Had loved each other. . . . Sir, thy countenance
Is changed.

MITHRIDATES.

      No, no! Enough! I shall at once
Send him to thee. Go. Time is precious. I
Must use it well. I see thou wilt comply
Willingly with my wishes. I am glad.

MONIME (*to herself, going*).
O gods! Can I have been deceived, betrayed?

                [*Exit* MONIME.

MITHRIDATES.

They love each other. They have tricked me thus.
Oh, thou shalt pay for all, thou traitorous,
Ungrateful son—pay with thy life! I know
How thy renown and manly valour's show
Have won my soldiers' hearts. False wretch, I mean
To smite thee with unerring blows. 'Tis, then,
Needful to rid myself of malcontents,
The better to destroy thee, sending hence
The most rebellious, and keep near my side
Those I can trust. Yet here I must not bide.
I will display an angry face to none,
But go on feigning as I have begun.

ACT IV

Monime *and* Phaedima *are discovered.*

MONIME.

Phaedima, in the gods' name, do the thing
I ask. Go, find out what is happening
And then come back and tell me. I know naught,
But cannot reassure my heart. Ah, what
Countless dreadful suspicions torture me!
Why tarrieth Xiphares? and why doth he
Delay his urging of the suit which has
His father's sanction now? His father, as
He left me, said that he would send him here;
But he perhaps was feigning. I should ne'er
Have failed to deny all. Did the King feign?
And I, my thoughts disclosing to him then . . .
Couldst thou forsake me, heaven, in such a strait?
And is it possible that to his hate
I indiscreetly have exposed my lover?
Ah, dear prince, when thou soughtest to discover
My secret in thy great love's urgency,
Full twenty times I all too cruelly
Refused to tell it to thee. I even tried
To punish thee for tearing what I would hide
Out of my heart. But when perhaps thy father
Distrusts thee—when thy very life, say rather,
May be in danger—then I speak straightway,
And, being too easily deceived, betray
To him at whose breast he should launch his blow.

PHAEDIMA.

Nay, madam, be more just to him. Would so

Renowned a monarch stoop to tricks like this?
What need to employ subterfuge was his?
Thou wert about to go, unmurmuring,
Before him to the altar. Would the King
Slay a son whom he dearly loves? So far
His promise and what since hath happened are
Quite in accord. He told thee that a great
Design would 'gainst his will necessitate
His leaving thee to-morrow. This design
Alone claims all his thoughts; and that the time
Of his departure may be earlier,
He himself on the shore hath in his care
All things; he fills with soldiers all the ships;
And Xiphares everywhere attends his steps.
Is it thus a rival in his fury acts?
Are the King's words belied by any facts?

MONIME.

Yet Pharnaces, imprisoned by his command,
Finds him a rival cruel and unrestrained.
Will he deal kindlier with Xiphares?

PHAEDIMA.

He punishes Rome's friend in Pharnaces.
Love hath but small part in his just complaints.

MONIME.

I credit, all I can, thy arguments.
They soothe a little the anguish that I feel.
But Xiphares remaineth absent still!

PHAEDIMA.

What folly of fond lovers, who would have
All else give way to accord them what they crave,
Who, chafing 'gainst the slightest obstacle . . .

MONIME.

Who could imagine such a miracle,
Phaedima? After two whole years of grief,
Whose weight thou knowest, I once more can breathe
Joy's breath.
                    Prince, shall I see myself thy wife?
Does my love not endanger now thy life?
Shalt thou see duty, shall I see honour, approve
Now finally a so long resisted love?
And can I henceforth tell thee every day
I love thee? Why dost thou e'en yet delay
Thy coming . . .

                              [*Enter* XIPHARES.

                    I was speaking, sir, of thee
And wishing in my heart thou mightest be
With me, to . . .

XIPHARES.

            I have come to say good-bye.

MONIME.

"Say good-bye"? Thou?

XIPHARES.

            For all eternity.

MONIME.

What! I was told . . . Alas, I was betrayed!

XIPHARES.

I cannot guess what hidden foe hath made
Our secret known, thereby accomplishing
My ruin and perhaps thine; but the King,
Who would not believe Pharnaces, hath now
Learned of our inmost feelings. 'Neath a show
Of fondness he conceals his plans; but I,

Who was beside him reared from infancy,
Only too well can read his countenance.
I see impending vengeance in his glance.
He sends away all those whom harm to me
Might in their grief arouse to mutiny.
In his feigned kindliness constraint appears.
Arbates hath himself confirmed my fears
Briefly. He found a chance to speak to me
And said, with tearful eyes: "Save thyself; flee;
For he knows everything." These words made me quake
With terror for thee, and for thy dear sake
Alone I have come hither. I am afraid
Of what thou wilt thyself do. To persuade
And on my knees to beg thee to have some
Regard for thine own safety, I have come,
My princess. Thou art in one's hands who ne'er
Hath shrunk from shedding blood, however dear.
I could not tell thee to what cruelty
Hath Mithridates oft by jealousy
Been driven. Perhaps his anger threatens me
Only. Perhaps he fain would show to thee
Mercy when he hath slain me. Deign, oh, deign
To accept it, I beseech thee, nor again
Enrage him by refusing to be his.
The less thou lovest him, the more need there is
To try to please him. Then dissemble; strive.
Remember that he is my father. Live;
And let the tears that, in thy love, will flow
Be all that my misfortunes cost thee.

MONIME.

Oh,

I have destroyed thee!

XIPHARES.

Ah, thou true of heart,
Monime, think not that thou the reason art
For my disaster. Not thy love alone
Hath caused my ruin. I am clearly one
Hounded by Fate; 'tis Fate that robbed me of
My father's love, made him my rival, drove
My mother to revolt, and now doth raise
A secret foe who me and thee betrays
Alike in this dread hour.

MONIME.

Dost thou not know,
Then, even yet, who is thy secret foe?

XIPHARES.

To crown my grief, madam, I know him not.
How gladly would I pierce, before I got
My death, that false and treacherous heart of his!

MONIME.

Well then, sir, I must tell thee who it is.
Seek not elsewhere the foe that did such harm
To thee. Strike. No respect should stay thine arm.
I am the traitor. Thou shouldst punish me.

XIPHARES.

Thou!

MONIME.

Oh, if thou but knewest how craftily
The cruel man wrought until I had confessed
My love! What great affection he professed
For thee! How well he would be satisfied
To see thee be my husband, me thy bride!

Who would not have believed . . . ? But no, my love
Should more have dreaded to make hazard of
Thy life, however much he feigned good will.
The gods, whose guidance I have followed ill,
Thrice in my heart warned me to hold my peace.
I should have done so still,—should without cease . . .
I know not what . . . I should at least have been
Less baleful to thee. I should with fear have seen
The King's envenomed kindness. I, if thou
Sparest me, will punish mine own self, I vow.

XIPHARES.

What! is it thou, is it thy love that hath
Exposed me to the fury of his wrath?
Does my misfortune spring from that sweet source?
Hath too great love laid bare our hearts perforce?
And canst thou blame thyself for making me
Happy? What else would I? Adoring thee,
I shall die proudly. A quite different fate
Confers on thee a crown. Then, madam, wait
No longer to submit to it, nor shun
The marriage that will seat thee on a throne.

MONIME.

Thou'dst have me wed a man so odious,
Whose cruel love for ever parteth us?

XIPHARES.

Remember, thou wert ready heretofore
To obey him, wed him, and see me no more.

MONIME.

Did I then know all his barbarity?
Wouldst thou indeed desire that after I

Have seen thee pierced and mangled by his blows,
Sanctioning his mad rage I should then espouse
This tyrant at the altar,—that I should
Place in his hand, still reeking with thy blood,
My hand, the hand of her who loves thee so?
Try to protect thyself from him. Go, go,
And waste no time here arguing with me.
Heaven will teach me what my course should be.
How if he came, great gods, and took thee by
Surprise? Some one is coming now. Go. Fly.
Preserve thy life whatever happens. Wait
At least until thou knowest of my fate.

[*Exit* XIPHARES.

PHAEDIMA.

Oh, what a dreadful risk for him to take
Here, madam! It is the King!

MONIME.

Quick, help him make
Good his escape unseen. Go. Leave him not.
Bid him do nothing to decide his lot
Till he discovers what hath been mine own.

[*Exit* PHAEDIMA. *Enter* MITHRIDATES.

MITHRIDATES.

Come, madam, come. A reason known to none
Compels me to depart more speedily.
Hence, while my troops, ready to follow me,
Re-embark in our ships, to go where'er
Their king may lead them, this is the time to swear
Oaths at the altar which will fulfil my fond
Promise to thee and by an eternal bond
Unite us.

MONIME.

    Us, my lord?

MITHRIDATES.

               What! darest thou
Hesitate, madam?

MONIME.

             Didst thou not, only now,
Forbid all thoughts of such a union?

MITHRIDATES.

                     Oh,
I had my motives, then, for doing so!
Let us forget them, madam. Now think but of
How best to be responsive to my love.
Thy heart, remember, is my property.

MONIME.

Why, then, sire, hast thou given it back to me?

MITHRIDATES.

What! for my false son hast thou such desire
As to suppose . . .

MONIME.

         Thou hast deceived me, sire!

MITHRIDATES.

Traitress! it well becomes thee to talk thus,
Who, cherishing a love so infamous,
When I was lifting thee to glory's height,
Hatched 'gainst me treachery as black as night.
Hast thou forgotten, false, ungrateful woman,
More in thy soul my foe than any Roman,
From what exalted rank I deigned to stoop

To raise thee to a throne far past thy hope?
    See me not vanquished, hunted, as I am;
See the once dreaded conqueror, great of fame.
Remember with what ardour my heart burned
For thee in Ephesus, and how I spurned
The daughters of a hundred kings for thee
(Who gladly would have been allied to me)
And at thy feet laid realms innumerable.
    Oh, if another love's resistless spell
Then unto all my favours made thee blind,
Why didst thou go so far from home to find
A hated husband? Why didst thou not speak
Before thou camest here? Didst thou wait, to break
This bitter news to me, till hostile Fate
Had taken from me all else and, 'neath the weight
Of countless evils crushed, I saw in thee
My only blessing which might comfort me?
Yet when I fain this outrage would forget
And from my heart shut out all sense of it,
Thou darest to call up the past again
Before mine eyes; thou darest to blame me, when
'Tis I who have been wronged!
                      I see that thou
With fond hopes for a traitor even now
Beguilest thy heart. O great gods, how ye try
The soul of Mithridates! It is by
What secret spell that I am made to stay
This wrath so stern and swift to punish. Nay,
Lose not the moment's chance that I allow.
For the last time, come, I command thee. Draw
No fruitless perils on thy head for one
Whom thou wilt see no more, my upstart son.
Boast not thy love of him; it is my right.

Lose thou his memory, as thou shalt his sight,
And moved henceforth by gratitude alone
To me, deserve the mercy thou art shown.

MONIME.

I have not forgotten, sir, thy favours. They
Should truly have made me subject to thy sway.
However great my lineage formerly,
Its distant glory hath not dazzled me.
Respectfully do I recall how far
Above my birth thy nuptial grandeurs are;
And though my feelings formerly inclined
Unto thy son, the foremost of mankind
Save thee, when once I wore this diadem
I gave him up, gave up all thoughts of him.
To sacrifice ourselves we both agreed.
Far from my sight, he would, as I had bid,
Fly to forget me. Love's hid flame would die.
Nor could I even lament my destiny,
Since, having renounced my dearest hopes, I now
Brought happiness to a hero such as thou.
    None, sir, but thee—yes, none but thee—hath torn
My heart from that obedience it had sworn.
This fated love which I had triumphed o'er,
And which I deemed would be revived no more
For I would ne'er again its object see—
Thy trickery hath discovered it in me.
I have confessed it; I must reverence it.
Useless would be thine efforts to forget;
And this avowal which thou didst compel
Must in my heart henceforth for ever dwell.
I would always think thee of my faith unsure;
And the grave, sir, would be easier to endure

Than that man's couch who thus hath treated me,
Who took advantage of me ruthlessly,
And who, to my eternal shame, could fan
My cheeks to crimson for another man!

MITHRIDATES.

This is thine answer, then? And though it offend me,
Wilt thou refuse the honour I extend thee?
I wait, not yet resolved. Consider well.

MONIME.

Nay, sir, in vain thou thinkest to make me quail.
I know thee—know the doom that I invite—
And see what woes upon my head shall smite.
But my resolve is fixed. 'Twill not grow weak.
Judge of it, seeing how I dare to speak
To thee and how put off that modesty
Which I till now have worn continually.
Thou hast employed my hapless arm to run
A dagger through the bosom of thy son.
I have revealed the innocent secret of
His heart, and if it cost his father's love
Alone, 'twould kill him, sir. My fealty
Or love shall ne'er reward a treachery
So cruel. Decide, then. Slay one who defies thee.
Assume the power o'er me that none denies thee.
I shall await my death—which thou'lt decree.
　　I ask but one thing ere I go from thee
(To innocence I owe this justice, still):
Believe that only I oppose thy will,
Unseconded, and that it would be done
Completely, had I hearkened to thy son.

　　　　　　　　　　　　　[*Exit* MONIME.

MITHRIDATES.

She leaves me! And in craven silence I
Appear to sanction her audacity!
It seems to lack but little that my heart
Should blame me as too cruel, and take her part.
Am I, then, Mithridates? and is this
Monime? Nay, nay, for one so conscienceless
No thought of love or pardon entertain.
My wrath returns. I am myself again.
Let us, ere we depart, immolate three
Ingrates at once. We go to Rome, and we
Shall by this sacrifice make heaven propitious.
We should. We can. Those who might be seditious
For their sake are at sea. Without defence
Are they. Come, let us make no difference
Now between those I love and those I hate.
First Xiphares himself shall meet his fate.

    What am I saying? Have my senses flown?
Thou meanest to slay—whom? Wretched man, thy son!
Him whom Rome fears, who can avenge his sire!
Wherefore slay one whose aid my plans require?
With so much lost whereof my downfall reft me,
Do I now have too many friends yet left me?
Nay, I should keep his love for me alive.
My need is an avenger, not a wife.
Is it not better, since I cannot have her,
To give her up to him—whom I would favour
To bind him to me? Let us give her up.

    Vain effort of a heart that seeks to dupe
Itself, but doth in this way only learn
How weak it is! Fiercely its passions burn
Still. I adore her. Far from banishing . . .

    Oh, but her crime is past all pardoning!

What pity makes mine anger hesitate?
Have I not punished treachery far less great?
O Monime! O my son! vain rage, and ye
Proud Romans, how triumphant ye would be
If ye but knew my shame, and tidings true
Bore news of my base inward strife to you!
What pains I took, fearing domestic treason,
To guard my life against all kinds of poison!
I learned by long and arduous work at last
To neutralize even the deadliest.
Ah, how much better, wiser, happier course
It would have been to learn to stay the force
Of love's assaults and to protect a heart
Already chilled by age from love's keen dart!
From these dire toils, how can I e'er get free?

[*Enter* ARBATES.

ARBATES.

Sire, all thy troops refuse to go with thee.
Pharnaces keeps them here; they learned it from
Him that thou wouldst renew the war with Rome.

MITHRIDATES.

Pharnaces?

ARBATES.

He corrupted his guards first,
And at the very name of Rome dread pierced
The boldest hearts—such perils, they conceive,
Face them. Some vehemently refuse to leave.
Others, who had embarked, leap overboard
Or threaten, each with brandished spear or sword,
The sailors. Chaos reigns on every hand;
And, far from listening to us, they demand

Peace, and themselves talk of surrendering.
Pharnaces heads them, ever flattering
Their wishes, promising in Rome's name this peace
They ask.

MITHRIDATES.

The traitor! Quick! let Xiphares
Be summoned; let him follow me and be
His father's rescuer.

ARBATES.

I know not what he
Intends, but he impetuously hath sped
Down to the port already, and 'tis said
That, followed by a band of trusty friends
He was seen mingling with the rest. Here ends
My knowledge of the matter.

MITHRIDATES.

What is this
That thou hast told me! Ah, since thus it is,
Perfidious youths, my vengeance was delayed
Too long. But I am not at all afraid
Of aught ye do. Despite their insolence,
The rebels would not dare to face my glance.
Let me but see them: I will sacrifice
These froward sons of mine before their eyes.

[*Enter* ARCAS.

ARCAS.

The rebels and the Romans, sire, a host,
With Pharnaces surround us. All is lost.

MITHRIDATES.

The Romans!

ARCAS.

On the shore the Romans throng.
Thou'lt be besieged within these walls ere long.

MITHRIDATES.

Gods! Haste we, then. But hearken . . .

[*He whispers to* ARCAS. *Exit* ARCAS.

If doomed I be,
It shall not, faithless princess, profit thee.

[*Exit.*

ACT V

Enter Monime, *distractedly, closely followed by* Phaedima.

Phaedima.

Ah, madam, whither rushest thou? What blind strife
Within thy soul hath thus against thy life
Armed thy hand? Couldst thou towards thine own self be
So ruthless as to fashion impiously
A noose out of the fillet on thy brow?
Seest thou not that heaven, less cruel than thou,
Itself hath broken this noose which thou didst tie?

Monime.

Why with such mad persistence dost thou try
To make me live despite me, following
My footsteps? Xiphares now is dead. The King
In his despair no longer looks for aught
But certain death. For thy presumption, what
Motive hast thou? Dost thou intend to give
Me up to Pharnaces, false woman?

Phaedima.

                    Live
At least till news more to be trusted hath
Confirmed to us his hapless brother's death.
In the confusion of which we have just heard
Is it not hard to learn what hath occurred?
At first a slanderous rumour, as thou know'st
Ranged Xiphares among the rebels' host.
Now art thou told that these same mutineers
Have turned against him their disloyal spears.
Judge one tale by the other. Lend an ear . . .

Monime.

Xiphares lives no longer: that is clear.
The outcome is but what I could foresee.
Even had these tidings dire not come to me,
I would be all too certain he is dead
Because I know how much the Romans dread
His courage and his name. Ah, Rome which long
Hath thirsted for the blood of one so strong
And noble now accounts her triumph sure.
What hostile arm henceforth can challenge her?
But how can I dare thus to shift the blame
On others, wretched woman that I am!
What! would I fain not see that it was I
Who have destroyed him, not acknowledge *my*
Guilt in all his misfortunes? I have armed
'Gainst him so many murderous hands. Unharmed,
How could he have escaped their countless blows?
Did I not to his father's wrath expose
His life? I made them jealous of each other,
So that to shun the Romans and his brother
Were not enough. To light the flames that scorch
Them all, a fatal fury and a torch
Of discord, it is I, I, who have come,
Shaped and bred by the demon god of Rome!
And I still live? I wait till Pharnaces,
Bathed in their blood, returns with some of his
Good friends, the Romans?—wait till he displays
His fratricidal joy before my face?
Despair can find more than one road to death.
Yes, to no purpose thy cruel succour hath
Now closed my swiftest way to the grave's peace.
I shall achieve it even in thine arms' embrace.

               [*She gazes at the fillet in her hands.*

Thou fateful fabric, luckless diadem,
Witness of all my woes and source of them,
Fillet, which many a time my tears would stain,
Couldst thou not end my life and all its pain,
And do me thus at least one boon? Away!
Never again let eyes of mine, I say,
Behold thee! There without thine aid shall be
Some other means found that will rescue me!
Curst be the day,—the blood-stained hand be curst,—
That ever on my forehead placed thee first!

PHAEDIMA.

Some one is coming, madam! Some one is
Coming.
                              [*Enter* ARCAS, *with a cup.*
        'Tis Arcas, and I hope that his
News will dispel thy fears.

MONIME.

                    Is it all over,
Arcas? Hath Pharnaces . . .

ARCAS.

                    Nay, to discover
Aught that hath happened, madam, do not ask
Of me. I have been given a grim task.
This poison tells thee what the King's will is.

PHAEDIMA.

Ill-fated princess!

MONIME.

        Acme of all bliss!
Give it to me! And, Arcas, tell the King,
Who sends it to me, that ne'er could anything

His kindness hath bestowed upon me be
So dear and welcome as this is to me.
At last I can breathe freely, saved by heaven
From those who with their unsought aid have striven
To force me still to live. For once I can
Be mine own mistress and my fate ordain
As I may choose.

PHAEDIMA.

Alas!

MONIME.

Repress thy cries
And mar not with unworthy tears or sighs
The beauty of this happy moment. If
Thou lovedst me, Phaedima, better had thy grief
Been shown when with a title fraught with woe
Thou sawest me honoured and I had to go,
Torn from my sweet home, to this savage shore.
Return now to our fair Greek land once more,
And if my name is still remembered there,
Phaedima, tell what thou hast seen; declare
To all the story of how I trod the path
Of duty.
And thou, dear hero, whom the wrath
Of jealous Fate did from this aching heart
Of mine, that so adored thee, ever part,
And (though I am about to die) with whom
I dare not ask that even in one tomb
We finally may be united, pray
Accept the sacrifice of my life, and may
This draught of poison make the atonement owed
By me, to expiate my lover's blood!

[*She raises the cup.* ARBATES *bursts into the room.*

ARBATES.

Stop! Stop!

ARCAS.

What is it thou wouldst do, Arbates?

ARBATES.

Stop! I bring orders here from Mithridates.

MONIME.

Oh, let me . . .

ARBATES (*dashing the cup from her hand*).

Hold, I say! And let *me* now
Carry out the King's wishes. Live.

And thou,
Arcas, to Mithridates run, and tell
The news of the success that crowned my zeal.

[*Exit* ARCAS.

MONIME.

O cruel Arbates, thou hast unto what
Exposed me? Is my punishment, then, thought
Too little? Does the King begrudge a death
So sudden unto me, and would his wrath
Have me die more than once, ere 'tis content?

ARBATES.

Thou soon shalt see him, and I am confident
That thou wilt weep for him no less than I.

MONIME.

What! is the King . . .

ARBATES.

The King's last hour draws nigh.
Never will he behold another sun,

Madam. I left him bleeding, borne upon
A litter by some soldiers; and, with these,
Beside him comes the sorrowing Xiphares.

MONIME.

Xiphares! O great gods! Am I awake?
I scarce dare trust mine ears, the while I shake
As with a palsy. Xiphares lives?—for whom
I wept . . .

ARBATES.

He lives, with glory crowned, o'ercome
With grief. The tale that he was dead had flown
Like wildfire. Thou wert not the only one
Needlessly frightened by it. The Romans spread
The story, shouting it, and thus dismayed
The hearts of all. The King, himself deceived,
Shed tears, and thenceforth, as he now believed
Defeat sure for his arms and being upon
Every side hard pressed by his recreant son,
Devoid of hope of rescue, and to death
Resigned, and seeing (to increase his wrath
And misery) his own standards 'gainst him borne
Beside the Roman eagles by his forsworn
Troops, he aspired unto no higher aim
Than in some manner to avoid the shame
Of falling alive into the hands of foes.
First he availed himself of poisons, those
He thought the surest and most virulent.
He found them all harmless and impotent.
"Vain help!" he cried. "I carefully protected
Myself 'gainst each of them, and thus rejected
Unwisely the recourse I might have had
To them. Let us now turn to surer aid

And seek a death more harmful unto Rome!''
  He spoke, and bade the palace gates be thrown
Wide, in defiance of the multitude
Thronging against them. When the Romans viewed
That countenance whose rage so oft had filled
Their ranks with terror, thou couldst have beheld
The sight of them all drawing back apace
To leave 'twixt them and us an ample space,
And some e'en then fled in their panic fear
Back to the vessels that had brought them here.
But—must I tell it, O heaven!—reassured
By Pharnaces, and with their hearts restored
To boldness by their shame's awakening,
They found fresh courage; they attacked the King,
Whom some few men with me defended still.
  Who could describe what feats incredible,
What blows struck by him with fierce-flashing eyes,
Then for the last time were to signalize
The arm of this great hero and to be
The last of all his exploits! Finally
Worn out, and covered o'er with dust and blood,
Behind a barrier of dead foes he stood.
Now other troops approached us. To unite
With them, the Romans waited, ceased to fight;
They would o'erwhelm, together, Mithridates.
  And he said unto me: " 'Tis enough, Arbates.
Too long hath my blood-frenzy made me strive.
They must not, above all, take me alive.''
Therewith he plunged his sword into his breast.
But death recoiled, played false, nor yet released
His mighty soul. All drenched with gore he fell
Back in my arms, strengthless, vexed that life still
Lingered, and chafing at so slow an end.

Again he lifted his now feeble hand
And, pointing to his heart, seemed to implore
Of me the favour of a blow more sure.
I, meanwhile, by o'ermastering grief possessed,
Was minded to pierce, rather, mine own breast,
When loud cries suddenly now rent the air.
I saw—who would have thought it?—everywhere
The Romans, vanquished, routed, put to flight,
Seeking their ships, with Pharnaces, to quit
These shores, and my bewildered faculties
Perceived the victor—it was Xiphares!

MONIME.

Just heaven!

ARBATES.

Xiphares had remained always
Loyal, but in the thickest of the fray's
Welter had been surrounded by a band
Of mutineers, by Pharnaces' command.
Yet he escaped out of their hands at last,
Cut down the most rebellious, won the rest
Back to their fealty, and with godlike power
And glad delight, even in that fearsome hour,
O'er countless dead, blood-stained and glorious,
He towards his father hewed a path victorious.
Imagine how his joy gave place to grief.
His own hand would have stretched him, without life,
At the King's feet; but men were quick and stayed
His madness. The King looked at me and said,
In that grim moment, speaking with great pain:
"If there be yet time, run and save the Queen."
Suspecting secret orders, I at these
Words trembled for both thee and Xiphares.

Exhausted though I was, my zeal and fear
Gave me new strength wherewith to hasten here;
And I am happy amid all our woe
To have parried, for you both, death's threatened blow.

MONIME.

Dazed though I am by what I have just heard,
At this great king's sad end my heart is stirred
To pity. Would to heaven that in his fate
I myself had not had a part, and that
As a mere witness of what wrought his doom
I could without guilt grieve for it. He doth come.
New turmoil racks me as I look upon
The dying father and the weeping son!
    [*Enter* MITHRIDATES, *borne by guards, and* XIPHARES.
Ah, sire, can this be true, as now appears?

MITHRIDATES.

Be silent, both of you, and restrain your tears.
(*To* XIPHARES) From thy devotion and her heart's tender-
    ness
I expect other feelings than distress.
My glory, rather, claims your admiration.
Sully it not with sighs and lamentation.
    I have avenged mankind as far as lay
Within my power, and death alone doth stay
My efforts to that end. An enemy
Both of the Romans and of tyranny,
I never bowed unto their yoke that shames
The wearer, and among the famous names
Of those whom hate for them hath made so known
I dare to flatter myself that there is none
From whom their victories were more dearly bought
Nor who hath more misfortunes on them brought.

'Twas not the gods' will that I should achieve
My purpose and amid Rome's ashes breathe
My last breath. But some joy at least have I,
In dying, to console myself: I die
Ringed round with enemies that I have slain,
In their loathed blood I bathed my hands amain;
And I last saw the Romans in full flight.
　　To my son Xiphares I owe this sight.
He spares their presence to my darkening gaze.
All my great empire, in its palmiest days,
Would be too little to repay that boon.
　　　　　　　　　　　　[*He turns to* MONIME.
　　And now, instead of sceptre, crown, and throne,
I have but thee. Naught else to me is left.
Let me, then, madam, make of thee a gift;
And all that for myself I claimed from thee,
I ask for Xiphares instead of me.

MONIME.

Live, my lord, live for the world's sake. Upon
Thy life her liberty depends, alone.
Live; triumph o'er a beaten enemy.
Avenge . . .

MITHRIDATES.

　　　　　Nay, all is over, madam; I
Have done with life.
　　　　　　　　My son, for your own selves
Seek safety now, and think not of aught else,
Nor dream thou couldst make good this land's defence
Against a foe in numbers so immense.
Soon will their legions, goaded on by shame,
Return and crush whoe'er opposes them.
Lose not the time still left thee, ere they come,

In paying unneeded honours to my tomb.
So many lifeless Romans here will be
Sufficient tribute to my memory.
Conceal your names and persons for a time.
Go; save yourselves.

XIPHARES.

What! fly and leave the crime
Of Pharnaces, sire, and the Romans' pride
Unpunished? They shall soon . . .

MITHRIDATES.

Nay, I forbid
What thou intendest. Be it soon or late,
Pharnaces will be punished; as to that,
Trust Rome.

But now my strength is almost gone.
I feel that I am dying. Come close, my son.
In this fond last embrace, take in my stead
The soul of Mithridates.

[*He embraces* XIPHARES, *and falls back on the litter.*

MONIME.

He is dead.

XIPHARES.

Ah, madam, as in grief now let us be
In marriage united; and then seek with me
In every land for all who, moved by hate
Of Rome, will help us to avenge his fate.

IPHIGÉNIE
(IPHIGENIA)

INTRODUCTION

THE appraisal of *Iphigénie* has varied strangely. Though it did not create a sensation like *Andromaque* when first presented, of all the tragedies of Racine it was the most universally admired in his lifetime. In the eighteenth century, Voltaire regarded it and *Athalie* as the supreme achievements of French drama; in the nineteenth, Sainte-Beuve quoted approvingly a friend's opinion that it ranks second only to *Athalie* and higher than *Andromaque, Phèdre,* and *Britannicus* among its author's "five masterpieces"; and this great critic himself held that as a finished and effective work, best exhibiting the beauties characteristic of Racinian tragedy, it has a right to stand first.[1] Yet to-day it is not generally classed with *Andromaque, Britannicus, Phèdre,* and *Athalie,* but as one of Racine's plays of the second grade. Such was the position assigned to it by N. M. Bernardin (with *Bajazet* and *Mithridate*), by Mary Duclaux (with *Mithridate,* above *Bajazet*—but all three below *Bérénice*!), and by Emile Faguet (immediately below "the four miracles"). Jules Lemaître went so far as to say that if we had to lose two of the secular tragedies of Racine (disregarding, of course, the immature productions before *Andromaque*) he would least unwillingly sacrifice *Mithridate* and *Iphigénie,* for beyond all the rest they smack of the pseudo-classical age in which they were written; and he appears to value *Iphigénie* even less than *Mithridate.*

[1] *Portraits Littéraires,* Paris, Garnier, vol. i, p. 114. This statement occurs in a study dated January 15, 1844. Earlier Sainte-Beuve had judged differently—and better. In December, 1829, he wrote (*op.cit.,* p. 85): "*Britannicus, Phèdre, Athalie* . . . these are the three great dramas of Racine, below which his other master-works take their places"—a dictum with which I entirely agree.

In reality, aside from its style, which is somewhat "stately," *Iphigénie* is not more romanesque than most of Racine's other dramas, but less so. Returning in this play, for the first time since *Andromaque*, to a subject treated by one of the great Attic masters, its author seems, as was the case in his maiden effort of *la Thébaïde*, to be trying to reproduce a classical tragedy on the French stage with the least modification that would make it acceptable to his public. And it is to be doubted whether he came so near to doing this even in *Phèdre* as he did here except in the part where Eriphyle is concerned. Scene after scene is derived from Euripides' *Iphigenia in Aulis*.[2] Many speeches have the true classic note. Clytemnestra's indignant appeal to her husband does not suffer when compared with the one in Euripides; though somewhat more rhetorical than its Greek analogue, it is perhaps even more moving, and it works up to a more impressive climax.

The Iphigenia of Racine, however, is a quite different per-

[2] Both plays open with a dialogue between Agamemnon and a faithful attendant, whom he informs of the plan to sacrifice Iphigenia and dispatches with a letter countermanding his summons of her. (The imitation in this scene is close.) After an interval, there is in both a colloquy between the King and some one who is determined that the sacrifice shall be carried out (Menelaus in one play, Ulysses in the other) ; and in both, this talk is interrupted by the arrival of Clytemnestra and Iphigenia, destroying Agamemnon's last hope of averting the girl's death. Both present the meeting of father and daughter in a number of brief speeches, largely questions and answers, on the part of each—he in agony which he attempts to dissemble, she happy in seeing him again but puzzled by his mood. In both plays, Agamemnon bids Clytemnestra not to go with Iphigenia to the altar, and they have a dispute over this. In both alike the revelation of his real purpose is made to Clytemnestra, Iphigenia, and Achilles by the domestic who was given the never-delivered letter and who now seizes the chance to disclose all, and the Queen kneels to Achilles and begs his aid. Lastly, in both plays Agamemnon comes to fetch Iphigenia when she has not gone to him, and Clytemnestra calls her and shows him that they know the truth; then both mother and daughter try unsuccessfully, each with a single long speech, to persuade him to relent.

A few passages in *Iphigénie* are based on the *Iliad*. For the most part they are in connection with Achilles.

son from the shrinking and afterwards heroic child of the
Iphigenia in Aulis. She is a grown woman, a gracious, self-
possessed princess, who is prepared, throughout, to let herself
be sacrificed if it is indeed her father's will, and whose ac-
quiescence springs from filial devotion and not from any fervour of patriotism. Though such a characterization of Iphigenia loses the effect produced by her sudden change in the
Greek play, which is one of the most heart-stirring things in
literature, it is a quite legitimate and well-executed variant.[3]

The love between her and Achilles is not the sheer romanesque invention that traditional criticism has pronounced it.
Any one who reads Euripides intelligently ought to see that
before the end of his tragedy Iphigenia is consciously or un-
consciously half in love with the splendid young hero who
has offered himself as her champion, and that Achilles is
wholly in love with Iphigenia.[4] Racine neither invented their
love nor derived it necessarily from Rotrou's *Iphigénie*, where
it also appears, just as he did not invent or derive from Rotrou
that of Antigone and Haemon in *la Thébaïde*; in each case
he merely expanded and emphasized a "heart-interest" that
was in his original—as almost any author of to-day, no less
than one in Racine's day, would be sure to do in treating a
Greek subject. Actually, by representing Iphigenia as already
betrothed to, loved by, and loving Achilles before the action
of the play begins, he is not as romantic as Euripides, who
with greater dramatic effectiveness makes their love be born

[3] A similar conception of her character is found in a play on the same
subject by Rotrou. Racine owes little if any other debt to that drama.

[4] "The gods would make me happy," he tells her, "if I might win
thee for my bride. . . . A yearning for thy love lays hold on me the more
that I have seen thy nature, how noble is thy heart. Look now; I fain
would save thee—fain would bear thee to my home." *Iphigenia in Aulis*,
ll. 1404-1405, 1410-1413.) And not the least of the reasons that persuade Euripides' heroine to accept her doom is the fear that Achilles
will come to harm in defending her.

of the girl's peril and felt only in the moment when it is hopeless. What Racine's changes do accomplish is to give their love
a more prominent place in his play than it had formerly held.

His Achilles himself is also based on the classical sources.
If he is not the Achilles of Homer, he at least comes as near
the popular conception of him, derived from the *Iliad*, as would
have been possible in the Age of Louis XIV. As in Homer, he
is brave, impetuous, hot-tempered, eager to win glory; also he
is something of an egotist, as in Homer—and in the extant
text of *Iphigenia in Aulis*. In that play, Achilles first consents
to defend Iphigenia not so much out of pity as because of his
anger at the unauthorized use of his name to decoy her to her
death; he cares nothing for the fate of any mere girl. This
touch, if not an interpolation as F. Melian Stawell has per-
suasively argued,[5] is a characteristic example of Euripides'
disillusioning treatment of the heroes of legend. Racine has
softened it, but has not wholly omitted it. Though his own
Achilles, too, is preoccupied with the fact that his name has
been thus vilely used, the excuse can be made for him that he
is so sure of his ability to save Iphigenia that he takes it for
granted and therefore gives free scope to his resentment of
the outrage done him. Yet even at best it is an unlovely trait
in him that he thinks, at such a time, of his own wrongs instead of Iphigenia's, and that he looks at almost everything
primarily in relation to himself.[6]

---

[5] *The Iphigenia in Aulis of Euripides*, New York, 1929, p. 112.

[6] This defect in him is to some extent a defect in the play; for Racine,
unlike Euripides, can have had no reason to cheapen the character of
Achilles. Far, then, from departing unduly from his sources, he has here
followed them "not wisely but too well."

Nor is this the only instance in which he has done so. When his Clytemnestra, like the Clytemnestra of Euripides, kneels before Achilles and
begs him to protect her daughter, her action and her words too (though
she does remind him that he and Iphigenia are betrothed) seem more
appropriate to the situation in the Greek drama, where he is a stranger,

The fact is that Racine's Achilles is no insipidly stereotyped figure of a young "hero" and lover, no "Timocrate" or "Astrate"—not even a Xiphares or a Bajazet. He employs, of course, the language of gallantry in speaking of love (as every one does in the tragedies of the period) but he is well and consistently individualized. True, when Iphigenia refuses to let him shield her and thus defy her father's orders, he exclaims that she is inspired more by hatred of himself than by filial respect; this, however, is not merely an instance of the habitual tendency of the characters in romanesque plays to impute the worst possible motive to anything that displeases them in the conduct of those whom they are represented as "loving." Racine here has at the same time followed convention and rationalized and transcended it. He has made the hackneyed thing the natural and characteristic thing. Such an outburst is natural and characteristic in Achilles; it does not give utterance to his real belief, but is simply an explosion of his baffled anger at Iphigenia's obstinacy. Not for a moment does he lapse from his determination to save her, and it should be realized that it is he who, in the event, does save her: with a small band of soldiers he breaks through the mass of men about the altar and, holding off the entire army, effects a delay which gives Calchas time to learn and declare the true will of the gods. Such an Achilles need not be judged unworthy of his name.

The Agamemnon, the Clytemnestra, and the Ulysses of *Iphigénie* are in the same way essentially transcripts from the

---

than here where the presumption is that he will be concerned, without urging, over the fate of his plighted bride.

Again, the whole project of the marriage between Iphigenia and Achilles at the end of the war, clashes with the common knowledge that he is fated to die in the expedition. Racine should have suppressed that detail of the story. But this inconsistency would probably not be noticed in presentation.

Greek. The most prominent trait in Agamemnon is pride of
authority; but Racine has made his character somewhat more
"sympathetic" by the invention of his renewed efforts to save
his daughter when the time for her sacrifice arrives. Clytemnestra is depicted as less intractable than in Euripides:
she finally bows to Agamemnon's command that she shall not
witness the wedding of Iphigenia; and indeed it would have
been shocking to a French audience in the days of the *grand
monarque* if she had defied the will of her husband and king
as she does in the Greek play. Racine's Ulysses, like the traditional Odysseus, sets public interest above all else, yet he is
not wantonly cruel; when the sacrifice of Iphigenia is no
longer required, it is he who hastens to bring the good news
to her mother.

The romanesque element in this play is in fact mostly con-
fined to that portion of it which deals with Eriphyle, whom,
alone of the important dramatis personae, Racine created
practically out of whole cloth and introduced into the action
—because he felt that his public would find the slaughter of
so blameless a heroine as Iphigenia unendurable and yet
could not accept the alternative version of the Greek legend,
according to which she was saved miraculously. Thus thrown
on his own resources without the guidance of the classics,
Racine promptly reverted to the literary fashions of his time.
That Eriphyle, as well as Iphigenia, is in love with Achilles,
and that her unrequited passion breeds in her a deadly jealousy, is a complication thoroughly characteristic of French-
classical drama. The only genuine confidant in *Iphigénie* (for
Arcas appears but briefly in this function, and so does Aegina) is Doris, to whom Eriphyle unbosoms herself—somewhat against likelihood when she tells of her secret love
though she thinks it shameful and though it is for the man
who killed Doris' father.

Not only is the role of Eriphyle in the play conventionally romanesque; it begets romanesquely conventional conduct in others. How insane is Agamemnon's choice of a story to prevent Iphigenia from coming to Aulis: that Achilles had changed his mind about marrying her, and that Eriphyle was said to be the cause of his loss of ardour! It had every prospect of resulting in serious complications with Achilles, and there was no necessity for it. Many other pretexts were possible—for instance, that the young hero had been summoned to the aid of his father, Peleus, which was indeed the case; even some distorted report of the intended sacrifice itself would have been safer. But a French dramatist in the seventeenth century was sure to select a reason involving a second woman and furnishing an occasion for jealousy. The violent outburst of this passion to which Iphigenia presently gives vent seems somewhat out of character, as also does her immediate acceptance, with apparently no surprise, of the idea that Eriphyle loves Achilles and has captured his heart—out of character, that is, except according to the conventional romanesque notion that every one in love is prone and prompt to be violently jealous on every possible occasion.[7] That a misunderstanding as to the object of Achilles' affections should arise out of the situation in which he and the two

---

[7] Sarcey maintained that the reproaches heaped upon Eriphyle by Iphigenia are not spoken in anger but in tearful distress, for only thus would they be natural to her. In proof that they should be so interpreted, he offered line 711, "Vous triomphez, cruelle, et bravez ma douleur" ("Thou triumphest, cruel girl, and mockest my woe"—not "rage," but "woe," "*douleur*"). But he overlooked the fact that immediately afterwards (ll. 715-718) she threatens her "rival" with Agamemnon's vengeance:

> Thou art too quick, however, to exult.
> This Agamemnon, whom thou dost insult,
> Commands all Greece; he is my father; he
> Loves me. My sorrows wound him more than me.

women are placed, is an inevitable detail of romanesque tragedy.

But Eriphyle, no more than Achilles, is a featureless puppet of conventional design. If she does not belong to the heroic world of the distant past, she looks towards the future. She is the feminine counterpart of the Orestes of Racine's *Andromaque*, anticipating like him (as Lemaître pointed out in regard to them both) the morbid heroes of nineteenth-century romanticism, who are imbued with the idea that they are the especial victims of relentless fate, who derive a melancholy pleasure from this distinction, and who think it justifies them in any conduct. Eriphyle recalls in lingering detail—her relish of it is a daring touch for the decorous Racine—that she was carried off insensible by Achilles and recovered consciousness to find herself held fast in his bloody arms. Her jealousy is sharpened by the envy which she, a girl of unknown parentage and doubtful estate, who has been reared under another's roof and on another's bounty, feels towards the favoured child of fortune to whose happy home she is consigned when a captive's lot has just been added to her already full store of ills. "If she hates Iphigenia"—I translate from Félix Hémon's well-stated analysis of her character— "it is not only because Iphigenia is the betrothed of Achilles, but because she is the daughter of Agamemnon, is a princess respected by all, loved, worshipped, for whom the present is bright and the future more glorious still." As a self-pitying egoist, Eriphyle craves the affection that she has never received, and whose imagined sweetness, which she has missed, she continually dwells upon. The monstrous ingratitude and treachery with which she repays all the great kindness shown her are the measure of the deep wells of bitterness in her soul.

Eriphyle, if considered only as a character and apart from

her introduction of a marring element into the play, is not a blemish there, but one of the chief excellences.

Next to the romanesque features of *Iphigénie*, its theme itself has most often been the target for adverse criticism. That the Olympian gods demand a human sacrifice is an initial assumption too barbarous to be made by civilized Christian audiences, we are told. But the fact is that the idea of human sacrifice was no less revolting to intelligent Athenians of the fifth century B.C. than to the contemporaries of Racine or even to us, and Euripides' tragedy on the same subject was eminently successful when it first appeared and has not diminished in fame since that time. No inconceivable moral problem is posed in either the Greek play or the French; the sacrifice of Iphigenia is not represented as being actually desired by the gods, but as being made the price for the taking of Troy, and thus an obstacle to the destruction of that city, which they, traditionally, loved. Agamemnon is at liberty, his army is at liberty, to give up the war instead.[8] Unless such a course is indeed an alternative which they are free to choose, and not merely an impious refusal to obey the will of heaven, there can be no real indecision for Agamemnon, and his indecision is the very core of both dramas.

Moreover, the idea of human sacrifice is not so strange to us that we cannot project ourselves imaginatively into a situation dealing with it. The parallel between us and the Greeks of Euripides' time is peculiarly close in this respect. Just as human sacrifice, an atrocity which they would never

---

[8] This is not so evident in Racine as in Euripides, for the characters in *Iphigénie* often express the contrary view as a result of misgivings or wishes. But we are not obliged to agree with them, and their interpretation of the quoted words of the oracle, though possible, is not the natural one. The signs with which the gods receive the sacrifice indicate nothing more than their acknowledgment of its consummation and their readiness to keep their side of the bargain.

have dreamed of perpetrating, was familiar to them as a rare but well-known detail in their ancient, semi-sacred legends, whereas other sacrifices held a prominent place in their religion,—so, too, is human sacrifice familiar to our minds because of the Old Testament stories of Jephthah's daughter and Abraham-and-Isaac, and the idea of propitiatory sacrifice is basic in Christianity.[9] And we have the legends of Greece besides as part of our own mental background—tales that we have known from childhood. It is true that the Greeks of Euripides' day themselves believed in the Olympian gods concerned in the story of Iphigenia, and we do not; but our disbelief in them does not hinder our appreciation of the tragedies of the Attic dramatists, and there is no reason why it should hinder our appreciation of *Iphigénie*.

Emile Faguet argued that Racine was grievously at fault in not making the prophet Calchas one of the dramatis personae and indeed the central figure in his play.[10] But Calchas does not appear in Euripides' play, either. The same critic also deplored the assignment to so unimportant a character as Arcas of the important function of disclosing the intentions of Agamemnon to Clytemnestra, Iphigenia, and Achilles; Arcas, he said, is too *"vulgaire"* a personage to be worthy of this revelation and the fine *coup de théâtre* that it makes. Yet the same function is discharged in Euripides by the corresponding character, who is not given there even a name. The most terrific revelation and the most tremendous *coup de théâtre*, perhaps, in the whole range of drama is the disclosure of the parentage of Oedipus in Sophocles, and it is

---

[9] Such a sacrifice must have seemed still less unnatural to the age of Racine, a period of greater religious faith—and superstition—than ours. In this connection, Lemaitre has noted the alleged belief of Madame de Montespan that the blood of an infant child, shed by a recreant priest, would preserve for herself the love of Louis XIV and rid her of Madame de Fontanges. (*Jean Racine*, Paris, 1908, p. 243.)

[10] See Faguet's *Propos de Théâtre*, vol. iii, Paris, 1906, p. 82f.

effected by a nameless herdsman, who speaks, in all, twenty-
five complete lines and four incomplete lines. I cannot help
suspecting that this last criticism of Faguet's was inspired
by some survival, conscious or unconscious, in him of the
old notions of decorum and degree, those fetishes of pseudo-
classical *littérateurs*, in deference to which Corneille changed
the opening of the *Cid*—"because Elvira was not of sufficient
dignity to be seen in conversation with the Count de Gormas."

Why, then, does *Iphigénie* enjoy no higher esteem to-day
than it does? Why is it now produced only at rare intervals?
Mainly, I think, for two reasons—reasons which no one has
mentioned, yet by which I believe people have been uncon-
sciously influenced in their attitude towards this drama.

In the first place, Racine has never elsewhere followed so
closely another play that was the source of his own, yet in no
important respect has he surpassed or indeed equalled his
Attic model. We are instinctively dissatisfied, even if we do
not realize why, with an imitation that contributes practically
nothing of superior value to previous treatment of the same
theme. The *Iphigenia in Aulis* of Euripides, judged by any
plausible reconstruction (such as F. Melian Stawell's) of
its corrupt text, is a very great play; it is not one of the half
dozen Greek tragedies which constitute together with Shakespeare's four tragic masterpieces the supreme achievements
in the dramatic literature of the world, but it stands in a
group immediately below these. Its failure to rival them is in
large measure due to a certain lack of unity, a shift in interest and emphasis, that would seem almost unavoidable
with its subject matter. A similar fault is to be found in another tragedy of approximately the same degree of greatness
and by the same author, the *Hippolytus*, from which Racine
derived his next play. But whereas in *Phèdre*, as I point out

in my study of that drama, he corrected the chief imperfection of his Greek original, in *Iphigénie* he worsened it.

Unity of a sort is of course not wanting in either his or Euripides' version of the affair at Aulis; in both plays the issue is whether or not Iphigenia will be sacrificed. But this would appear, in the first three-quarters of the *Iphigenia in Aulis*, to depend on Agamemnon; he is on that account the central figure, and the all-important question is, What will he decide to do? Then, after line 1275, when he has declared his unalterable purpose and gone finally away, it is Iphigenia herself who becomes the central figure, and the question is thenceforth, What will she herself do? Now in Racine's *Iphigénie* also, the problem of Agamemnon's choice remains long dominant—though not so completely as in Euripides, for Iphigenia's misunderstanding about Achilles and her consequent jealousy divert attention from her danger, on which it ought to be fixed. But Agamemnon's decision is reached at the end of Act IV; he determines to save his daughter if he can. Thereupon the question becomes merely one of whether or not she can succeed in escaping from the camp; and then, when this proves impossible, of whether Achilles can persuade her to accept his protection; and then of whether he will save her in spite of herself;—and then at the last, to crown all, she fortuitously owes her life to the recoil of Eriphyle's wickedness upon her own head, a surprise-ending! There is plenty of action, excitement, suspense, and strong emotion in the fifth act of *Iphigénie*, but not the substance of great drama.[11]

[11] Not only is the material in this act melodramatic in itself, but its manipulation is that of melodrama. Clytemnestra was hardly the sort of woman to faint; her reported swoon is but a transparent device to cause and explain her absence when Achilles finds Iphigenia. She appears as soon as he is gone; had she been present earlier, during the contention between the lovers, there is no saying what would have been the result. It is pure chance and a matter of a few minutes that she was not present.

A second reason for the relative disregard of this play in modern times is the fact that it contains none of Racine's finest characters. Among its dramatis personae there is no one comparable to Achmet or Roxana in *Bajazet*, or to Mithridates or Monime in *Mithridate*. Such figures challenge the skill of great actors and actresses, and invite critical study. The fascination they exert makes one return again and again to a play in which any of them appears, and perhaps grow to love it in spite of its blemishes; the praise of them reflects glory upon it.

But *Iphigénie* is nevertheless, we should not fail to realize, superior to both *Mithridate* and *Bajazet*. Though it has in it no remarkable piece of characterization, it is peopled with a larger number of well-conceived, thoroughly individualized men and women than any other tragedy of Racine. There are six of them: Agamemnon, Achilles, and Ulysses; Clytemnestra, Iphigenia, and Eriphyle.[12] These characters, as Faguet observed, clash continually—Achilles with Agamemnon, Clytemnestra with Agamemnon, Ulysses with Agamemnon, Iphigenia with Eriphyle, Iphigenia with Achilles. The tension, therefore, is almost as incessant as in *Andromaque*. *Iphigénie* certainly cannot compare in structural excellence with that miracle of plot-design, nor can it boast such exquisite poetry; and Hermione is one of the greatest creations of Racine. But on the other hand, *Iphigénie* exhibits much less of pseudo-classicism in language and sentiments and method of treatment than *Andromaque*, and much more that is truly classical and thus harmonious with its subject; and it is marred by no character like Andromache herself, for whom sympathy is required yet whose code and conduct, rightly

---

[12] *Britannicus* and *Athalie* have only five each (if the unsatisfactory prince Britannicus and the little-developed Joash are excluded from the reckoning, as they should be), the rest in no instance more than four.

judged, are both wrong and absurd. On the whole, one may, perhaps, fairly conclude that though *Iphigénie* is far inferior to *Britannicus*, not to speak of *Phèdre* and *Athalie*, it deserves a place with *Andromaque* just outside the circle of dramas that can properly be called "great."

CHARACTERS IN THE PLAY

AGAMEMNON, *King of Argos and Mycenae, leader of the Greek army against Troy.*

CLYTEMNESTRA, *his wife.*

IPHIGENIA, *his daughter.*

ACHILLES.

ULYSSES.

ERIPHYLE, *a young girl taken prisoner by Achilles at Lesbos.*

ARCAS
EURYBATES } *servants of Agamemnon.*

AEGINA, *attendant of Clytemnestra.*

DORIS, *friend and fellow-captive of Eriphyle.*

Guards.

The scene is laid in the camp of the Greek army at Aulis. In the foreground is an open space; in the background are tents, one of them Agamemnon's.

The name "Eurybates" is accented on the second syllable. All the other names are accented on the next to the last syllable.

IPHIGENIA

ACT I

*The first faint light of morning is visible in the sky. During
the course of the Act, it gradually grows brighter.*
AGAMEMNON *is discovered, bending over* ARCAS, *who has
been sleeping on the ground before the King's tent.*

AGAMEMNON.

Yes, it is Agamemnon; 'tis thy king
That wakes thee. Recognize whose voice doth ring
Now in thine ears.

ARCAS (*starting up*).

'Tis thou, my lord, indeed!
So long before the dawn? What urgent need
Hath roused thee? This dim light had scarcely shown
Thy face to me. Thine eyes and mine, alone,
Are open yet in Aulis. Didst thou hear
Some sound of wind? Doth heaven grant our prayer
This night? (*Listening*) Nay, all things sleep, all are at rest—
The army, and the winds, and Neptune's breast.

AGAMEMNON.

Happy is he with lowly lot content,
Free from the yoke 'neath which my neck is bent
By pride and power,—who lives in the obscure
Station assigned unto him, thus secure!

ARCAS.

How long, sire, hast thou spoken words like these?
The gods, who give thee whatsoe'er might please
Thy heart, have by what secret injury

Made thee, when thou art crowned with honours, see
With scorn and bitterness what they have done
For thee? King, father, happy husband, son
Of Atreus, thou dost rule the richest lands
In Greece. Thy line on every side descends
From Jove; with that same source whence thou hast sprung
Thy marriage links thee further; and now young
Achilles, whom so many oracles
Extol,—whose valour will work miracles,
They promise,—woos thy daughter, and would light
His nuptial torch at burning Troy. What sight
So glorious, what triumph, sire, so great
As here is thine? A thousand ships await—
With twenty kings upon them, by this strand—
Only a wind, to sail 'neath thy command.
This lengthy calm doth, it is true, delay
Thy conquests, all too long hath barred thy way
To Ilium. Three months have the winds been chained.
Midst all thine honours, a man thou hast remained;
And Fortune, which hath ever changed its face,
Ne'er promised thee an unmixed happiness.
Soon . . . But yon letter tells thee of what dire
Mishap, to cause the tears thou sheddest, sire?
Is it the babe Orestes who is dead?
For Clytemnestra dost thou weep instead,
Or Iphigenia? What is written there?
I pray thee, let me know.

AGAMEMNON (to himself).

Nay, I will ne'er
Consent to such a thing! Thou shalt not die.

ARCAS.

My lord!

AGAMEMNON.

Thou seest me grieve. Now learn thou why,
And judge if this should be a time of rest
For me, good friend. Thou well rememberest
When first our ships at Aulis gathered. We
Seemed to be summoned by the winds to sea.
We would set forth; a thousand cries of joy
Already carried threats to distant Troy,
When a most shocking marvel cut them short:
The favouring breeze failed us while still in port!
We had to turn and back to Aulis creep,
With feeble oars troubling the waveless deep.
A portent so astounding turned my thought
Unto the goddess worshipped in this spot.
With Menelaus, Nestor, and Ulysses
I prayed to her with secret sacrifices.
What was her answer? How was it with me
When I through Calchas heard her cruel decree?
  "Ye muster against Troy your might in vain
  Unless with sacred, solemn rites the blood
    Of a young girl of the same strain
    As Helen's doth in Aulis stain
  The altar of Diana. If ye would
    Obtain the winds which heaven denies
To you, 'tis Iphigenia ye must sacrifice."

ARCAS.

Thy daughter!

AGAMEMNON.

Dazed, as thou canst guess, I stood.
Those dreadful words seemed to freeze all my blood.
Voiceless was I, and would be yet, had not

A thousand sobs made passage of my throat.
I blamed the gods, and on their altars swore
To disobey them; I would hear no more.
Why did I then not yield to love's dismay,
And send the army home that very day?
Ulysses seemed to agree with what I said,
Letting my words' first torrent rage unstayed;
But soon, as crafty as he ever was,
He spoke of honour and our country's cause,
This host, these kings subject to my commands,
And empire promised Greece in Asian lands—
What figure I would cut, to immolate
Unto my child the welfare of the State
And back to Argos go, with infamy,
To grow old there amid my family!

    I myself—I confess it with some shame—
Was charmed by power and grandeur; and the name
Of king of kings and leader of all Greece
Flattered my heart in its vaingloriousness.
To crown my misery, the gods every night
When woe was eased by sleep, however light,
Came to avenge their altars for the blood
Denied their claims, reproaching me who could
Be swayed by impious pity, brandishing
Their bolts before mine eyes and threatening,
With hand upraised, to punish such a sin
If I were stubborn. Arcas, I gave in,
And, vanquished by Ulysses and my fears,
Ordered my daughter's sacrifice, in tears.

    But from her mother's arms I had to tear her.
How heartless was my stratagem, to snare her!
I feigned to speak now for Achilles, who
Loves her. To speed her coming, I unto

Argos wrote that this warrior, though most fain
To set forth with us, wished to see again
My daughter and, ere going, marry her.

ARCAS.

Hast thou no fear of his hot temper, sir?
Thinkest thou this hero, whom both love and right
Would arm, will quietly let thee expedite
Thus, by his name's misuse, that sacrifice
And see his loved one slain before his eyes?

AGAMEMNON.

Achilles was not here. Peleus, his sire—
Thou wilt remember—did his aid require
Against a neighbouring foe, and called him hence;
And there seemed, Arcas, every evidence
This war would make his absence be, perforce,
Longer. But who can stay a torrent's course?
Achilles goes to fight, and triumphs at once;
And scarce could tidings unto us announce
His victory ere he came back yesterday
At nightfall. Yet still stronger reasons stay
My hand. My daughter hastens to her death.
She draweth near and no suspicions hath
Of what awaits her. She perhaps doth find
Joy in the thought her father is so kind!
My daughter . . . 'Tis not only for that name
She beareth, which hath such a sacred claim
Upon me, that I mourn, nor for her youth,
Nor for my blood in her. I mourn, in truth,
Her countless virtues and our love, no less—
My tenderness for her, her duteousness
Towards me, and in her heart a reverence
For me that naught can shake—to recompense

Which better, I in former days did give
My promise. Nay, I never shall believe,
Just heaven, that thou didst approve of this
Insensate, cruel, and horrible sacrifice.
Thine oracle hath doubtless sought to test me,
And if I dared obey it, thou wouldst blast me.

    Arcas, 'tis thou whom I have chosen to tell
These things to. Thou herein must show thy zeal,
Prudence, and skilfulness in serving me.
The Queen, who well had known thy loyalty
In Sparta, set thee in the place which thou
Hast ever since had near my person. Now
Take thou this letter; go without delay
To meet her, following post-haste the way
That doth to Aulis from Mycenae lead.
When thou hast found her, bid her to proceed
No further, and give this missive unto her
Which I have written her. But do thou beware
Of straying. Take with thee a trusty guide.
If once my daughter should set foot inside
This camp, e'en then she is as good as dead.
Calchas, who waits for her, will make instead
Of our sad tears the voice of heaven be heard;
And to religion's claims, the Greeks, thus stirred
Against us, all will hearken timorously.
Those, too, that being ambitious, hate to see
My greatness, will again aspire and hence
Intrigue against me—take from me, perchance,
The power which so offends them.

                          Go, I say,
And save her from my weakness. Come what may,
Though, do not lose discretion in thy zeal
And my grim secret unto her reveal.

If it be possible, let my daughter ne'er
Be undeceived and learn the peril here
Unto which I exposed her. Spare me thus
A mother's frenzied cries, and let thy voice
Confirm what I have written. To turn back
Daughter and mother, too—so wronged, alack!—
I write them that Achilles' mind is changed
And he would have this marriage, first arranged
At his love's urgency, now be deferred
Till his return. Thou canst add: thou hast heard
The cooling of his love is thought to be
Caused by young Eriphyle, she whom he
In Lesbos took, and whom he, having brought her
To Argos captive, left there with my daughter,
Himself. That is enough for thee to say.
As to all else, be silent. Now the day
Grows bright about us. Some one comes, e'en now.
I hear sounds. 'Tis Achilles. Go; haste thou.
O gods! Ulysses cometh with him.

[*Exit* ARCAS. *Enter* ACHILLES *and* ULYSSES.

(*To* ACHILLES) What,
Sir! Can success have with such swiftness brought
Thee back here? Of thine unfledged valour these,
Then, are the trial flights? What victories
Will follow such brave deeds? All Thessaly
Either subdued or pacified by thee,
And Lesbos, too, conquered while thou didst wait
For the host to sail—these things, which would be great
Displays of any other's martial powers,
Only amuse Achilles' idle hours.

ACHILLES.

Sir, speak less highly of such slight success.

May heaven, which detains us in this place,
Soon open nobler fields to me, whose breast
Thrills at the glorious prize thou offerest.
But can I credit a report which quite
Surprises me and fills me with delight?
Deignest thou, sir, to speed my wishes, then?
Am I so soon the happiest of men?
'Tis said that Iphigenia is being brought
To Aulis, and that her lot and my lot
Are now in marriage to be linked together.

AGAMEMNON.

My daughter? Who hath told thee she comes hither?

ACHILLES.

What is there to astonish thee in this?

AGAMEMNON (*aside to* ULYSSES).

Gods! Hath he heard of my grim artifice?

ULYSSES (*to* ACHILLES).

Sir, Agamemnon rightly is astounded.
Forgettest thou by what ills we are hounded?
Oh, what a time for marriage to be proposed!
When to our ships the sea is ever closed,
All Greece despairs, the army wastes away,—
When to appease the wrath of heaven may
Require the blood we prize all else above,—
Achilles, only he, doth think of love!
Is it his wish to flout the public fear?
And shall the leader of the Greeks prepare
Such nuptials' pomp and feasts, and so provoke
The Fates? Ah, is it thus the woes our folk
Now suffer, sir, can to compassion move
Thy soul, and thus thou dost thy country love?

ACHILLES.

On Phrygian fields our deeds will testify
Which loves her more, Ulysses—thou or I.
Till then I leave thee to parade thy zeal.
Thou canst pray, all thou wishest, for her weal;
Heap high with offerings and drench with blood
The altars; o'er the victims' entrails brood,
Thyself, to find from them the reasons why
The winds are stilled. But in such matters I
Rely on Calchas. Let me quickly, sir,
Conclude a marriage that cannot rouse the ire
Of heaven. A warlike ardour fills me, which
Prevents all sloth, and I will on this beach
Rejoin you soon. Great would be my regret
If any warrior's foot save mine were set
First on the plains of Troy.

AGAMEMNON.

              Why must it be,
O heaven, that thou in secret jealousy
Barrest to heroes such as these the way
To Asia? Have I witnessed their display
Of noble fervour, and yet found no cheer
For my sick heart?

ULYSSES (*aside*).

Gods! what is this I hear?

ACHILLES.

My lord, what meanest thou by such words?

AGAMEMNON.

                    That now,
Princes, all, all of us, must hence withdraw;
That we too long have let vain hopes abuse us,

Waiting for winds which heaven doth refuse us.
The gods protect Troy, and with many a presage
Their wrath forbids us thither to seek passage.

ACHILLES.

What dread signs prove to us their enmity?

AGAMEMNON.

Consider what they have foretold for thee.
Why shut thine eyes? 'Tis known, through thee must come,
So they decree, the fall of Ilium.
But as such glory's price, 'tis known, they have
Marked out upon the plains of Troy thy grave.
Thou wouldst live happily for a long time
Elsewhere, but there must die in youth's fair prime.

ACHILLES.

Then all the kings that to avenge thee came
Will go home, laden with eternal shame;
And Paris, in his love triumphant, will
Possess unpunished thy wife's sister still?

AGAMEMNON.

Nay, hath thy valour, which outstripped us, not
Sufficiently avenged our honour's blot?
The fate of Lesbos, all laid waste by thee,
Leaves the whole region of the Aegean Sea
Aghast. Troy saw the flames, and the waves bore
Wreckage and bodies to her shores. Yet more,
A Helen of her own she doth lament,
Whom thou hast captive to Mycenae sent;
For I can doubt not that what this fair maid
Tries vainly to keep secret is betrayed
By both her youthful beauty and her pride.

Her very silence tells us she doth hide
The fact she is a princess, now, from us.

ACHILLES.

No, no; all this is too ingenious.
Thou probest too deeply heaven's mysteries.
Shall I be stayed by empty threats like these
And flee from all the high renown that waits
For me if I but follow thee? The Fates,
'Tis true, aforetime to my mother said,
When with a mortal husband she had wed,
That I must choose either long years and tame
Or else a brief life and enduring fame.
But since in each case I must presently
Come to the tomb, would I prefer to be
A useless burden upon the earth, to save
Too carefully the blood a goddess gave
To me, wait with my father for an obscure
Old age, and having shunned thus (to secure
Such length of life) all knowledge of the path
Of glory, die—forgotten after death?
Let us not raise unworthy obstacles.
When honour speaks, we need no oracles.
Heaven our life and span of days commands,
But our fair fame, sire, lies in our own hands.
    Why fret o'er what the gods may cause to ensue?
Let us attempt to be immortal, too,
Scorn Fate, and rush where valour offers one
A destiny as noble as their own.
That is at Troy; my heart pants to be there;
And, warn me as they may, my single prayer
Is for a wind to waft me thither soon;
And though I had to undertake alone

This siege, I with Patroclus still would go
Now to take vengeance for thee. But not so
Be it; 'tis into *thy* hands that this task
Hath been consigned by Fate. I only ask
The honour, sire, of following thee. No more
Do I now urge thee, as I did before,
To sanction my love's impulses, which were
About to take me far away from here.
That same love, zealous for thy glory, sire,
Would have me also by my example fire
The hearts of all and ne'er will let me leave thee
Unto the timid counsels that some give thee.

[*Exit* ACHILLES.

ULYSSES.

Thou hearest, my lord. Whate'er it costs him, he
Would go to Troy, fulfil his destiny.
We feared his love; and 'gainst himself he has
Now armed our hand by his mistake.

AGAMEMNON.
Alas!

ULYSSES.

What augureth that sigh? Is it a plaint
Breathed by a father's heart, which groweth faint?
Must I believe a single night could shake
Thy purpose? Was it, then, thy soul that spake
Just now to us? Take thought. Thou owest, sir,
To Greece thy daughter. Thou didst promise her
To us; and on the strength of this thy pledge
Calchas, whom daily all the Greeks besiege
For counsel, hath foretold that sure it is
That favouring winds will blow anon. If this

Proveth untrue, dost think he will remain
Silent and thy attempts will not be vain
To make him let the gods appear to be
Liars, instead of laying the blame on thee?
And who can say how far the host, whom thou
Defraudest of their victim, may allow
A wrath to go which they deem justified?
Force not a maddened people to decide
Between the gods and thee. Beware their choice.
    Was it not thou, my lord, whose urgent voice
Summoned us all to sail to Xanthus' strand,
Appealing, town by town throughout the land,
Unto the oaths all Helen's suitors swore
When all Greece, as thy brother did, of yore
Sought her in marriage from Tyndareus,
Her sire? Whoe'er for husband she might choose,
We promised to defend their nuptial ties,
And if some ravisher e'er stole his prize,
Our hands would bring to him that villain's head.
But would the compact which our love then made
Have been respected when that love was gone,
Were it not for thee? Thou torest us—thou alone—
From new loves, madest us leave our children dear
And wives. And when we are assembled here
From every side and can no longer see
Aught save the honour of avenging thee,—
When we select thee, whom we recognize
As being the author of this great emprize,
To be our leader,—when the kings who might
Dispute that rank are ready in the fight
To pour forth all their blood in serving thee,—
Doth Agamemnon renounce victory—he,
He only—and doth he not dare to buy

With even a little blood a fame so high?
Daunted at the first step, doth he assume
Command of the army but to send it home?

AGAMEMNON.

Ah, sir, how easily when without the woe
That overwhelms my heart, thy heart can show
Its loftiness! Yet if thou sawest thy son
Telemachus, with the fatal wreath upon
His head, approach the altar, we straightway
Would see thee then exchange, in sore dismay
At such a sight, these scornful words for tears,
Feel all the grief that now in me appears,
And rush 'twixt him and Calchas' hand abhorred.

    Sir, thou well knowest that I have given my word;
And if my daughter comes, I must allow
Her sacrifice. But if despite me now
A happier fate makes her in Argos stay,
Or stops her on the road, grant that I may
No longer strive to have here rites so fell,
But dare to look upon this obstacle
To them as sent to save her from the knife
By some kind god who watches o'er her life.
Thy counsels have had o'er me too much sway.
I blush . . .

                   [*Enter* EURYBATES.

EURYBATES.

    Sire . . .

AGAMEMNON.

    Oh, what comest thou to say?

EURYBATES.

The Queen, whose haste hath been outstripped by mine,

Will soon thy daughter to thine arms consign.
She now draws near, but for some time was lost
In the woods round the camp of the Greek host.
Scarce were we able amid that darkling shade
To find again the path from which we strayed.

AGAMEMNON.

Good heavens!

EURYBATES.

    She bringeth with her here, as well,
Young Eriphyle, who in Lesbos fell
Into Achilles' hands, and who hath come,
She saith, to Aulis seeking to learn from
Calchas about herself, whereof is known
Nothing. The news of their approach hath flown
Already everywhere, and an admiring crowd
Views Iphigenia's beauty and with loud
Cries prayeth heaven for her happiness.
Some towards the Queen to pay their homage press,
While others ask of me what brings her here;
But one and all say that since heaven hath ne'er
Beheld a king more gloriously enthroned
Or equally with its secret favour crowned,
Ne'er was a father happier than thou.

AGAMEMNON.

Enough, Eurybates. Thou mayst withdraw.
The rest is my concern. I must take thought
Thereof.

       [*Exit* EURYBATES.
   Just gods, 'tis thus ye bring to naught
All that my futile prudence can contrive,
Making your vengeance sure! Could I e'en grieve

Freely, tears could allay my sufferings
In part at least. Sad destiny of kings!
Slaves that we are to Fortune's cruelties
And men's opinions, we have witnesses
On every side, who watch upon us keep,
And the most wretched dare the least to weep.

ULYSSES.

I am a father, sir, and weak like thee.
I put myself in thy place easily.
I shudder at the blow that makes thee groan;
Nor do I blame thy tears, I add mine own
To them. But there is left thee no excuse
Of which thy love can rightly yet make use.
The gods their victim have to Calchas brought.
He knows it; he awaits her; and if aught
Do ye delay, he will himself appear
Before thee, with a loud voice claiming her.
We are alone still. Let the tears, then, flow
Which on thy loved one's fate thou must bestow.
Weep for her, weep—or cease from sorrowing,
And think instead what honour thence will spring.
See 'neath our oars the Hellespont all white,
False Troy in flames, her captive people's plight,
Priam before thee bowed, Helen restored
Again by thine own hand unto her lord,—
And see thy ships with garlands at the stern
Crowned when to Aulis they with thee return,
And all the glory to be had therefrom,
The eternal theme of centuries to come!

AGAMEMNON.

I know how vain my efforts are, and hence
I yield and let the gods slay innocence.

The victim soon will in thy footsteps walk.
Go. But see to it that Calchas does not talk.
Help me to keep this fatal secret so,
Nor let her mother near the altar go.

ACT II

ERIPHYLE *and* DORIS *are discovered.*

ERIPHYLE.

Come, Doris; let us not be in their way.
While in the arms of sire and husband they
Vie in displaying love, let us not remain
But give my sadness and their joy free rein.

DORIS.

What, madam! always thinking of thy woe?
Wilt thou see only grounds for tears? I know
All is displeasing to a captive's eyes.
In slavery's chains there are no joys to prize.
But in that dreadful time when we sailed o'er
The waves, borne off by Lesbos' conqueror,
And in his ship, a timid prisoner, thou
Sawest the blood-stained victor, less than now
Thy face was wet with tears and thou didst less
Often yield utterly to thy distress.
All smiles upon thee at the present time.
Iphigenia's heart is bound to thine
By true affection. Pitying thy sighs,
She looks upon thee with a sister's eyes;
And even in Troy itself thy lot would be
Less fortunate. Thou hadst a wish to see
This Aulis, where her father called her; thou
Hast arrived here in Aulis with her now;
Yet for some reason which I cannot conceive,
As we drew nearer, thou the more didst grieve.

ERIPHYLE.

Nay, could sad Eriphyle, dost thou deem,
Look on their happiness with tranquil mien?
Thinkest thou my misery will vanish, where
Good fortune is which I can never share?
A daughter in her father's clasp, I see;
Her regal mother's only pride is she—
And I, whom always some new evil harms,
Consigned from infancy to strangers' arms,
Was given life's gift, and live, yet know not still
Either a father's or a mother's smile.
I know not who I am, and, worst of all,
Must never know; for a dire oracle,
When I desired to learn whence I derive,
Told me I could not do so and survive.

DORIS.

Nay, nay, to learn this thou shouldst stop at naught.
An oracle always loves to hide its thought.
It never hath one meaning, plainly shown.
Losing a false name, thou'lt regain thine own.
Thus Eriphyle, we might say, will cease
To be; no other danger wilt thou face.
Thou knowest thy name was changed in infancy.

ERIPHYLE.

Naught else about myself is known to me.
Thy hapless father, who knew all the rest,
Would tell me no part of it—not the least.
In Troy, where I was waited for, said he,
My proper station would be accorded me,
And in recovering name and rank I would
Find that I was of most exalted blood;

And I e'en then envisioned that great city.
  But heaven sent the warrior without pity,
Achilles, unto Lesbos; all gave way
Before his dire attack; thy father lay
Dead 'neath the heaps of slain, and I was one
Of those in chains, still to myself unknown.
Of all my promised greatness, there doth abide
In me, the slave of Greeks, only the pride
Of noble lineage which cannot be proved
Is mine.

DORIS.

  How cruel the hand which hath removed
One who well knew thine origin must appear
Unto thee, madam! Calchas, though, is here,
Who can see plainly all that heaven leaves dim—
Yes, the famed Calchas. The gods speak to him;
And, thus instructed, he knows everything
That yet hath been or future days will bring.
Could he be ignorant of who gave thee birth?
Thou hast of friends, even in this camp, no dearth.
When Iphigenia and Achilles wed,
He will provide a home for thee, she said,
Binding with oaths her words before me spoken.
She asks this of him as his love's first token.

ERIPHYLE.

What wouldst thou think, Doris, if I confessed
Their marriage to be far the bitterest
Of all my woes?

DORIS.
What, madam!

ERIPHYLE.

                  Thou in great
Amazement seest my grief doth not abate.
Listen, and be amazed that I live on.
To be a stranger and a slave unknown
Is but a small thing. That destroying curse
Of wretched Lesbos, that Achilles, source
Of thy woes and of mine, whose crimson hand
Bore me off prisoner, slew thy father, and
Thus robbed me both of him and of the chance
To learn my birth, and who to me should hence
Be wholly odious—even his name—is of
All mortals he whom I most dearly love.

DORIS.

Oh, what is this thou sayest!

ERIPHYLE.

                 I would tell
Myself continually that I could conceal
My weakness by eternal silence. Now
My heart, being too full, doth overflow,
And once for all I speak to thee hereof.
Ask me not on what hope this fated love
Was based, whereby I found myself possessed.
I would not blame therewith regret expressed
At some time by Achilles—so unto me
It seemed—which merely was in courtesy
To me in my misfortune. Heaven is taking
Without a doubt a savage joy in making
The shafts of all its hate rain down on me.
Shall I recall the fearsome memory
Of the sad hour which brought us slavery's doom?

In the cruel hands that plucked me from my home
I long unconscious and in darkness lay.
At last my sad eyes sought the light of day,
And seeing myself clasped by an arm all smeared
With blood, I trembled, Doris, and I feared
To look on a fierce conqueror's visage grim.
I went on board his vessel, loathing him,
Averting ever my horror-stricken gaze.
But I beheld him finally. His face
Had not a vestige of ferocity.
Upon my lips did my reproaches die
Unuttered, and I felt my heart declare
For him, against myself. I then and there
Forgot my anger and could only weep.
I willingly went with him in the ship.
I loved him first in Lesbos, and I still
Love him in Aulis. Iphigenia will
Vainly offer me protection and
Stretch forth to solace me a helping hand.
Dread consequence of the madness torturing me:
I clutch that offered hand only to be
Armed against her and take her unaware,
To thwart her happiness that I cannot bear.

Doris.

How could thy helpless hate achieve that end?
Were it not better if thou hadst remained
Within Mycenae's walls, to shun thereby
The torments which thou findest here and try
To overcome a love thou needs must hide?

Eriphyle.

I fain had stayed there, but whate'er betide,
Doris,—however dread a sight and sore

To me would be her triumph on this shore,—
I had to bow to Fate, which drives me ever
Onward. A secret voice bade me come hither
And told me that by doing so perchance
I could bring with me my inheritance
Of evil,—that perchance, being near those
Too happy lovers, some shadow of my woes
From my unwanted presence might on them fall.
That is what leads me here, and not at all
Impatience to discover unto whom
I owe a life so wretched. But my doom
Would in their marriage find its own decree.
If they indeed wed, all is o'er for me:
I will die, Doris,—die this very day,—
And in the dark grave hide my shame away
Nor seek for parents whom I know not of,
And whom I have disgraced by my mad love.

DORIS.

Oh, how I pity thee! What tyranny . . .

ERIPHYLE.

With Iphigenia comes Agamemnon. See!
[*Enter* AGAMEMNON *and* IPHIGENIA.

IPHIGENIA.

Sir, whither hurriest thou? What urgent need
Now makes thee hasten elsewhere with such speed
From our fond arms? What means this sudden flight?
Respectfully I let the Queen's delight
At seeing thee be given free scope; but may
I not detain thee briefly and display
My joy in turn? May I not . . .

AGAMEMNON.

What wouldst thou?
Embrace thy father, child. He loves thee, now
And always.

IPHIGENIA.

Ah, how precious unto me
That love is! And how good it is to see
Both thee thyself and this new greatness which
Invests thee with such splendour, vast and rich!
What power and glory! I had already heard
The wondrous tale thereof; but I am stirred,
When mine own eyes behold so glad a sight,
Much more now by amazement and delight.
How Greece reveres and loves thee! Oh, what bliss
To be the child of such a sire it is!

AGAMEMNON.

Daughter, thou hast deserved a happier sire.

IPHIGENIA.

To what more happiness couldst thou aspire?
What greater honours could a king be given?
I deem I should but render thanks to heaven.

AGAMEMNON (*aside*).

Great gods! How can I tell her she must die?

IPHIGENIA.

Thou turnest away thy face and seemest to sigh.
Only with pain thine eyes now fall on me.
Did we come here from home unbidden by thee?

AGAMEMNON.

Ever, my child, mine eyes look on thy face

With love; yet now, with change of time and place,
My joy is marred by cruel anxiety.

IPHIGENIA.

Father, forget thine office while with me!
I know how hard 'twill be, to be so long
Parted. Does it appear, then, to thee wrong
To treat me for a moment as thy dear
Daughter? Thou seest that none else is here
But a young princess unto whom I have made
Boast of thy fondness for me. Of my aid
And thy indulgent love of me I o'er
And o'er assured her, telling her what great store
Of happiness was my proud possession hence.
What will she think of the indifference
Thou showest towards me? Have I aroused in her
A false hope? Is there nothing that will clear
Thy brow, so clouded o'er with troubled thought?

AGAMEMNON.

My daughter . . .

IPHIGENIA.

Yes? Go on, sir.

AGAMEMNON.

I cannot.

IPHIGENIA.

Perish that Trojan prince who causes us
So much unhappiness!

AGAMEMNON.

'Twill cost our house,
To conquer and to slay him, many a tear.

IPHIGENIA.

The gods protect thy life with special care.

AGAMEMNON.

The gods are cruel and lately to my prayers
Have been deaf.

IPHIGENIA.

Calchas, I am told, prepares
A solemn sacrifice.

AGAMEMNON.

Would that I might find
Earlier some means to make them less unkind!

IPHIGENIA.

Will it be offered soon?

AGAMEMNON.

Sooner than I
Wish.

IPHIGENIA.

Shall I be allowed to join in thy
Devotions? Will thy family with thee bow
Beside the altar?

AGAMEMNON (*aside*).

Alas!

IPHIGENIA.

Why art thou
Silent?

AGAMEMNON.

Thou shalt be there, my child. Good-bye!

[*Exit* AGAMEMNON, *hastily.*

IPHIGENIA.

What does a welcome such as this imply?
A secret horror makes my blood run chill.
I fear, despite myself, some unknown ill.
Just gods, ye know whose safety I implore.

ERIPHYLE.

How now! when all the cares which must hang o'er
His head so weigh upon him, doth a slight
Coldness suffice to fill thee with such fright?
Alas, then, to what sighs am I condemned—
I, whom my parents left and never claimed,
A stranger everywhere, who even perchance
At birth has never had a loving glance!
If now thy father is unkind, at least
Thou still canst weep upon a mother's breast;
And for what sorrows can thy tears be shed
Which may not by a lover be allayed?

IPHIGENIA.

Sweet Eriphyle, thou art nowise wrong.
Achilles' love would dry mine eyes ere long.
That love, a daughter's duty, and his high fame
Give him my heart, which he can justly claim.
But of himself what must I now conceive!
This lover no one could persuade to leave
These shores, such eagerness was his to wed me,
Wherefore a message from my father bade me
Come here,—hath he shown any wish to see
Her whom I thought he awaited rapturously?
For my part, as these last two days we drew
Nearer the place which I so longed to view,
I was upon the lookout ceaselessly
For him; all roads that led from Aulis I

Searched every moment with my timid glance;
My heart, to seek him, flew far in advance;
I asked whoever on the way did meet me
About Achilles. He was not there to greet me
On my arrival, when I reached this spot
At last without him. He alone was not
Present; I scarce could penetrate the crowd
Of strangers. Agamemnon, sad of mood,
Seemeth afraid to speak his name before
My face. What is he doing? Who will explore
And solve this mystery for me? Shall I find
Achilles like my father cold, with mind
Preoccupied? Are the cares of war enough
To extinguish in a single day all love
And tenderness from their hearts? But no—I thus
Wrong him with needless fears. Myself it was
To whom Greece owes his aid against her foes.
He was not one of Helen's suitors, those
Who all in Sparta to her father gave
Their oath. He is alone of Greeks no slave
Thereof, unbound by any pledge. If he
Sails against Ilium, this he does for me
And fain would carry, for his reward, the name
There of my husband; he naught else doth claim.

       [*Enter* CLYTEMNESTRA.

CLYTEMNESTRA.

Daughter, we must without delay be gone
And save by flight thy fair fame and mine own.
I am no more surprised that, so distrait,
Thy father seemed to see us with regret.
Attempting to protect thee from the shame
Of being rejected, he had, ere we came,

Sent me this letter early in the day
By Arcas, who, because we lost our way,
Then failed to find us and hath given it
Only now unto me. Let us, I repeat,
Save our smirched honour. Achilles changed his mind
About your marriage now, and hath declined
The honour granted him. He now doth wish
To wait till his return.

ERIPHYLE (*aside*).
What!

CLYTEMNESTRA.
Thy cheeks flush
Crimson, I see, at such an insult. Thou
Must arm with noble pride thy bosom now.
I gave my sanction to this ingrate's wooing
And plighted thee to him in Argos, doing
This gladly that thou mightest wed with one
Of fame so glorious and a goddess' son;
But since his base repentance of his choice
Belies the blood ascribed him by men's voice,
We must show who we are, serene of mind,
And see in him the lowest of mankind.
Shall we, by lingering, make him think that we
Wish—and await—his heart's return to thee?
Let us break off the marriage he would postpone.
My plans have to thy father been made known,
And I delay only till he shall come
To say good-bye. To leave at once for home
I go to make all ready.

(*Turning to* ERIPHYLE) I urge not thee,
Madam, to follow us, for thou wilt be

In dearer hands. Thy secret aims are clear.
It was not Calchas whom thou soughtest here.

[*Exit* CLYTEMNESTRA.

IPHIGENIA.

Hearing these words, in what cruel plight I find
Myself! Achilles now hath changed his mind
About our marriage. I must go back home
Humiliated, and thou hast hither come
To seek not Calchas but another?

ERIPHYLE.

I
Do not know, madam, what thou wouldst imply.

IPHIGENIA.

Oh, thou canst understand me well enough
If thou desirest to. Fate hath robbed me of
A husband. Wilt thou abandon me to-day
In my misfortune, madam? Thou couldst not stay
Without me in Mycenae. Without thee
Must I from Aulis go?

ERIPHYLE.

I wish to see
Calchas ere I leave here.

IPHIGENIA.

Then why dost thou
Not let him know it?

ERIPHYLE.

In but a moment, now,
Ye will be on the Argos road again.

IPHIGENIA.

A moment sometimes can make all things plain.
But I am pressing thee too hard. I see
That which I never wished to think of thee.
Achilles . . . Thou dost long for me to go.

ERIPHYLE.

I? Thou suspectest me of being so
Perfidious? I, I could love a fierce
Conqueror, who always to mine eyes appears
Covered with blood,—who, torch in hand and made
Mad by the lust to kill, in ashes laid
Lesbos . . . ?

IPHIGENIA.

Oh, yes! false wretch, thou lovest him.
Those same fierce features which thy words so limn,
Those arms which thou hast seen by gore made red,
Lesbos, that torch, those ashes, and those dead
Are things which stamped his image in thy heart;
And far from hating to think of them, thou art
Fond of telling me of them o'er and o'er.
Already in thy forced laments I more
Than once ought to have seen—and I did see—
Thine inmost feelings; but I invariably
Would in my easy kindliness replace
The veil thus lifted for a little space.
Thou lovest him. And I? How could I be
So fatally deluded as to take *thee*,
My rival, in my arms? Who else would do
Such a thing? Trustingly, I loved thee, too.
This very day I promised thee the aid
Of my false lover. This, then, is the glad

Triumph for which I was from Argos brought!
I must myself follow thy chariot.
I can forgive thee for thy selfish love
And for the loss of him thou robbest me of;
Yet that thou didst not warn me of the snare
Set for me, and hast let me come so far
From my Greek home to seek the ungrateful man
Who waited only to renounce me—can
This outrage, traitress, e'er be pardoned thee?

ERIPHYLE.

Thou givest me names bewildering to me,
Madam; for these till now I never heard.
Heaven, though long unkind to me, hath spared
Mine ears such words, to which I am not used.
Lovers' injustice, though, must be excused.
But what wouldst thou have had me warn thee of?
Couldst thou believe Achilles e'er would love
Rather than Agamemnon's daughter one
Without a name, of whom all that is known
E'en by her is that she was born of those
Whose blood he longs to shed, his hated foes?

IPHIGENIA.

Thou triumphest, cruel girl, and mockest my woe.
Till now I had not fully felt this blow.
Thou hast compared thy exile's lot and my
Eminence but to enhance thy victory.
Thou art too quick, however, to exult.
This Agamemnon, whom thou dost insult,
Commands all Greece; he is my father; he
Loves me. My sorrows wound him more than me.
My tears had touched his heart before they fell.
I heard the sighs he vainly sought to quell.

Alas! I blamed his sadness when first meeting me
Here and his lack of tenderness in greeting me!

[Enter ACHILLES.

ACHILLES (*to* IPHIGENIA).

Then 'tis true, madam, and 'tis thyself I see!
I thought that the whole camp must surely be
Mistaken. Thou in Aulis? Wherefore? What
Made Agamemnon tell me thou wert not?

IPHIGENIA.

My lord, be reassured. Thou shalt obtain
What thou wouldst. I shall soon be gone again.

[Exit IPHIGENIA.

ACHILLES.

She flees from me! Am I awake? Delusion,
Perchance, or dream is this? In what confusion
Her flight hath plunged me!
            (*To* ERIPHYLE) Madam, I do not know
Whether Achilles can before thee show
Himself without offence; but if thine ears
Are not intolerant of an enemy's prayers
(And he hath oft pitied his prisoner)
Thou knowest what reason led her footsteps here;
Thou knowest . . .

ERIPHYLE.

            What, sir! Dost thou not know it, too—
Thou, who for the past month hast pined here, who
Thyself hast caused and hastened their coming hither?

ACHILLES.

For the past month I have not been here, either.
I only yesterday returned here.

ERIPHYLE.

What!

When Agamemnon to Mycenae wrote,
Did not thy love, thine own hand, guide his pen?
What! thou who didst adore his daughter then . . .

ACHILLES.

Thou seest me more than ever now attracted
By her charms, madam; and if I had acted
As I have wished, I would myself have come
To her in Argos ere she had left home.
Yet now she flees from me! What is my crime?
I find no friends here. At this very time
Calchas, Ulysses, Nestor—they all use
Every vain trick of eloquence to oppose
My love and seem to take the stand that I
Must needs renounce it or not satisfy
Honour's demands. What schemes could have been laid
Here? Without knowing it, have I been made
The laughing-stock of the army? I will go
And wring from them this secret I must know.

[*Exit* ACHILLES.

ERIPHYLE.

Gods, who behold my shame, where can I hide?
Thou'rt loved, proud rival, yet art tearful-eyed.
Must I endure thy triumph and insults, both
At once? Ah, rather . . . But either I am loath
To put aside false hopes which I have nursed,
Doris, or else a storm, ready to burst,
Hangs o'er their heads. I am not blind. Their bliss
Is not assured yet. Iphigenia is
Deceived; she from Achilles' presence flies;

And Agamemnon utters groans and sighs.
Then let us not abandon hope. If Fate,
Hostile to her, joins forces with my hate,
I shall find ways to profit well thereby—
Not weep alone nor without vengeance die.

ACT III

AGAMEMNON *and* CLYTEMNESTRA *are discovered.*

CLYTEMNESTRA.

We were about to go, sir. Justly wroth,
I soon would have been far away from both
Achilles and the camp. My daughter came
With me; she would in Argos weep her shame.
But he himself, astonished that we fled
So suddenly, found us just then and stayed
Our steps, and with such oaths as could not fail
To win belief convinced me all was well.
The marriage that 'twas said he would postpone
He urges now, and seeks thee to disown
The lying rumour, full of rage and love,
Eager to learn who was the author of
That story and confound him. Then dismiss
These notions that have marred our happiness.

AGAMEMNON.

'Tis enough, madam; I am content to take
His word now, recognizing the mistake
Which had misled me, sharing thy delight
With all my heart. Calchas, then, shall unite
Him, as thou wishest, to my family.
Send thou thy daughter to the altar. She
Will find me there, awaiting her. But ere
We proceed further, thus with no one near
I for a moment want to speak to thee.

  To what place thou hast brought her, thou canst see.
Here naught to marriage, all to war belongs:

The tumult of a camp, everywhere throngs
Of soldiers and of sailors, bristling spears
And darts about the altar—all appears
Quite suitable for Achilles, but nowise
A proper spectacle for my queen's eyes.
And shall the Greeks behold their king's wife thus
Amid surroundings most unmeet for us?
Wilt thou herein be ruled by me? Allow
Iphigenia to her bridal now
To go accompanied by thy women, not
By thee.

CLYTEMNESTRA.

      To go without me, sayest thou? What?
Shall I entrust my child to others' care,
Not see that done for which I did prepare?
When I from Argos have to Aulis brought her,
Shall I not to the altar lead my daughter?
Ought I to be farther from Calchas' side
Than thou? Who else will give away the bride?
Who order the procession rightly?

AGAMEMNON.

      Thou
Art not in Atreus' palace. Thou art now
In an armed camp . . .

CLYTEMNESTRA.

      Where all to thy commands
Submit; where Asia's fate into thy hands
Is given; where 'neath thy sway I see all other
Greeks; and where Thetis' son will call me "mother."
In what proud palace could I seem—whate'er
Its splendours—greater in estate than here?

AGAMEMNON.

In those gods' names who are the authors of
Our race, grant, madam, this favour to my love!
I have my reasons.

CLYTEMNESTRA.

In those same gods' name,
Rob me not of so sweet a sight! What shame,
Sir, can my presence here bring unto thee?

AGAMEMNON.

I hoped thou wouldst reply more graciously;
But since the force of logic cannot sway thee,—
Since my entreaty hath no power to stay thee,—
Thou hast heard, madam, what I would have thee do.
I wish it, and I now command it, too.
Obey me.

                      [*Exit* AGAMEMNON.

CLYTEMNESTRA.

Why is Agamemnon so
Cruel and unjust he will not let me go
To the altar? Doth he know not, in the pride
Of his new rank, who *I* am? At his side
Am I not fit to stand, does he dare think?
Or, of his power still doubtful, doth he shrink
From showing Helen's sister here? Yet how
Is it needful *I* should hide? Upon my brow
By what injustice ought her shame to sit?
No matter. He so wills, and I submit.
Daughter, thy happiness consoleth me
For all. Heaven gives Achilles unto thee,
And I am overjoyed to hear men talk
Of thee as . . . Here he is.

                      [*Enter* ACHILLES.

ACHILLES.

Nothing could balk
My ardent wishes, madam; and the King
Desires naught more explained. On witnessing
My transports, he believed I was sincere
And unto what I said scarce lent an ear.
Embracing me, he as his son-in-law
Accepted me, with few words. But hast thou
Learned what good fortune thou hast brought with thee
Unto the camp? The gods consent to be
Reconciled. Calchas hath proclaimed, at least,
That in an hour they will be appeased,—
That Neptune and the winds, to do our will,
Only await the blood his hand shall spill.
Even now every ship, with all sails spread,
Is turned towards Troy, relying on what he said.
For mine own part, though heaven would be most kind
Unto my love if still we had no wind,—
Though with regret this blessed shore I quit
Whereon my nuptial torch shall soon be lit,—
Must I not welcome any chance so good
To go and seal our bond with Trojan blood,
To bury 'neath Troy's ruins the disgrace
Of those henceforth allied to me in race?

[*Enter* IPHIGENIA, ERIPHYLE, DORIS, *and* AEGINA.

(*To* IPHIGENIA) Princess, my happiness depends on thee.
Thy father waits to give thee unto me
Before the altar. Come, and there receive
A heart that worships thee.

IPHIGENIA.

With the Queen's leave,
Sir—for 'tis not yet time for us to go—

I ask from thee a promise which will show
Thy love for me, and hence which thou shouldst grant.
I this young princess unto thee present.
Her noble lineage in her face appears.
Her eyes continually are wet with tears.
Thou knowest her misfortune, for it hath
Its source in thee; I later in blind wrath
Increased it. May I not, by timely aid,
Atone for what I have unjustly said?
I speak for her. Naught more can *I* do. None
But thee, sir, can undo what thou hast done.
She is thy captive; and her chains, which pain
My heart, will fall at thy command. Thus, then,
Let us begin this happy day, that she
May find herself no longer doomed to be
Our slave. Show all men that I am to wed
A prince who would not merely fill with dread
The human race, nor would to fire and sword
Confine his fame, but gladly doth accord
To his wife's prayers mercy in victory
And, softened by the sight of misery,
Can imitate the gods from whom he sprang.

ERIPHYLE.

Yea, sir, make less my soul's most grievous pang.
In Lesbos I became thy prize of war,
But thou wouldst press a captor's rights too far
To add the torment which here rends my breast.

ACHILLES.

What torment, madam?

ERIPHYLE.

　　　　　Aside from all the rest,
Couldst thou impose on me a deadlier woe

Than mine when thou to my sad eyes dost show
The happiness of those who injured me?
I hear the threats against my country, see
An army setting out against her, fierce
For slaughter, and now see—a sight to pierce
My heart—a marriage which will give to thee
The torch that will consume her utterly.
From thee and Aulis let me go, alone,
For ever wretched and for aye unknown,
To hide a fate so worthy of regret,
Whereof not half thou knowest even yet.

ACHILLES.

Nay, nay, fair princess, come with me. Thou must
Come, that before the eyes of the Greek host
I now may set thee free. My happiest hour
Shall gladden thee with liberty once more.

[*Enter* ARCAS.

ARCAS (*to* CLYTEMNESTRA).

Madam, beside the altar now the King
Awaiteth Iphigenia. Everything
Is ready for the rites. I come for her.
   (*Turning to* ACHILLES) Nay, rather do I come to beg
     thee, sir,
To save her from him.

ACHILLES.

Arcas, what dost thou

Mean?

CLYTEMNESTRA.

Gods! What would he tell me?

ARCAS (*to* ACHILLES).

I see now
No one who can defend her except thee.

ACHILLES.

Against whom?

ARCAS.

I speak out unwillingly.
I have kept silent as long as e'er I dared;
But fillet, knife, and pyre are all prepared,
And though on mine own head the stroke should fall,
I needs must speak.

CLYTEMNESTRA.

I tremble. Tell me all,
Arcas.

ACHILLES.

Whate'er this be, speak. Let thy heart
Fear naught.

ARCAS.

Thou art her bridegroom;—and *thou* art
Her mother. Send her not unto her sire.

CLYTEMNESTRA.

Why should we fear him?

ACHILLES.

Why dost thou desire
That I should trust him not?

ARCAS.

Because 'tis she
Whom he would offer on the altar.

ACHILLES.

He?

CLYTEMNESTRA.

His daughter?

IPHIGENIA.

My own father?

ERIPHYLE.

Gods! What news!

ACHILLES.

Mastered by what mad frenzy could he choose
To arm his hand against her? Who without
Horror could hear of this?

ARCAS.

Would I could doubt
Its truth. By Calchas' voice the oracle
Demands her. There is no acceptable
Victim but her, he says; and the gods, who
Always protected Paris hitherto,
Promise us winds and Troy at this sole price.

CLYTEMNESTRA.

The gods command foul murder, then?

IPHIGENIA.

Ye skies
Above, what have I done that I must be
Consigned to such a fate?

CLYTEMNESTRA.

Now do I see
The reason I was forbidden to go near
The altar!

IPHIGENIA (*to* ACHILLES).

'Twas *this* wedding, then, that here
Awaited me!

ARCAS.

Thus did the King devise,
Feigning this marriage, to make thee come. Likewise
All the camp was deceived, and is e'en yet.

CLYTEMNESTRA (*to* ACHILLES).
Sir, I must needs throw myself at thy feet.

ACHILLES (*raising her*).
Nay, madam!

CLYTEMNESTRA.
Vain my greatness; think thou not
Of it; this sad abasement suits my lot.
Most fortunate if these tears can make thee feel
Pity, a mother can before thee kneel
Without shame. 'Tis thy bride, alas, men snatch
From thee. I brought her here, pleased at this match.
'Twas thou we sought, sir, on this fatal shore.
Thy name led her to death. Must she implore
The gods for justice, with her arms around
Their altars, for her sacrifice festooned?
She hath but thee alone; thou art for her
Sire, husband, gods, and sanctuary, sir.
I in thy glance read how these wrongs aggrieve thee.

My daughter, with thy bridegroom I shall leave thee.
Sir, stay with her, I beg of thee, and wait.
To my false husband I shall hasten straight.
He cannot face my wrath; his will must bow.
Calchas must find some other victim now,
Or, if I cannot save thee from the knife,
My child, they first will have to take my life.

[*Exeunt all but* ACHILLES *and* IPHIGENIA.

ACHILLES.

I have stood speechless, rooted to this spot.
Was it to me she spake, and knows she not
Achilles? Can thy mother think she must
Beg *me* to save *thee*, humble herself in the dust—
A queen, before me—wronging me with her fears,
And have, to touch my heart, recourse to tears?
Who could desire thy safety more than I?
Ah, surely, she might on my troth rely!
I, too, am outraged; and whate'er be done,
I will keep safe a life linked with mine own.
But my just anger moveth me to do
More than defend thee,—to avenge thee, too,
And swiftly punish that vile stratagem
Which dared make use against thee of my name.

IPHIGENIA.

Ah, stay, my lord, and hearken to me, I pray!

ACHILLES.

What! shall a tyrant flout me in this way?
He sees me fly to right his sister's wrong;
He knows I voted for him first among
All the Greeks, causing him to be elected
O'er twenty kings who might have been selected,
Instead, our leader; and for the reward
Of all my efforts, of all wrought by my sword,—
For the sole recompense of a victory which
Would alike give him vengeance, bring him rich
Booty, and crown him with undying fame,—
I was content and proud to bear the name
Of Iphigenia's husband and, in fine,

Asked of him only that thou mightest be mine.
Yet he to-day, bloodthirsty and forsworn,
Not love alone and natural ties doth scorn,—
Not only fain would with one mortal blow
Thy reeking heart upon an altar show
To me,—he hides this sacrifice beneath
Pretended marriage rites and to thy death
Would have thee led by me myself, by me
Have the blow struck unwittingly, have me be
Hence not thy bridegroom but thy murderer.
    And had I come but one day later here,
How hadst thou fared in these cruel nuptials? How?
Why, helpless in their frenzied hands, e'en now
Beside the altar, wouldst thou seek in vain
For me and, smitten without warning then,
Fall, blaming for the fraud my name and me!
Full satisfaction for such treachery,—
Such danger unto thee,—I must demand
Of him before the eyes of all the land.
Madam, thou art involved, too, in what blots
Thy husband's honour, and shouldst approve my thoughts.
He who hath treated me with such disdain
Must learn whose name he thus hath dared to stain.

IPHIGENIA.

Oh, if thou lovest me and will grant to her
Who loveth thee one final favour, sir,
Now is the time to prove this unto me;
For he thou meanest to beard, this enemy
Cruel and unjust and bloodthirsty, is still,
Forget thou not—yes, do whate'er he will,
Forget thou not—my father.

ACHILLES.

He, thy father?
After his horrible design I, rather,
Shall know him as thy would-be murderer.

IPHIGENIA.

I say again, he is my father, sir—
A father whom I love, whom I adore,
Who loves me, too, and never hath before
To this day shown me any sign of aught
But tenderness. My heart, from childhood taught
To reverence him, can only be distressed
By anything that even in the least
Offendeth against him; and far from my
Being transformed so suddenly that I
Approve the fierce flame of thy passion's fit,
And far from with mine own words fanning it,
Know this: that love as great as mine for thee
Was necessary to enable me
To suffer all those odious names which thou
Didst in thy love insult him with just now
Before my face. And why dost thou believe
That he is cruel and savage, and does not grieve
At what awaiteth me? What father would
Willingly give up his own flesh and blood?
How could it be that he would take my life
If he were able to save me from the knife?
I have beheld his tears, be thou assured.
Must thou condemn him ere he hath been heard?
Alas! when he is crushed beneath such weight
Of horrors, must he also bear thy hate?

ACHILLES.

How now! with things to dread at every turn,
Are these the ones that cause thee most concern?
A cruel man (what else call him?) doth intend
To sacrifice thee, slain by Calchas' hand;
And when I shield thee from him with my love,
His peace of mind is all thou thinkest of?
Thou'dst silence me, pity him and excuse him?
For him thou tremblest, thinking I abuse him?
Sad outcome of my efforts! Is that the whole
Success gained by Achilles in thy soul?

IPHIGENIA.

O heartless man! hath this love which thou fain
Wouldst doubt waited till now to be made plain?
Thou sawest how calm, how little moved was I
On being informed that I was doomed to die.
I never blenched. Would that thou mightest have seen
How utter, earlier, my despair had been
When from a false report, just after we
Reached here, I heard thou wert untrue to me!
How turmoiled were my thoughts! I with what floods
Of bitter speech railed against men and gods!
Then wouldst thou have perceived, though I had ne'er
Told thee so, that thy love was much more dear
To me than life. Who knows? my happiness
May even have angered heaven by its excess.
It seemed to me so beautiful a love
Had lifted me all mortals' lot above.

ACHILLES.

If I am dear to thee, my princess, live.
                    [Enter CLYTEMNESTRA and AEGINA.

CLYTEMNESTRA.

Sir, we are lost unless thou canst contrive
To save us. Agamemnon fears to see
Me now. He shuns me and denies to me
All access to the altar. Everywhere
Guards placed by him prevent my going there.
He flees me, for my grief he dares not face.

ACHILLES.

Well then, I, madam, needs must take thy place.
He shall see *me*. *I* will speak with him now.

IPHIGENIA.

Ah, madam . . . Ah, my lord, where goest thou?

ACHILLES.

And what unjust thing wouldst thou ask of me?
Have I to fight first always against thee?

CLYTEMNESTRA.

My child, what is thy wish?

IPHIGENIA.

                         In heaven's name,
Madam, restrain him that his frenzy's aim
May not be carried out. Do not allow
A meeting so unfortunate.
    (*Turning to* ACHILLES) Sir, thou
Too bitterly wouldst upbraid my sire. I know
How far the rage of one in love will go;
And jealous would my father, if defied,
Be of his power. Too famous is the pride
Of Atreus' sons. Let tongues less bold, sir, speak
To him. He will himself come soon to seek

For me, most certainly, in his surprise
At my delay. Then will he hear the sighs
Of a grief-stricken mother; and to what
May I not be inspired then by the thought
I might prevent the tears ye both would shed,—
Might end your throes of anguish, and, instead
Of dying, live for thee?

ACHILLES.

Well, this alone
Contents thee; so thy will must needs be done.
Both of you give him counsel that will avail;
Make him know reason; persuade him without fail
For your own sakes, for mine, and even for his.
But I waste time in idle talk like this.
Deeds and not words are needed now from me.

(*To* CLYTEMNESTRA) Madam, I shall do all I possibly
Can do to serve you. To your tent repair,
And take some rest. Thy child shall live, I swear.
Believe at least that while I still draw breath
The gods will vainly have decreed her death.
Better than Calchas I herein foretell
The future—mine the surer oracle.

ACT IV

ERIPHYLE *and* DORIS *are discovered.*

DORIS.

What art thou saying? Ah, what strange, mad thought
Can make thee envy Iphigenia's lot?
She is to die an hour from now, or less;
Yet ne'er, thou tellest me, hath her happiness
Made thee more jealous. Who will believe that,
Madam? What heart so wild . . .

ERIPHYLE.

                    I never yet
Have uttered truer words. My sad soul, torn
By many cares, was never so forlorn
And envious of her felicity.
Fortunate danger! Hope that cheated me!
Hast thou not seen her triumph—how deeply moved
Achilles is? *I* saw—what too well proved
The fact thereof—and I have fled that sight.
This hero terrible, who fills with fright
All other mortals,—who of tears doth know
Nothing save those that he hath caused to flow,—
Who 'gainst them steeled his heart from childhood's years,—
Who even sucked the blood of lions and bears
If what is told be not a lie,—through her
Hath finally now learned what it is to fear.
She saw him weep; she saw his face turn pale.
And thou dost pity her, Doris! How much bale
Would I not wish were mine, if I might vie
With her for such tears? Even if I had to die
Like her within an hour . . . What do I say—

"Die"? Never think that she will die. Nay, nay!
Deemest thou Achilles, sunk in shameful sleep,
Could, without vengeance for her, blench and weep?
Achilles can avert her fate at will.
Thou'lt find that heaven gave us this oracle
To augment her honour and my agonies
And make her fairer in her lover's eyes—
Naught else. What! seest thou not all that is done
For her? By few the gods' decree is known;
For, though the pyre is heaped, the victim's name
To all the camp a secret doth remain.
Canst thou not see this silence indicates,
Doris, that still her father hesitates?
What will he do? What heart unless of stone
Can bear what his shall be assailed with soon:
A mother's rage, a daughter's tears, the cries
And the despair of all his family, ties
Of blood, sights that would naturally dismay him,
Achilles' threats, who would if need be slay him?
No, heaven, I tell thee, hath but futilely
Condemned her. I alone am, and shall be,
Unfortunate. Ah, if I followed now
My impulses . . .

DORIS.

What course considerest thou?

ERIPHYLE.

I do not know what stays me from straightway
Going in my anger to tell all I may,
Revealing what the wrathful gods have said
And publishing abroad what plots are laid
Most wickedly to rob them of their due
And cheat their altars.

DORIS.

What a thing to do,
Madam!

ERIPHYLE.

Oh, Doris, what entrancing joy!
How thick would every temple smoke in Troy
With incense, if, embroiling all Greece, I
Could in revenge for my captivity
Arm Agamemnon 'gainst Achilles, so
That in their mutual hate they would forego
Strife with my country, and could turn their swords
Which they had sharpened against her, through my words,
Against each other!—if I could thus destroy
This entire army for the sake of Troy!

DORIS.

I hear some one approaching. . . . 'Tis the Queen.
Control thy feelings, madam, or go within.

ERIPHYLE.

Come, then. To balk this cursed marriage, let us
Give my rage scope, wherein the gods abet us.
[ERIPHYLE *and* DORIS *retire into the tent assigned to them.*
Enter CLYTEMNESTRA *and* AEGINA.

CLYTEMNESTRA.

Aegina, I cannot endure that sight.
My daughter, far from weeping and without fright
At death, would fain excuse her father and
Have me in my distress respect the hand
That is to pierce her heart. O filial love
Which naught can shake! And for reward thereof
The barbarous wretch—to face him here I wait!—
E'en now at the altar blames her being late,

And soon will come to ask the reason why,
Thinking he still can hide his perfidy.
Here he is. Let us not denounce him yet,
But see if he persists in his deceit.

[*Enter* AGAMEMNON.

AGAMEMNON.

What art thou doing, madam? Why doth this place
Nowise present thy daughter to my gaze
With thee? I sent by Arcas word to thee
To send her to me. Why delayeth she?
Is it thou who stayest her? Wilt thou not obey
My lawful wishes? Can she not walk her way
To the altar save beside thee? Speak!

CLYTEMNESTRA.

If she
Must go, my child is ready. But what of thee?
Hast thou, my lord, nothing to stay thee?

AGAMEMNON.

I,

Madam?

CLYTEMNESTRA.

Hast thou prepared all, carefully?

AGAMEMNON.

Calchas is ready, and the altar, too.
I have done all that duty bids me do.

CLYTEMNESTRA.

Thou tellest me nothing of the victim, sir.

AGAMEMNON.

What wouldst thou say? What jealous care doth spur . . .

CLYTEMNESTRA (*raising her voice*).
Come, daughter, come! For thee alone they wait.

[*Enter* IPHIGENIA.

Come; thank thy father, who hath for thee so great
A love that he himself will lead thee now
To the altar.

AGAMEMNON.

What is this? What meanest thou?
My child, thou weepest, and thy downcast eyes
Seem ill at ease to meet mine own. What sighs
Are these! But they both weep—daughter and mother.
Oh, wretched Arcas, thou hast betrayed me!

IPHIGENIA.

Father,
Do not be troubled. Thou art not betrayed.
When thou commandest, thou shalt be obeyed.
My life is *thy* gift. Thou wouldst have it back.
Thou needest but only speak thy will, and take.
With no more shrinking glance nor heart more loath
Than if I wedded him thou didst betroth
To me, I would bow down a guiltless head,
A willing sacrifice to Calchas' blade,
And, reverencing the blow decreed by thee,
Give thee again that life thou gavest me.
     Yet if my filial obedience
Deserves, thou thinkest, a different recompense,
And if thou pitiest a mother's grief,
I shall say frankly that just now my life
Seems amid such fair honours to be set
That I would fain not lose it, but would regret
That, snatching it, a cruel destiny
So soon after my birth should make me die.

A daughter of Agamemnon, she I am
Who was the first to call thee by the name
Of "Father," who brought joy unto thine eye
So long and made thee thank the gods on high
For that dear name, and whom thou wouldst caress,
Nowise ashamed to exhibit tenderness
For thine own child.
        Alas, I numbered through,
With joy, the lands thou goest to subdue,
And even now, foreseeing Ilium's fall,
Was planning a triumphant festival!
I little dreamed that, to begin thy task,
My blood would be the first which Fate would ask.
    'Tis not from dread of what is threatened me
That I recall thy past love unto thee.
Fear naught; I, who am jealous for thy fame,
Will ne'er make such a father blush with shame;
And if I had only my life to shield,
Deep in my breast these memories would be sealed.
But on my lot, thou knowest, sir, my mother's
Happiness doth depend,—also my lover's.
A prince well worthy of us thought the day
Had come which was to join our hands for ay.
Sure of my plighted heart already, he
Deemed himself blest; thy pledge for this had we.
He has learned thy purpose, now; judge of his fears.
Here stands my mother, and thou seest her tears.
Forgive me for thus having tried to keep
Unshed those which my death must make her weep!

AGAMEMNON.

My daughter, 'tis too true. I do not know
For what crime the gods' wrath would have blood flow
Upon an altar here, but they require

A victim, and have named thee in a dire
Oracle. To defend thy life from their
Decree, my love did not await thy prayer.
I shall not tell thee how long I held out
Against that savage hest, but do not doubt
The love to which thou didst thyself just bear
Witness. This very night, as thou didst hear
Perchance, I have revoked the order I
Was forced to write. Such was thy victory
Over the good of Greece. My rank, my life
Itself I risked to save thee from the knife
Of Calchas. I sent Arcas forth to tell
Thee not to come here. It was the gods' will
That ye should fail to meet. They brought to naught
The efforts of a hapless sire who sought
To rescue one whom they condemned to die.
    Upon my feeble power do not rely.
What could restrain a people's lawlessness
When heaven doth smile on their blind zeal's excess,
Freeing them from a yoke deemed burdensome?
My child, we must submit. Thine hour hath come.
Remember in what station thou wert born.
    I give thee counsel which I myself, forlorn,
Can scarcely follow. Thou scarcely more than I
Shalt, from the blow that is to smite thee, die.
Show in thy death from whom thou hadst thy birth.
Make the gods blush for dooming such great worth.
Go; let the Greeks, who wish thee to be slain,
Perceive in thy shed blood our royal strain.

CLYTEMNESTRA (*to* AGAMEMNON).

Thou showest thyself not false to a fell brood.
Yes, thou'rt of Atreus' and Thyestes' blood.
Butcher of thine own daughter, for the rest

Thou only needest to set a dread repast
Before her mother. Barbarous monster, this,
Then, is thy fine, fair-seeming sacrifice!
    Did not the horror of that dire command,
When thou didst sign and seal it, stay thy hand?
Why put feigned sadness on before our eyes?
Thinkest thou to prove thy love by tears and sighs?
Where are the struggles thou didst undertake?
What streams of blood hast thou shed for her sake?
What carnage doth of thy resistance tell?
What field bestrewn with dead bids me be still?
    Those are such proofs as I must have, cruel man,
That thy love sought to save her. She must be slain—
So a grim oracle decreeth? Nay,
Do oracles say all they seem to say?
Is heaven, just heaven, with a murder pleased?
By innocent blood is it to be appeased?
If Helen's kin for Helen's sin ye slaughter,
In Sparta seek Hermione, her daughter.
Let Menelaus at such a price redeem
His guilty wife, who is too dear to him.
But thou—what madness makes thee sacrifice
Aught thine? Why must thou expiate her vice?
And why must I thus cause my heart to bleed,
And pay for her mad loves with my pure seed?
    What say I? She who giveth strife such cause,—
Who troubleth Europe's peace and Asia's,—
This Helen,—is she worth high deeds of fame?
How often hath she dyed our cheeks with shame!
Ere thy poor brother wedded her, withal,
Theseus had taken her from her father's hall;
Unpublished nuptials placed her in his bed,
Thou knowest—so Calchas many times hath said—

And that a princess was the fruit of these,
Whom she hath hidden from the eyes of Greece.
    Oh, no, a brother's love, his honour stained,
Are the least things by which thou art constrained.
Thy thirst for sovereignty, which naught can slake,
Thy pride, that twenty kings serve thee and quake,
The rule entrusted thee, who all devisest—
These are the gods to whom thou sacrificest,
Hard heart! Thou dost not spurn the task now set
For thee; thou makest a virtue out of it!
Fearful that some should envy thee thy powers,
Thou fliest to pay for them with blood of ours,
And fain by such a price wouldst terrify
Whoe'er might challenge thine authority.
    Are fathers, then, like that? Ah, all my reason
Totters, confronting this inhuman treason!
A priest, amid relentless warrior bands,
Will lay upon my child his wicked hands,
Will pierce her breast and seek, with curious eye,
From her yet-throbbing heart some augury. . . .
And I, who brought her here, so loved, elate—
I shall go back alone and desperate;
And I shall see the roads still perfumed sweet
With flowers that were strewn before her feet!
Nay, 'twas not for her death I brought her here,
Or Greece shall have *two* victims! Neither fear
Nor duteous respect can force me hence.
She must be torn out of mine arms' defence,
Bleeding. Thou savage husband, sire accurst,
Come, take her from her mother if thou durst!
    (*Turning to* IPHIGENIA) As for thee, go within, my
        daughter, and
For one last time obey still my command.
                    [*Exeunt all but* AGAMEMNON

AGAMEMNON (*to himself*).

I could not have expected I would hear
Less frenzied words. 'Twas these that I did fear.
Yet I were happy had my tortured soul
Nothing to dread but such vain cries of dole.
Alas, great gods, who gave me this cruel hest,
Why was a father's heart left in my breast?

[*Enter* ACHILLES.

ACHILLES.

A very strange report hath reached mine ear.
I deemed it little worthy of credence, sir.
The tale is told—and this with horror I
Repeat—that Iphigenia is to die
To-day by thine own orders, and that, steeling
Thy nature against every human feeling,
Thou wilt thyself place her in Calchas' hands;—
Yet more, that I—because by promised bonds
Of marriage with me she hither was enticed—
Am party to her being sacrificed,
And that, with both of us duped by that ruse,
Thou puttest my name to this most shameful use.
What sayest thou, my lord, in answer? What
Am I to think of all this? Wilt thou not
Silence such ugly rumours, which must grieve
Thine outraged heart?

AGAMEMNON.

I do not have to give
Account, sir, of my plans. My daughter still
Herself is ignorant of my sovereign will.
When the time comes for her to learn it, I
Shall tell the army what her destiny
Will be, and thou wilt hear it then.

ACHILLES.

I know
Too well the destiny thou wouldst bestow
Upon her.

AGAMEMNON.

If thou knowest it, why ask *me*?

ACHILLES.

"Why ask"? O gods! Can I believe it of thee,
That thou wouldst dare avow so foul a crime?
Deemest thou that I will aid thy purpose grim
And let thee slay thy child before my sight,—
That love and honour will consent to it?

AGAMEMNON.

Nay, thou who speakest to me so threateningly,
Hast thou forgotten that it is to me
Thou speakest?

ACHILLES.

Hast thou forgotten who it is
I love and whom thou plannest to sacrifice?

AGAMEMNON.

And who hath placed my family in thy care?
Must I, except with thy consent, not dare
Dispose of mine own daughter? Am I, then,
No more her father? Art thou her husband? Can
She not . . .

ACHILLES.

Nay, she is no longer thine.
I will not, since she hath been plighted mine,
Submit to being cheated. While there remains
A single drop of blood still in my veins,
Since thou in plighting her to be my wife

Gavest unto me all her further life,
I will defend the rights which thou didst swear
Were mine. Was it not to wed me she came here?

AGAMEMNON.

Blame, then, the gods who at my hands require
Her death. Blame also Calchas and the entire
Army, Ulysses, Menelaus, and, more
Still, thine own self.

ACHILLES.

Myself?

AGAMEMNON.

Thou, given o'er
To dreams of Asian conquest, who each day
Complainest of heaven for causing our delay,—
Thou, who, much vexed at my well-founded dread,
Through the whole camp hast thine own frenzy spread.
I offered thee a course which would have brought
Safety to her; but thou couldst think of naught
But Troy. I would have closed to thee the path
Thou fain wouldst take. Well, have thy will. Her death
Will open it for thee.

ACHILLES.

Just heaven! Must I
Hear and endure these words? To perfidy
Shall insults, too, be added? I would go hence—
I, I, thou sayest?—at her life's expense?
And what wrong hath Troy done me? What thing calls—
What interest—to me to assail her walls?
Deaf to a goddess-mother's warning voice
And a distracted sire's, I made it my choice

Thither to go, regardless of the doom
Oft promised their son there—and all for whom?
Did ships from the Scamander e'er descend
Upon the shores of my Thessalian land?
Did e'er some ravisher to Larissa come
And steal my wife or sister from my home?
What grudge have I, what losses of my own?
Thou barbarous wretch, I go for thee alone,—
Thee, to whom only I, of these collected
Greeks owe naught,—thee, who wert through me elected
Their leader and mine, too,—thee, whom my hand
Avenged in blazing Lesbos ere this strand
Saw thine assembled army!
                       And for what
Purpose did we all flock here? Was it not
To restore Helen to her husband? Since
When was I deemed so helpless in defence
Of what is mine as to let any one
Deprive me of a wife I love? Hath none
Except thy brother who endures the shame
Of outrage to his love the right to claim
Vengeance for such offence? Thy daughter was
Loved by me, and I sought her love. My vows
Were made to her alone. Moved by the charms
Of our prospective marriage, I promised arms,
Ships, soldiers—all unto my bride-to-be,
And unto Menelaus naught. If he
So wills, let him pursue his ravished wife
And seek a victory that would cost my life.
I know not Priam, Helen, or Paris. 'Tis
Thy daughter's hand I wish for, and at this
Price only will I now set forth.

AGAMEMNON.

Then fly.
Go back home to thy Thessaly. Hereby
Do I myself release thee from thine oath.
No lack of others in thy stead, less loath
To show respect for my authority,
Will come and win the laurels promised thee,—
Will by the greatness of their exploits bend
Fate to their will and witness Ilium's end.
I see too well the price that would be paid—
Shown by thy insolence—for thy haughty aid.
Thou settest thyself up as the arbiter
Of Greece already, and—to hear thee, sir—
Her kings have given me but the empty name
Of leader. Boasting thy prowess, thou dost claim—
If I have understood aright what thou
Hast said to me—that all must march, must bow,
Must tremble 'neath thy sway. A service made
The grounds for a reproach becomes instead
An offence unto us. Less do I care
For valour than obedience. Go. I fear
Thy helpless anger not at all, and I
Break every tie between us.

ACHILLES.

For one tie
Be thankful—all that now restrains mine ire.
I still respect Iphigenia's sire.
Without that name, this lord of kings perchance
Would find such words his final utterance.
I say but one thing more; hear, heed it, thou.
I have thy daughter and my honour now

Both to defend. If her thou meanest to slay,
Thy sword must through my body carve its way.

[*Exit* ACHILLES.

AGAMEMNON (*gazing after him*).

And thou hast thus made her destruction sure.
My child herself, unaided, moved me more.
Thinking thou couldst, by being insolent,
Daunt me, thou hastenest what thou wouldst prevent.
  Let us defy him. No more doubts! Concern
For mine own honour, now at stake, doth turn
The scale. Achilles' threats decide all. Here
Pity would seem the consequence of fear.
  Ho, guards!

[*Enter* EURYBATES *and guards*.

EURYBATES.

My lord.

AGAMEMNON (*to himself*).

What is it that I intend
To do? How can I give this dire command
To them? Thou must prepare for what dread strife,
O heartless man! Who is this foe whose life
Thou yieldest to them? A mother doth await
My coming, one who will in such a strait
Defend her daughter quite unflinchingly
Against a murderous father. I shall see
My soldiers, not so cruel as I, respect
Their king's child, whom her clasping arms protect.
Achilles threatens me and flouts me. Is
My daughter's duteous love made less by this?
Hath she attempted to escape the altar?
Hath she made any moan or seemed to falter

At prospect of the blow I wish to deal
To her? "Wish"? Nay, what could such impious zeal
Gain me? What pray for in my sacrifice
Of her? However glorious the prize
That was proposed, what laurels ever could
Please me if they were watered by her blood?
Would I fain move the immortal gods on high?
What gods could be more cruel to me than I?
No, no, I cannot do this. Let us yield
To blood-ties and affection, nor be filled
Longer with shame at just compassion. She
Shall live. . . .
                But stay! Does royal dignity
Matter so little to me that I should
Accord the victory to Achilles proud?
He in his arrogance, thus increased, will deem
That I gave in to him—was afraid of him . . .
    With what vain cares my soul is occupied!
Can I not strip Achilles of his pride?
My daughter shall bring naught to him but grief.
He loves her; she shall be another's wife.
    Eurybates, fetch me the Princess here—
The Queen, too. Tell them they have naught to fear.
                      [*Exit* EURYBATES.
    Great gods, if in your anger ye wish still
To take her from me, what, to thwart your will,
Can all the efforts of weak mortals do?
My love avails her nothing against you;
It furthers her destruction. This I know.
But, O great gods, a victim treasured so
Requireth that ye confirm your harsh decree
And ask her death a second time of me.

[*Enter* Clytemnestra, Iphigenia, Eriphyle, Doris, *and*
 Eurybates.

(*To* Clytemnestra) Go, madam, go. Guard carefully her
 life.
I give thy child again to thee, dear wife.
I entrust her to thee. Take her with all speed
Far from this dangerous place. Arcas will lead
My guards, accompanying you. I willingly
Pardon his fortunate breach of faith to me.
All hangs on secrecy and dispatch. Not yet
Hath Calchas or Ulysses spoken. Let
Naught be known by them of your flight. Conceal
Thy daughter. Let all think I keep her still
Here in the camp and thee alone have sent
Back home. Away! May heaven be content
With my tears shed already, and let not
My sad eyes see her more in this dread spot.
　　Guards, follow the Queen.

Clytemnestra.

Ah, my lord!

Iphigenia.

Oh,
My father!

Agamemnon.

Foil blood-thirsty Calchas. Go,
I say! I, to assist you, will beguile
His mind with some excuse, and have, meanwhile,
The fatal preparations all suspended,
Claiming a respite till this day be ended.
　　[*Exeunt all but* Eriphyle *and* Doris.

Eriphyle.

Come with me, Doris. Our path lies not there.

Doris.

Wilt thou not follow them?

Eriphyle.

Oh, I can bear
No more! Achilles' love, in her defence,
Hath wrought this change. I will not carry hence
A helpless rage and bitterness, to nurse.
No further talk of this! I must perforce
Destroy her, or else die. Nay, come! I shall
Go straight to Calchas. I will tell him all.

[*Exeunt.*

ACT V

IPHIGENIA *and* AEGINA *are discovered.*

IPHIGENIA.

Go back, Aegina, to my mother. Cease
To attempt to keep me here. We must appease
The wrath of heaven. Because we would deny
The gods my blood, see what a stormy sky
Lowers over us. Consider the Queen's plight.
Behold how all the army blocks our flight.
How insolently soldiers everywhere
Brandish before our faces sword and spear.
Our guards were driven back; she fainted—we
To far too much expose her. Let me flee
From her,—nowise await her powerless aid
But take advantage of her swoon instead.
My father, even, alas!—this needs must I
Tell thee—though trying to save me, bids me die.

AEGINA.

Thy father? What! how could this be?

IPHIGENIA.

Perchance
Achilles' too great zeal in my defence
Hath angered him. The King, at any rate,
Hateth him and would have me share his hate.
He orders me to sacrifice mine own
Feelings, through Arcas making his will known
To me. Aegina, he forbade me e'er
To speak of him.

AEGINA.

Oh, madam!

IPHIGENIA.

How severe
A doom for me! He whom I love thus banned!
The gods are kinder; they but my life demand.
Let us die, then. But what is this I see?
Ah, heaven! Achilles?

[*Enter* ACHILLES.

ACHILLES.

Madam, follow me.
Fear not the clamour nor the impotent
Numbers of those who crowd around this tent.
Show thyself and, awaiting not my blows,
Their surging throngs will part and ne'er oppose
Thy passage through the press. Patroclus and
Some other captains under my command
Bring thee the flower of my Thessalians. All
The rest have 'neath my standard formed a wall
Of steel to guard thee, through which none can pierce.
Take refuge from thy persecutors fierce
Behind it. Let them come to seek thee now
Among Achilles' tents. . . . Is it thus that thou
Greetest my efforts? What! to my appeal
Are tears thy only answer? Dost thou still
Put trust in them? The crucial moment nears.
Thy father hath already seen thy tears.

IPHIGENIA.

I know it well, and my sole hope doth lie
Now in the blow by which I am to die.

ACHILLES.

Thou, die? Nay, do not use that word again.
Hast thou forgot the vows that bind us twain?
Forgot—to bring such vain talk to an end—
My happiness doth on thy life depend?

IPHIGENIA.

Heaven on a life so luckless doth not base
Achilles' destiny and happiness.
Our love deceived us. 'Tis the Fates' decree
That thou far happier through my death wouldst be.
Think of the honours to be reaped, my lord,
That victory will to thine arm accord.
This field of glory, which ye all seek, would
Be barren if not watered by my blood.
Such is the gods' will, to my sire disclosed,
Which, deaf to Calchas, he in vain opposed.
With one united voice was heaven's hest
Against me by the Greeks made manifest.
Go forth; I offer too great obstacles
To thy renown. Fulfil the oracles
About thee. Be that hero promised Greece.
Direct thy wrath against her enemies.
Already Priam blenches, and Troy fears
My sacrifice, trembling to see thy tears.
Go; and within her walls, bereft of men,
Make Trojan widows weep my death. Serene
And in this hope content, I lose my life.
If fated not to be Achilles' wife,
I trust that memories will in times to come
Link me with his immortal deeds, my doom
Be known to have made possible his glory

And e'er be told as prelude to its story.
Farewell, Prince. Mayst thou live, thou worthy seed
Of the immortals.

ACHILLES.

I will not hear or heed
Such words! Thou vainly triest by this farewell
To serve thy sire and cheat my love. With skill
Too cruel, thou, bent on death, dost vainly try
To make me, for my fame's sake, let thee die.
These laurels, conquests, honours awaiting me—
I find them every one in serving thee.
And who would care aught for my favour if
I, soon to wed thee, cannot save thy life?
My love, my fair fame, both require that thou
Shalt live. Come, madam; so believe, and now
Follow me.

IPHIGENIA.

I? Rebel against my own
Father? Deserve the death I sought to shun?
Lose filial respect? And my supreme
Duty . . .

ACHILLES.

Thou'dst follow a husband given by *him*.
That is a title he will vainly seek
To rob me of. Is it alone to break
Oaths that he swears them? Say thyself, thou whom
So stern a duty keepeth here for thy doom:
When unto me he gave thee, was he not
Thy father? Only when he hath forgot
He is, and ceased to be that, thou obeyest
His strict commands. Come; thou too long delayest,
My princess, and I fear . . .

IPHIGENIA.

How now! Yet worse,
Sir, wouldst thou go so far as to use force?
Couldst thou, thus hearkening to thy passions mad,
This crowning woe to my afflictions add?
Less precious than my life my honour is
To thee? Oh, spare poor Iphigenia this!
Subject to orders which must be revered
By me, I did too much even when I heard
Thy words. No further press thy victory
Unfairly, or by mine own hand set free
From the disgrace which unto me thou'dst bring,
I of my life shall make an offering
To save myself, in this strait, from thine aid.

ACHILLES.

Well, then, I say no more. Obey, cruel maid.
Embrace a death which seems so fine a thing
To thee and sweet. Unto thy father bring
A heart wherein, hearing thy words, I see
Less reverence for him than hate for me.
My soul is seized with righteous rage. Lo, I
Like thee go to the altar, but I fly
Thither, madam. Is heaven athirst for gore?
That altar never will have reeked with more.
To love's blind fury I will set no stay,
The priest will be the first whom I shall slay;
The funeral pyre, by these hands overthrown,
Shall swim in those men's blood who craved thine own;
And if amid the dread confusion thy
Father himself should, smitten, fall and die,
Then, seeing the fruit of thy obedience,
Know that thou speddest the blows that took him hence.

[*Exit* ACHILLES.

IPHIGENIA.

Ah, sir! Ah, cruel . . . But he has fled, is gone.
O thou who wishest my death, I am here, alone.
Strike, end, just heaven, my life and my dismay!
Launch now thy shafts, which only me will slay.

[*Enter* CLYTEMNESTRA, AEGINA, EURYBATES, *and guards.*

CLYTEMNESTRA.

I will defend her against all the host.
Cowards, ye fail your queen when needed most.

EURYBATES.

Nay, madam; thou hast but to order it,
To see us fight and die here at thy feet.
But from our feeble strength what canst thou hope?
Can we defend thee? Can a handful cope
With such great numbers? This no longer is
An ineffectual mob here gathered; this
Is the whole army, whom religious zeal
Hath blinded. No more pity do they feel.
Calchas alone reigns here, alone commands.
Piety claims an offering at his hands.
The King beholds himself stripped of his power.
He bids us yield. All else must yield before
Achilles, but Achilles 'gainst this storm
Himself would vainly wish to oppose his arm.
What will he do? Who can disperse our foes,
Whose surging waves would o'er his head soon close?

CLYTEMNESTRA.

Then let them prove on me their impious zeal
And rob me of the few years left me still!
Death, death alone, can break the embrace wherewith
My arms shall hold and shield her—naught but death.

My soul shall from my body part much rather
Than I would ever let . . . My child!

IPHIGENIA.

Oh, mother,
Under what baleful planet didst thou bear
This hapless object of a love so dear?
But what canst thou do in our present plight?
Thou hast the gods and men alike to fight.
Wilt thou confront a frenzied multitude?
Go not amidst an army who, imbued
With madness, 'gainst thy husband all rebel;
Nor stubbornly resist alone their will
About me, lest, haled in unseemly wise
By soldiers' hands, thou offer to mine eyes,
As the sole fruit of efforts vain by thee,
A sight far bitterer than death to me.
Go; let the Greeks achieve their purpose, and
Do thou at once leave this unhappy strand.
The pyre that doth await me is near by.
Linger not, or its flames thou wilt espy.
One thing more: if thou lovest me, by that love
A mother feels, I beg of thee above
All else, blame not my father with my death!

CLYTEMNESTRA.

By whom thy heart to Calchas given . . .

IPHIGENIA.

What hath
He not done, trying to give me back to thee!

CLYTEMNESTRA.

Treacherous and cruel was his deceit with me.

IPHIGENIA.

He renders to the gods what he received
From them. Ye by my death are not bereaved
Of all the offspring of your mutual love.
Your lives are linked by other fruit thereof.
Your eyes shall still behold me in my brother,
Orestes. Ah, may he bring to his mother
Less pain! Thou hearest the camp's impatient roar.
Please, take me in thine arms this one time more,
Madam; then with thine heart which ne'er would falter . . .
[CLYTEMNESTRA *clasps her in a long, last embrace, then finally releases her.*
Eurybates, lead the victim to the altar.

               [*Exeunt* EURYBATES *and* IPHIGENIA.

CLYTEMNESTRA (*attempting to follow them*).

Thou shalt not go alone. I do not mean . . .
(*Recoiling*) But crowds press close all round and wall me in.
Traitors! Ye thirst for blood. Here is mine. Drink!
[*She tries repeatedly to find passage through other spaces between the tents.*

AEGINA.

Where rushest thou, madam? and what dost thou think
To do?

CLYTEMNESTRA.

   Alas! I spend my strength in vain.
Anguish, briefly escaped, racks me again.
Can I yet live, who die time after time?

AEGINA.

Ah, knowest thou whose the treason, whose the crime,
Madam? Knowest thou what deadly snake, unguessed,
Iphigenia took unto her breast?

'Twas Eriphyle, whom ye hither led,
None else, that unto all the Greeks betrayed
Your flight.

CLYTEMNESTRA.

O monster from Megaera sprung,
Born of her womb! monster whom hell hath flung
Into our arms! Oh, and shalt thou not die?
To punish her foul deed . . . But where shall I
Find for mine agony some vengeance meet?
To swallow up the Greeks and all their fleet,
Wilt thou, O sea, not open vast new deeps?
Or else when Aulis spews their thousand ships,
Which she hath harboured, forth in all their sin,
Will not the winds, the very winds till then
Long blamed for idleness, not cover thee
With wreckage? And thou, sun, who here dost see
And know the son and heir in his own right
Of Atreus, thou who didst not dare to light
The father's feast, turn back; thou wert taught how
To go that dread path then . . . But even now—
O hapless mother, O vaulted sky!—my daughter,
Crowned with the cursed chaplet, for her slaughter
Offers her bare throat to her father's knife.
Calchas will in her blood . . . Oh, spare her life,
Cruel men! Her blood is that of him whose power
Wields heaven's bolts. I hear the thunder roar
And feel the earth shake. Thunder? In that noise
Heed an avenging god's deep, awesome voice.

[*Enter* ARCAS.

ARCAS.

Doubt it not, madam, a god fights for thee.
Thy prayers are answered by Achilles. He

Hath broke through all the Greeks against him massed,
And reached the altar. Calchas stands aghast.
The sacrifice is interrupted. There
Are threats and rushing feet, swords flash, the air
Resounds. Achilles marshals all his friends
About thy daughter, men in her defence
Ready to die. Sad Agamemnon, who
Dares not approve hereof, to shun the view
Of slaughter he foreseeth in that place—
Or else to hide his tears—covers his face.
Come; speak, since he is silent; by some word
Of thine lend aid to thy defender's sword.
He longs to place, with hands which gore doth stain,
Her whom he loveth in thine arms again.
He himself bade me bring thee to him. Fear
Nothing.

CLYTEMNESTRA.

I, fear? Oh, let us hasten, dear
Arcas. No danger now can frighten me.
I will go anywhere. . . . But do I not see
Ulysses? Gods! 'Tis he. That tells her fate.
My child is dead, Arcas. It is too late!

[*Enter* ULYSSES.

ULYSSES.

Nay, thy child lives, and heaven is appeased.
Be of good cheer. The gracious gods are pleased
To give her back to thee.

CLYTEMNESTRA.

She lives! And thou
It is who comest to tell me of this now!

ULYSSES.

Yes, madam, it is I, who long did feel
That against her and thee I ought to steel
Thy husband's heart;—who caused your tears to flow
By my stern counsels, being always so
Concerned for the honour of our arms;—and who
Now come, when heaven smiles on us anew,
To heal all pain where I had dealt the wound.

CLYTEMNESTRA.

My child! Ye powers above! Prince, I am stunned.
What god hath saved her life? what miracle?

ULYSSES.

Myself thou seest, in this glad moment, still
O'erwhelmed with awe and joy—in ecstasies.
No day e'er seemed so fatal unto Greece.
Discord, already mistress here, had spread
Her blindness over all and given the dread
Signal for the beginning of the fray.
Thy daughter saw the dire sight with dismay,—
Saw the whole host against her, and on her side
Achilles; but Achilles had defied
Their numbers, and, though one against them all,
Was able in his fury to appal
The entire army and give even the gods
Divided counsels. Now already clouds
Of arrows filled the air; already blood,
The first-fruits of the impending carnage, flowed.
Calchas between them came. His eyes' wild glare,
His solemn mien, his bristling beard and hair,
All showed that he was mastered by the god
Wont to inspire him. Terrible, he stood.

"Hear me, Achilles! Hear me, all ye Greeks!"
He cried aloud to them. "Heaven, which thus speaks
Unto you at this moment through my voice,
Explains its oracle, declares its choice.
Another child of Helen's race it is—
Another Iphigenia, and not this—
Who on these shores must at the altar die.
Helen was unto Theseus secretly,
After he bore her off, in wedlock sealed.
A daughter thence was born, whom she concealed;
And Iphigenia was that daughter's name.
I myself saw this fruit of their love's flame
In those days, and foreboded for her life
A dismal future. Now unto the knife
Her evil fate and her own passions' curse
Have brought her hither, under a name not hers.
She sees me, hears me; she before you stands.
She is the offering that heaven demands."
　　Thus Calchas spake. Motionless and in awe,
The whole camp hearkened unto him, and saw
And looked at Eriphyle. She beside
The altar was, and in her thoughts did chide,
Perhaps, the tardiness of the sacrifice;
For she it was who went, some while ere this,
In haste to inform the Greeks ye sought to fly.
All marvelled at her birth and destiny;
Yet since her death was the price asked for Troy's
Downfall, the army with a single voice
Doomed her, and ordered Calchas to perform
The fatal rites. But when he raised his arm
To seize her, "Stay!" she cried. "No nearer come.
The blood of that heroic line wherefrom
Thou sayst I am descended doth not need

Thy impious hands to cause it to be shed"—
Then to the altar sprang, like one possessed,
Snatched the knife there, and plunged it in her breast.
   Scarce had her lifeblood flowed and stained the ground
When peals of thunder made the heavens resound,
The rustling winds began to blow, the roar
Of the sea answered them, the distant shore
Was white with foam, the pyre burst into flame,
Lightnings flared, the skies opened, and there came
Upon us all a holy awe which made
Our hearts serene. Bewildered soldiers said
That in a cloud Diana to that pyre
Descended,—then, rising from out its fire,
So they believe, bore back to heaven with her
Our offering and our prayers. Now all bestir
Themselves to set forth. Iphigenia alone,
Amid the general joy, weeps for her own
Enemy. Come, receive her from the hand
Of Agamemnon. Come, Achilles and
He are impatient to see *thee* again,
Madam; and once more reconciled, those twain
Are ready to confirm the alliance great
Which is to bind them fast.

CLYTEMNESTRA.

                   How can my debt
Unto the kindly gods be paid, O heaven,
And to Achilles meet reward be given?